A MAPP OF Yᵉ COVNTY OF ESSEX, WITH ITS HVNDREDS BY RIC. BLOME BY HIS Maᵗⁱᵉ COMAND.

# ESSEX HEYDAY

*By the same Author*

EPPING FOREST
THE ENGLISH COUNTRY PARSON

Hadfield · Walden · Harlow · Onger · Wicham · Harwich · Colchester

Epping · Ingerstone · Chelmsford · Rochford

Hare · Malden

Waltham Abby · Romford · Brentwood

Barking · Hornedon

Sea Ht. · Tilbury Fort

Grace

Thames River

# ESSEX HEYDAY

by

## WILLIAM ADDISON

With thirty-five illustrations
in collogravure

LONDON
J. M. DENT AND SONS LTD

Made in Great Britain
by
The Temple Press · Letchworth · Herts
Collogravure plates printed by
Harrison & Sons Ltd. · London
First published 1949

Is not old wine wholesomest, old pippins tooth-somest, old wood burns brightest, old linen wash whitest?  Old soldiers, sweetheart, are surest, and old lovers are soundest.

JOHN WEBSTER.—Westward Ho!, Act II, sc. ii.

# PREFACE

IN this sketch of social life in seventeenth-century Essex, national as well as local characters appear, seen in their homes and villages at the time when the county's life was most alert and vivid. Lords and their ladies, parsons, publicans, village weavers, and country gentlemen, mingle as freely as at a country fair. In so light a study it seemed unnecessary—undesirable even—to encumber the text with full biographical details each time a well-known name was mentioned. What a man has done in one place need not be relevant to what he does in another. When Tennyson had stayed at the Bull Inn, Woodbridge, FitzGerald tried to impress upon the landlord, John Grout, how greatly the house had been honoured. 'Daresay,' said John, when informed that his guest was poet laureate, 'but he didn't fare to know much about horses.'

To the social historian the Grouts may be as important as the Tennysons. Their records are not equally easy to find. Historical survival is the reward of private enterprise, not of communal endeavour, however worthy. So though innkeeping is the most public of businesses, and poetry the most private, ten pages can be written on a poet with less trouble than ten lines on a publican. For a balanced impression of the seventeenth-century scene, even in its livelier aspects, it is as necessary to subdue the eminent, on whom ample biographical material is available, as to advance the lowly, whose names and circumstances can only be discovered after patient search through public and private archives. Some readers, however, may wish to have more precise information about the chief persons mentioned, so biographical details not essential to the text, yet of interest from the county point of view, have been dealt with as refreshments might be dealt with at a country fair. They have been put into a separate booth at the back, a Who 's Who, or buffet of personalities, at which each may call for what he pleases.

In glancing through these chapters before they are committed to print I am conscious of my inability to acknowledge adequately all the help, advice, and facilities for research I have enjoyed while collecting material from so many varied sources, both public and private. Debt, it has been said, is a grievous bondage to an honourable man. It cannot be so described in this instance, for the only restriction has been my ability to use the material offered, particularly at the Essex Record Office, which now has a collection of approximately 1,500,000 individual documents earlier than 1889. Much of what is new in this book has come from that source, or is based on a perusal of material found there, and it is a pleasure to record the continuous and invaluable help I have had from the county archivist, Mr. F. G. Emmison, F.S.A., F.R.Hist.S., F.R.G.S., and his senior assistant, Miss H. E. P. Grieve, B.E.M., B.A., both of whom, by their infectious enthusiasm no less than by their expert knowledge, are doing so much for historical research in Essex.

W. A.

LOUGHTON,
   *January* 1949.

# CONTENTS

The map on p. 266, illustrating the siege of Colchester, is reproduced by permission of John H. Burrow & Sons, the plate facing p. 45 by permission of the Royal Commission on Historical Monuments, the others by permission of the Essex County Records Committee, to whom the author and publishers acknowledge their indebtedness.

# ILLUSTRATIONS

## COLLOGRAVURE PLATES

## LINE ILLUSTRATIONS

## CHAPTER I

## 'HAVE WITH YOU TO SAFFRON WALDEN'

So much those hours have freed
To blow away for memory's seed.
ANDREW YOUNG.

ESSEX is a county of contrasts. There is little that can be said of Chelmsford that is true of Chingford, or of Barking that is true of Braintree. Thaxted and Saffron Walden are in a different world from Ilford and West Ham; Southend and Colchester can hardly know each other. It is not distance that divides them but time. They belong to different centuries, and the old afford the surest pleasure. When the Essex man in exile thinks of his native county it is the Roothings, the Lavers, the Easters, the Wealds, the Colnes, and the Theydons he recalls—villages that are grouped like families on wide plains or in secluded valleys. Though humble, they belong to an ancient lineage. London now pours its surplus population over the border by the hundred thousand; but the Essex of the windmills, the weather-boarded cottages, the flint churches with homely porches, wooden towers, and slender spires is still there. It is the same low breezy land with a vast sky, against which oaks and elms, rising singly from the tangled growth of roadside waste, stand clear and challenging. Its beauty is of a vagrant kind: blown and beaten by the weather, but clean and healthy. With its corn-fields and thousands of acres of open nurseries where flowers are grown for seed, its fields in summer are as gay as a gipsy's kerchief.

This simple beauty of the Essex that lies between long arterial roads came to me with unusual freshness one autumn afternoon. I was motoring through lanes in the north-west corner, thinking of nothing in particular. The sun was a red disk behind trees from which the leaves were beginning

I

to fall. It was one of those days when nature's house seems
empty. The summer, the best in living memory, had gone;
the autumn was not yet in possession. It was a time like
that between night and day, between sleeping and waking,
and perhaps between life and death. Strange fancies take
life at such times. The mind is uncommonly sensitive. As
my car ran forward it seemed to be the one thing moving in
a pausing world, and it was through time, not space, that
I travelled. I had, as it were, caught the watchman off
guard and recovered the lost centuries.

In the south-west of the county no one could indulge such
fancies for more than a few seconds. But I was travelling
towards Saffron Walden, so it was easy to believe that inside
the scattered cottages and farmhouses, many of them dating
from the time that Arthur Wilson of Felsted, steward to the
Earl of Warwick, referred to as 'the wearing out of that old,
but glorious, and most happy Piece of Sovereignty, the late
Queen,' still lived the spirit of the seventeenth century, the
period that in so many ways was the county's heyday.

Buildings are among the best means we have to bring the
past before us, and the thought of Essex in its most daring
and exultant age set my imagination playing about Audley
End, the glory of Saffron Walden, a house that has so many
proud and beguiling memories that one might tell its old
tales again by the hour. It was of Audley End that James I
said it was too much for a king but might do very well for
a lord treasurer. To-day, though reduced in size, the west
front is still in full view from the Newmarket road, a memorial
to pride and ambition, and also to much that was noble in
the age it symbolizes.

Audley End takes its name from Thomas, Lord Audley
of Walden, Henry VIII's lord chancellor. Like so many of
Henry's favourites, he was an ambitious man whose com-
pliance could be bought, and seldom can a sovereign have
found an officer of state more subservient. He sanctioned
Henry's divorce from Catherine of Aragon, tried Anne
Boleyn and was present at her execution, carried through
Parliament the Act for dissolving the marriage with Anne

of Cleves, and two years later passed judgment on Catherine Howard, who succeeded her as queen. This loyal and obedient servant now rests in Saffron Walden church in the tomb he caused to be prepared for himself. The abbey at Walden, its lands and manor, had been granted to him by Henry VIII in 1538. 'In the feast of Abbey lands,' wrote Fuller, 'king Henry the Eighth carved unto him the first cut (and that, I assure you, was a dainty morsel).'

On the second of Elizabeth's two visits to the lord chancellor's abbey at Audley End she was the guest of one of the town's most distinguished sons, Sir Thomas Smith, her secretary of state and the author of *De Republica Anglorum*. Another remarkable but much less prudent local character, Gabriel Harvey, was in attendance, and the satirist Nash, who had long pursued him with raillery, seized upon the occasion for another outburst. He described Harvey as 'hobby-horse-revelling-and-domineering when the Queen was at Audley End, to which place Gabriel (to doe his countrey more worship and glory) came ruffling it out, huffty-tuffty, in his suit of velvet.' There are so many unpleasant shades at Audley End that we are grateful for this glimpse of the pompous but not unfriendly don. Gabriel Harvey has been laughed at for his pedantry, but all the mockery of lesser men cannot rob him of Spenser's tribute:

> Haruey, the happy aboue happiest men
>   I read: that sitting like a Looker-on
> Of this worldes Stages, doest note with critique pen
>   The sharpe dislikes of each condition:
> And as one carelesse of suspition,
>   Ne fawnest for the fauer of the great:
> Ne fearest foolish reprehension
>   Of faulty men, which daunger to thee threat.

A few self-conscious airs and graces are not unamiable—they are certainly not unusual—in a don of high renown. Perhaps in his official capacity he did strut a little ridiculously on his college stage; but did he not produce an apple that became the delight of Cambridge? Does that not entitle him to the reverence of all well-disposed sons of Adam who seek knowledge? To us he is the distinguished son of a rope-maker of Saffron Walden, 'a right honest man of good reckoninge,' whose name we find in many of our church-wardens' accounts against items for new bell-ropes. He is also one of our worthies. It is foolish to belittle either him or his achievement. Apart from the acrimonious exchanges with Nash, his life was an enviable one. His last years were spent comfortably in his native town, where he died in 1630 at the age of eighty-one. It is true that he lacked genius; but then, men of genius are rarely to be envied. They are driven too hard by their demons to get much pleasure from life. The scholar of sound reputation, with talents that bring him respect and good fellowship, has the happier lot. He is at ease on Parnassus. Of such was Gabriel Harvey.

But there does seem to have been a ridiculous strain in the Harveys. Gabriel had a brother named Richard, who, in a pamphlet dated from his father's house at Walden 6th December 1582, prophesied that various fearful happenings would befall the land on 28th April 1583, at high noon. The prophecy was not fulfilled and Richard, who was a curate, became a figure of ridicule. Nash joined in the fun. Was it possible for so foolish a curate to outlive his disgrace, he asked, and replied: 'It is, deare brethren, *vivit, imo, vivit*— he lives, verily, he lives—and, which is more, he is a *vicar*.'

Gabriel, the don, and Richard, the curate, had a sister named Mercy, whom Virginia Woolf describes in her essay *The Strange Elizabethans*, 'milking in the fields near Saffron Walden accompanied by an old woman, when a man approached her and offered her cakes and malmsey wine.' He had come from the young Lord Surrey, who, while bowl-ing at Audley End, had seen a gust of wind carry off her hat, and being one for whom

> A sweet disorder in the dress
> Kindles in clothes a wantonness,

had been overcome by desire for her. With the cakes and malmsey wine his servant brought gloves, a silk girdle, and a posy ring.

The story of Mercy and this young man of fashion is preserved in letters written to Gabriel by the milkmaid herself. At first she resisted the advances, knowing Lord Surrey to be married. 'Good lord,' she says she exclaimed when first he paid her his compliments, 'that you should seek after so bare and country stuff abroad, that have so costly and courtly wares at home!' But Lord Surrey persisted, and finally persuaded her to meet him alone at midnight in the house of a neighbour. There she found him 'in his doublet and hose, his points untrust, and his shirt lying round about him,' hoping, apparently, that a slight disorder in his own dress would affect Mercy as the disorder in hers had affected him. His unseemly intentions were soon made plain; but Mercy escaped, leaving the thwarted young gallant to curse her for an ill-mannered jade.

All this was in 1574, and on Christmas Eve of that year Mercy was again under promise, which had indeed been forced from her at the previous engagement, to meet her lover. She rose early that day, and by six in the morning had tramped through snow and flood seven dreary miles to save her honour. Of the spirit and dignity of this little country maid we have simple and becoming evidence in a letter she addressed to the nobleman who knew so little of her quality: 'The thing you wot of, Milord,' she wrote, 'were a great trespass towards God, a great offence to the world, a great grief to my friends, a great shame to myself, and, as I think, a great dishonour to your lordship. I have heard my father say, Virginity is y^e fairest flower in a maid's garden, and chastity y^e richest dowry a poor wench can have. . . . Chastity, they say, is like unto time, which, being once lost, can no more be recovered.'

A week later, on New Year's Eve, Gabriel was riding back to Cambridge when he fell in with a countryman bearing a letter addressed to himself, but which, when opened, was found to contain a love-letter from Lord Surrey to 'Mine Own Sweet Mercy,' and with it an English noble carefully wrapped in paper. These he handed back to the countryman with instructions to deliver them to his sister and bid her 'to look ere she leap.' 'She may pick out the English of it herself,' he added as he rode away.

As soon as he reached Cambridge he wrote a long letter to Lord Surrey, informing him that his sister's station in life was that of a maid, 'diligent and trusty and tractable,' in the household of Lady Smith at Audley End, that she belonged to an honest and respectable family who would never, if they could prevent it, see her preening herself as a nobleman's mistress.

It is rare indeed to find three members of an Elizabethan tradesman's family so buoyant and amusing as the Harveys of Saffron Walden. And how well they explain each other! Behind them is the hard-working rope-maker, proud to have sent three sons to Cambridge and to have seen two of them elected fellows of their college; proud, too, of his pretty daughter, and sufficiently pleased with his own success to have his fire-place adorned with a carving of himself, busily working at his craft. Gabriel, for all his success at Cambridge, was never ashamed of his home, and preferred to have his sister an honest milkmaid rather than a rich man's plaything. Hard work was ingrained in all of them. Gabriel's faults were one with his virtues, and the rope-maker's shop explains both. He had none of the advantages of birth that enabled some of his contemporaries to play the fool and yet capture the prizes, and consequently when he succeeded in making his mark he was inclined to crow about it. He had every reason to be proud of his achievement. He was a self-made man, and why should we mock him if, like most self-made men, he did show signs of unskilled labour at times? As for Richard, were not his prophecies the unguarded expression of the high-flown ambition of the lowly born? Perhaps Mercy's toying with her noble lover was the same. Her brothers had brains; she had beauty; would it be very wicked to yield? She decided it would, and turned her pride towards virtue instead, phrasing her defence more grandly, perhaps, than the circumstances required.

After keeping company with these lesser shades we turn

to a gloomier figure lurking in the shadows of this stately house, which early in the seventeenth century replaced the lord chancellor's abbey. It is the shade of its builder, Thomas Howard, first Earl of Suffolk, who cannot be represented as other than an extremely unpleasant person, though Fuller, it is true, describes him kindly as 'an hearty old gentleman, who was a good friend to Cambridge,' of which he was chancellor. He was the son of the fourth Duke of Norfolk and Margaret Audley, the lord chancellor's daughter; a parentage that gave him special claims to the favour of James I. His father had lost his life for plotting in the cause of the king's mother, Mary Queen of Scots, whom he had even aspired to marry after the death of his third wife. So when James became king, the Howards were among the first to receive honours, and Thomas, then Lord Howard de Walden, was created Earl of Suffolk. The new earl had distinguished himself in opposing the Armada. He had been admiral of the third squadron in the Cadiz expedition. But he never captured the popular imagination as did his younger brother, Lord William Howard, the 'Belted Will' of Sir Walter Scott, who was, in fact, born at Audley End.

Of the actual building of the mansion we know little. It was intended to surpass in magnificence every private residence in the kingdom. The cost was enormous, and it took thirteen years to build. When completed in 1616 it appears to have been comparable with Knole or Hatfield in splendour. The building we see now is only the part that stood along three sides of an inner court. The original surrounded two rectangular courts, approached through an elaborate gateway with four round towers. Corridors supported by alabaster columns formed wings to it north and south, and if the domestic and other offices are included, the whole covered an area of nearly five acres.

Neither the earl nor his countess ever found happiness there. In completing the house they achieved their ambition; but they had employed the most shameless methods in raising the necessary money. The countess had traded her influence at court, using Sir John Bingley as a bargaining agent. The procedure had been that if a young man of means was known to have ambitions he was interviewed by Sir John, and if he was ready to pay for it the countess's favour was his. It had amounted to a sale of offices so flagrant that Bacon had called the countess 'an exchange woman who kept a shop, while her creature, Sir John Bingley, cried "What d' ye lack?"' The earl had employed his own methods. Greed and the increasing demands of extravagant ambitions had involved both in a network of falsity from which eventually they struggled in vain to extricate themselves. They also became involved in one of the most sensational crimes in history, the Overbury case.

Sir Thomas Overbury, a poet and wit of repute in his day, was the intimate friend of Robert Carr, the handsome page upon whom James I bestowed honours so indiscriminately. Carr, by this time Viscount Rochester, became infatuated with the Earl of Suffolk's daughter, the Countess of Essex, whose lack of modesty scandalized even the uncensorious court of James I. Overbury did his best to stop the affair, telling his friend in the frankest terms what he and all who knew her thought of the lady, and in doing so used a word to describe her which, though doubtless appropriate, was extremely offensive. Rochester repeated this to his countess and she, not unnaturally, at once determined to destroy the friendship between her lover and the critical Overbury. To accomplish this she drew into the plot the king himself, the one other person who was so attached to Rochester that he was jealous of Overbury. First, an easy escape from a threatened trap was offered to the unwanted friend in the form of an ambassadorial appointment. When this was refused, a trumpery charge was produced and Overbury sent to the Tower. Lady Essex then got the governor of the Tower removed and a friend, Sir Gervase Elwes, put in his place. There was little hope of escape for Overbury under those conditions. When Sir Henry Wotton heard what had happened he shook his head and surmised that the poet would 'return no more to this stage.' He was right. On 15th September 1613 Overbury died. Nobody at the time thought it worth while to inquire into the circumstances of his death, and two months later Rochester, who had now become Earl of Somerset, was married with solemn pomp and ceremony to the lady for whose passion his friend's life had been sacrificed.

For more than a year afterwards all went well with the Suffolks and the Somersets. The Earl of Suffolk became lord treasurer. Audley End was far on the way to completion. With his son-in-law apparently so secure in the king's favour no one dared to withhold from the new lord treasurer anything he demanded. But the king found that Somerset was now too frequently occupied with his wife to have much time for his sovereign, and another young man caught his eye. This was his cup-bearer, George Villiers, afterwards Duke of Buckingham, who came to live at Boreham, near Chelmsford, when riches had been heaped on him. The Suffolks and the Somersets soon discovered that there was a rival party in the field. Then officers of the Tower began to whisper their secrets. The many enemies of the lord treasurer and his daughter and son-in-law realized that the time had come for them to put their heads together, and the circumstances leading up to the arrest of Overbury were investigated. Somerset and his lady, on a warrant from Lord Chief Justice Coke, were arrested. The earl was actually seized while at supper with the king at Theobalds. He appealed, it is said, for royal protection. But James knew the limits of his power.

'Gude faith, maun!' he exclaimed, 'I canna help it, for if Coke send for me I maun gang to him as well as you.'

At the trial a horrible story of slow poisoning was brought to light. Overbury had been attended by a jailer, one 'well acquainted with the power of drugs,' and a Mrs. Turner, who had been employed by the Earl of Suffolk as a companion for his daughter and later had acted as confidante and adviser in the delicate stages of the love intrigue. The young countess was said to have learnt most of her

lessons in depravity from the wicked Mrs. Turner, but with
such parents she was probably an apt pupil.   In the course
of the trial it was revealed that Mrs. Turner had been in the
habit of buying poisons from an apothecary named Franklin,
and that these had been served to the prisoner by his
warder in tempting dishes of food.   The four accomplices,
Elwes, the warder, the apothecary, and Mrs. Turner, were
all hanged.   Somerset and his wife were imprisoned for a
short time; but their lives were spared.   And in May 1616,
the year the house was completed, we read that 'the Lord
Treasurer and his Lady have gone to Audley End for shame
at the arraignment of their daughter and son-in-law.'

An amusing if irrelevant element was introduced into this
sordid story at the most solemn stage in the proceedings.
This shocking woman, Mrs. Turner, as Sir Walter Scott tells
us in *The Fortunes of Nigel*, brought into England a French
custom of using yellow starch, to which the lord chief
justice took strong exception.   So, in pronouncing judgment upon her, after telling her that she had been guilty of
the seven deadly sins, he accused her in solemn tones of this
additional guilt of yellow starch, and ordered that she should
be hanged in yellow starched cuffs and ruff, the which he
hoped she would be the last to wear.   Accordingly, when
the hour of her execution arrived, Mrs. Turner appeared at
the scaffold with her face rouged as for a festive occasion,
a ruff upon her neck and cuffs upon her wrists, stiffened to
perfection with the brightest yellow starch.

The lady who played the principal part in this melodrama,
the Earl of Suffolk's daughter, had been married to the
Earl of Essex, son of Elizabeth's favourite and himself
eminent later as commander of the Parliamentary army,
when she was thirteen.   The Earl of Suffolk's son and heir
took a younger bride, and a curious document connected
with this wedding is still preserved in the Audley End
archives.   It is the deed by which the Earl of Suffolk and
the Earl of Dunbar, who was lord treasurer of Scotland,
contracted terms for the marriage of Theophilus, afterwards
second Earl of Suffolk, with Elizabeth, the Earl of Dunbar's

youngest daughter, when the latter was only six years old. She was married at eleven.

With the reversal of fortunes that followed the disclosures of the Overbury case, inquiries began to be made into the Earl of Suffolk's conduct as lord treasurer. In 1618 he was charged with having embezzled sums of money received from the Dutch for the Cautionary Towns, and in the following year was imprisoned and fined £30,000. James, however, was still sufficiently friendly to get the figure reduced to £7,000 when the earl pleaded that he could not pay the sum demanded. The remainder of his life was spent under the burden of increasing debts. He died in 1626, and after his death the countess was obliged to hide from creditors. The second earl, who as a youth had figured prominently in all the tilts and tourneys of the court, held for many years the office of captain of the Band of Gentlemen Pensioners. In old age he became a pitiful figure, a sick man complaining bitterly about his poverty, until in 1640 he died, leaving a twenty-year-old son to succeed him in this unhappy earldom. The third earl lived quietly at Audley End, taking little part in national affairs during the civil wars, though he came under suspicion in 1647 and was imprisoned for a short time. At the Restoration this seems to have counted in his favour, for he was made lord-lieutenant of Essex and Cambridge, and in 1665 a gentleman of the bedchamber.

It is curious that although Audley End was completed in 1616 we have no description of it earlier than Evelyn's of 1654. He came to it from Cambridge, and saw the west front from the road, as we see it to-day, near enough to be distinct and distant enough to be in good perspective, with the Cam flowing through the park below it. He pronounced it a 'goodly palace,' and on closer view found it 'a mixt fabrick, between antique and modern, but observable for its being compleatly finished.' It was, he says, 'one of the stateliest palaces of the kingdom.' The gallery, in particular, he admired. He thought it the 'most cheerful, and . . . one of the best in England.' The rest he found answerable. The gardens, which he judged as an authority, he did not find in perfect order, though the park was 'nobly-well walled, wooded, and watered.' He noted, in particular, that there was a bowling alley, a popular feature of the day.

Pepys visited Audley End five years later. He was most impressed by the ceilings and chimney-pieces, which, along with the richly carved screen in the great hall, are still much admired features. In the cellars he drank the king's health and played on his flageolet, the vaulted cellars providing an excellent echo. The pictures, too, won from him a note of approval on this first visit. The next time he was there, on 7th October 1667, the house did not seem so fine as he had thought it eight years earlier, and he noted in particular that the ceilings were 'not so good as I always took them to be, being nothing so well wrought as my Lord Chancellor's are.' This is an interesting note, because between those two visits ornamental plaster-work had been at the height of its vogue, much of it the work of continental craftsmen who had come to England at the Restoration. It was not so novel to Pepys in 1667 as when he saw it in 1659. The staircase also he criticized. He thought it poor. And here again we have a sidelight on building development at the time. The Audley End staircase had been built just before imposing staircases came into fashion, though we find them at Hatfield and Blickling. Much of the furnishing seemed to him indifferent on this 1667 visit, and we might think him in a bad mood if it were not for his assurance that he was 'mighty merry,' and the delight he again found in the cellars, where 'my wife and I did sing to my great content. And then to the garden, and there eat many grapes, and took some with us: and so away thence exceeding well satisfied.'

These visits of Pepys to Audley End give us particular pleasure when we reflect that it was from there that the *Diary* went out into a delighted world in 1825 under the editorship of the third Lord Braybrooke. Pepys's library was bequeathed to Magdalene College, Cambridge, which had been refounded by Thomas, Lord Audley, and has been associated with Audley End ever since. Successive owners have the right to appoint its master, and that office was held by Lord Braybrooke's brother at the time the *Diary* was decipered by the Rev. John Smith and prepared for publication by his lordship.

Another significant entry in the *Diary* referring to Audley End appears against the date 7th March 1666. It informs us that 'The King and Duke are to go to-morrow to Audly End, in order to the seeing and buying of it of my Lord Suffolke.' They travelled, we learn, with 'a fine train of gentlemen,' so we can imagine the excitement they would cause in the neighbourhood. They were given a civic reception and the corporation presented the king with a silver cup filled with saffron, which cost them £20. Several years, however, passed before the house was conveyed to the Crown in a deed which declared 'that the King, upon his own personal view and judgment, had taken liking to the mansion called Audley End, with the park, out-houses, court-yards, orchards, gardens, stables, water-mills, and appurtenances, as a seat fit for His Majesty's residence; the ancient houses of the Crown having been in a great measure destroyed and demolished during the late times of usurpation, and therefore thought fit to purchase at the price of £50,000.' This purchase price, though not much more than a quarter of the original cost of the mansion, was never fully paid, and the Earl of Suffolk remained in possession of practically the whole of the estate. The arrangement probably pleased the earl well enough, because it shifted the enormous expenses of maintaining the house on to the royal purse, and gave him the £30,000 paid down when the conveyance was executed on 8th May 1669. It pleased the king no less, according to report, because it gave him a convenient place for the queen to be left in while he and his courtiers went on to the unrestrained pleasures of Newmarket, where other ladies awaited them. But Charles had, of course, his more honourable occasions there, and it is recorded that while in residence at the palace with his queen and court in 1668 he attended service in Walden church on 11th October.

There is an old story told in Saffron Walden of Queen Catherine of Braganza and her ladies going to Walden Fair disguised as country lasses and buying their fairings of yellow stockings and long gloves stitched with blue at one of the booths. Their foreign speech, it is said, betrayed them, and the country folk crowded round so rudely that they were obliged to retire. This was probably in 1670, and may have been the first time she visited the town. That year we find entries in the churchwardens' account books for money paid to the ringers when the queen came to town on market day.

When the place was returned to the fifth earl by William III in 1701 it was on condition that he waived his claim to the £20,000 still unpaid. The furnishings of the house, however, had not remained untouched. Tapestries valued at £4,500 had been removed and hung at Windsor, which by that time had been restored and had become the principal country palace of the king. But it is unlikely that the splendid mansion had ever been furnished and appointed in keeping with its grandeur as a building. None of the owners had been able to afford it. Sooner or later part of it had to be dismantled, and this process of reduction to manageable size began in 1721, when by the advice of Sir John Vanbrugh the kitchens, chapel, and the whole of the outer court were demolished. Further demolition was carried out about the middle of the century. Even the gallery that every one had admired so much was sacrificed. But in the second half of the eighteenth century this process of destruction was arrested by the Lord Howard de Walden who succeeded in 1762. At great cost he repaired and restored what was left. His successors, the Lords Braybrooke, descended in the female line from the third Earl of Suffolk, preserved and improved it with devoted care. But the social changes of the present century made even this smaller Audley End too large for its noble owner's use, and in 1948 it was bought by the Ministry of Works to be maintained as a national monument. Its glories recede. As the minds of old people turn to the memories of their youth, Audley End seems now to belong again to the pride and folly of the age that raised it. Nor is it alone in this. The pride of Audley End was matched, though not equalled, elsewhere in the county in the seventeenth century. No other age has left such lively memories.

## CHAPTER II

## A SCOT OUR KING!

A Scot our King!   That day
   Our cripple state will need a crutch.
What next?   In time a Scot will prate
   As primate of our Church.

OLD RHYME.

THE arrival of a Scots king after the long and glorious reign of Elizabeth could not be other than disturbing, and as much of his time was spent hunting in the Essex forests, either from Theobalds, the mansion he took from Cecil in exchange for the old palace at Hatfield, or from various country houses, Essex men were well aware of his presence. The Earl of Suffolk was not the only one to benefit from the change.   The air of the south—or some other beneficent force—so wrought upon the king's northern constitution that he produced new knights with alarming rapidity, advanced knights to baronies and barons to earldoms with equal enthusiasm, until men of weak memory were sadly confused on meeting an acquaintance to know how they should address him.   In 1611 he surpassed himself by creating an entirely new order of baronets.

Every one was kept on tiptoe, even to Cecil himself, who personally had secured the accession, and was therefore more favourably placed than any of his rivals, though it is true that his father, Elizabeth's Burghley, had been responsible for the execution of Mary Queen of Scots.   James was entertained at Theobalds at the end of his triumphal journey south, and was received with a brave display of loyalty. A hundred and forty men, dressed in blue liveries, came from the estates of Sir Edward Denny at Waltham Abbey, and the tribute was acknowledged the following year when Sir Edward was raised to the peerage.   Cecil received a barony at the accession, became Viscount Cranborne in

16

1604, and the following year Earl of Salisbury. Like the Earl of Suffolk he built his great house, and like him again he died a poor man. To Sir John Harington he wrote feelingly: ''Tis a great task to prove one's honesty and yet not spoil one's fortune. You have tasted a little hereof in our blessed queen's time, who was more than a man, and, in troth, sometimes less than a woman. I wish I waited now in her presence-chamber, with ease at my food and rest in my bed. I am pushed from the shore of comfort, and know not where the winds and waves of a Court will bear me; I know it bringeth little comfort on earth; and he is, I reckon, no wise man that looketh this way to heaven.'

Naturally the Scots fared better than the English in the new distribution of honours, and many of them, puffed up by the more bountiful fare served on English tables, developed, it is to be feared, the 'unco guid conceit o' themselves' that normally characterizes the Scot in his dealings with the Sassenach. Arthur Wilson, the worthy chronicler whose better acquaintance we shall make presently, tells us how sick the English were to see the Scots who came south in their blue bonnets strutting about in costly beavers, but it was left to a chaplain, who travelled in the king's retinue on one of the royal visits to Scotland, to express this feeling most delicately.

'First for their countrye,' he wrote, in a letter preserved at the Essex Record Office, 'I must confesse tis to good for those that inhabite yt and to bad for others to be at charges to conquer yt, the ayre might be houlsome but for the stinking people that live in yt, and the ground might be made fruitfull yf they had the wytt to manage yt, their beastes generally are small (weomen excepted) of which sorte there are not greater in the world. . . .'

He wondered 'that so brave a prince as Kinge James should be borne in so stinking a Towne as Eddenboroughe in lowsey Scotland.'

The honeycomb that another man eats never agrees with the stomach. Wilson slyly records that these new neighbours not only crept into English lordships but also into the beds of English ladies, provoking the just wrath of their rivals.

But the Scots were seldom rich, and James needed money. The advantages of the new knighthoods and peerages were usually reciprocal. James saw to that. Sometimes money changed hands; sometimes other services were performed or promised. In Essex, those in a position to offer the king good hunting were well placed for his favour. Francis Barrington, for example, who was knighted at Theobalds in 1603, received a baronetcy at once when that order was created in 1611. His family, who had long been settled at Hatfield Regis, or Broad Oak, had been woodwards of Hatfield Forest from the time of Ethelred the Unready until the office was abolished in the twenty-seventh year of Elizabeth's reign. Henry Maynard of Easton Lodge was another Essex landowner knighted at Theobalds in 1603. As he died in 1610 he could not receive a baronetcy, but his eldest son, William, was in the first list, and in 1620 became a baron. Sir John Petre, whose father had received more favours than most at the Dissolution, became Baron Petre of Writtle in 1603. On the whole, Essex families did well out of James, though some of them must have found their new honours expensive.

In the remarkable archives of the Barrington family, who had figured prominently in Essex life for more than six hundred years when the last Sir Francis Barrington died in 1836, there is a letter to Mr. Francis Barrington, apparently from his tailor, advising him how to dress when he went to Theobalds to offer his loyal service to the new king. After acknowledging the receipt of £20 conveyed by Lord Rich, his friend and neighbour, the letter proceeds: 'I have inquired concerning the manner of meeting the King, which is generally thought to be in black, without all cuttings; plain, which divers worshipful men of good quality have prepared for, some in black satin and some in velvet and other some in black stuff—furthermore for the coronation, for those which are in their robes have foot-cloths, and many others of good account have foot-cloths also, and

Audley End

Saffron Walden

some in rich sables also. Much white satin, and ash colour and suchlike colours, with much embroidering is prepared against the coronation also. Embroidering is now very dear. Also much gold lace is worn, which in my opinion is cheap and better. There is of divers sorts some trimmed with small gold lace and some broad. In my opinion of either side the panels with a cut in the middle is best. Nevertheless I would desire your worship send me how you would have it also. I have inquired concerning cloaks and can hear but of one rich cloak which is worn, but the most part be of black velvet or grogram or cloth, some with lace, some with borders, and most of them lined with rich stuffs, as cloth of gold and silver, and other with taffeta.' The spelling and punctuation have been modernized in this quotation, but the original form can be found by scholars in the *Transactions of the Essex Archaeological Society*, the 1884 volume. After one or two personal notes, the letter concludes by committing the worshipful Mr. Barrington to the protection of the Almighty and is signed 'Edward Shaw.'

Fine feathers may or may not make fine birds, but it is clear that the fine birds of Tudor and Stuart England wore fine feathers. There was no very marked sartorial development in James's reign. There was, if anything, a slight decline. The growth of the Puritan spirit was not conducive to display; and apart from dress, the new king, whose manners were by no means elegant, could not be expected to inspire so brilliant a court as had lately revolved round the ageing Gloriana. For all that, it could still be said of the Jacobean gentleman that

> His ruffe is set, his head set in his ruffe;
> His reverend trunks become him well enough.

He had none of the suavity of manner, assisted by the soft lace and velvet breeches, of the Restoration buck. James liked plenty of padding about his clothes because he was always afraid of the assassin's knife; but padding absorbed dust and was apt to get lumpy. Elegance came with Charles, if Van Dyck is to be trusted. The padding was then taken out, the whalebone thrown aside, the linen was soft and was allowed to show through the outer garments, the hair fell in locks about the shoulders, curled at the forehead, and hung in a pointed beard from the chin.   The scene at Theobalds would be of a sobered Elizabethan rather than of a Stuart character.

The new queen did not come to England with her husband. She was ill at the time of his accession.   But she followed as soon as she was able to travel, and at the border she was greeted by a number of English ladies who had gone north to escort her to London.   Among them was Penelope, Lady Rich, daughter of the first Earl of Essex and sister of Elizabeth's favourite.   She was the Stella of Sidney's sonnets. By this time she had deserted her husband, Lord Rich (of Leighs Priory, near Chelmsford, who in 1618 was created Earl of Warwick), for Lord Mountjoy, whom she took as her lover after Sidney's death.   Lady Anne Clifford recorded in her diary that the new queen vexed the great but elderly ladies of Elizabeth's court, who had travelled north at great risk to their health, by favouring 'my Lady Rich and such-like company.'   In view of that lady's character the feelings of respectable dowagers can easily be imagined.   Lady Rich, however, was already established in the queen's favour when the party reached London.   She was made a lady of the bedchamber, and in the late summer of 1603 James conferred on her 'the place and the rank of the ancientest Earl of Essex, called Bouchier,' to whom her father was heir. She therefore took precedence at court of all the baronesses in the kingdom.

The character of this fascinating but scandalous lady is a problem.   It is also of great importance in Essex history, because she was the mother of the second and greatest Earl of Warwick.   That she was brilliant is certain.   She had an extraordinary hold on men of letters.   Sidney's love has immortalized her.   After his death there was Mountjoy, and he also was a scholar.   She was one of the five ladies to whom Florio dedicated his translation of Montaigne's *Essays*, and in doing so he described her as 'one of those whose

magnanimity and magnificent frank nature have so be-
dewed my earth when it was sunburnt, so gently thawed
it when it was frost-bound, that I were even more senseless
than earth, if I returned not some fruit in good measure.'

Mountjoy basked with her in the sunshine of royal favour.
He was created Earl of Devonshire and Master of the
Ordnance of the Realm in the same auspicious year, 1603.
The following year he became keeper of Portsmouth Castle.
In 1605 Lord Rich divorced Penelope, and she and her lover
were free to marry. Though the canon law did not countenance such a marriage, it took place at the earl's house at
Wanstead, where Elizabeth's Leicester had married Lettice
Knollys in 1578, and the officiating clergyman was Laud
himself. It is not an event that the Church likes to remember. Laud, it must be said at once, was private
chaplain to the earl, and was persuaded to perform the
ceremony against his will. He did penance for it to the end
of his life, and always kept the anniversary of the wedding
as a solemn fast.

The sequel was both farcical and tragic. The king, who
had smiled on the lovers when they were living together
unmarried, now stormed at them for having broken a law
of his Church. He turned them out of his court and did
all he could to make them miserable. For a year after the
wedding they kept 'a sad house together' at Wanstead, and
in 1606 the earl died, a broken man, though not quite
forty-four. Penelope survived him only a few months. At
her death she was forty-five.

In 1616 Lord Rich, after offering his hand to several ladies
unsuccessfully, persuaded a rich widow in Lincolnshire, Lady
Saint-Paul, to marry him. The following year we find John
Chamberlain, in one of his letters, writing: 'Lord Rich is
said to be in great perplexity, or rather crazed in brain, to
see himself over-reached by his wife, who hath so conveyed
her estate that he is little or nothing the better by her, and,
if she outlive him, like to carry away a great part of his.'
This unhappy man was never equal to the part he was
expected to play in life. Captain Walter Devereux, in his

B

*Lives of the Devereux Earls of Essex*, describes him as 'rough and uncourtly in manners and conversation, dull and un-educated, proper in nothing but his wealth.' How could this man be expected to win the heart of Sidney's Stella? She was compelled to marry him simply because he was 'proper' in his wealth. She and Sidney were already lovers, but Sidney, though 'proper' in everything else, had no money. So far it was not an unusual story. Nor was it unusual for those who married where they did not love to love where they did not marry. The unusual features were the divorce and re-marriage, which, in the king's eyes, placed the deserted Lord Rich in the position of an outrageously wronged man. And so, after a while, and at the cost of £8,000, our clumsy Lord Rich was created Earl of Warwick, and took his place in a line with Beauchamps, Nevilles, and Dudleys. It was a topsy-turvy world.

In the November of 1605 James had more than a favourite's wedding to upset him. Thirty-six barrels of gunpowder were placed in readiness to blow up both him and his Parliament, and Essex was again in the picture. It was Lord Monteagle of Great Hallingbury Hall who received the warning letter that led to the discovery of the plot, and who, with his neighbour the Earl of Suffolk, then lord chamberlain, examined the cellars and found there the enormous piles of faggots. James, who was always nervy, was more wary than ever after that. He became less generous with his honours for a time, and put up the price.

James was a curious mixture of parsimony and generosity. One day he was at Whitehall with Sir Henry Rich, second son of Lord Rich and Penelope, and James Maxwell, a lord of the bedchamber, when porters passed by carrying £3,000 for the privy purse. Sir Henry whispered to Maxwell that he wished he had so much money. James heard the whisper.

'What says he? What says he?' he asked.

Maxwell told him.

'Marry shalt thou, Harry,' he said, and afterwards com-manded the porters to carry the money to Rich's lodging, accompanied by a note stating that His Majesty had far more pleasure in giving this money to his dear Harry, than Harry could have in receiving it.

This was in 1614, when Rich was a young man of twenty-four, with no special claims to the king's favour, except, perhaps, his youth and good looks. The king's weakness for young men is well known. It is made obvious in the career of Robert Carr, Earl of Somerset, and that of George Villiers, who displaced him as the king's prime favourite, and who bought Henry VIII's Beaulieu, or New Hall, Boreham, from the Earl of Sussex in 1620 for £30,000. There was no more astonishing rise to fortune under James than Villiers's, and to account for it there was only his handsome person, his elegant bearing and sprightly conversation. In addition to heaping honours on the handsome head of his beloved 'Steenie,' as Villiers was called by his sovereign, James bestowed honours wholesale on his family and friends, and allowed his mother to exercise an almost incredible amount of power. Villiers, from being a page in the royal household, became Viscount Villiers in 1616, Earl of Buckingham in 1617, Marquess of Buckingham in 1618, and Duke of Buckingham in 1623. After accomplishing the downfall of the Suffolks of Audley End he became the most eminent figure in Essex, as indeed at the court itself, when he settled at Boreham. His banquets were unsurpassed in sumptuous entertainment, and his equipage when he travelled along the London to Chelmsford road was the marvel of the day to the simple Essex country folk. Coaches had been introduced into England in 1580. They were usually drawn by two horses. But the coach in which Buckingham crossed Essex was always drawn by six horses. At the height of his power he was virtually ruler of England.

Unlike Carr, Villiers was able to survive marriage, even though it was to the Roman Catholic Lady Katherine Manners. Gondomar, in fact, the Spanish ambassador, nearly succeeded in persuading Buckingham to declare himself a Roman Catholic, and it is said that Laud, who was an Essex country parson—rector of West Tilbury from 1609 to 1616—was called in and had to exercise all his tact and eloquence to hold the king's favourite in the Church of which the king was head. But the most foolish and distressing part of the business was that the king's dotage on his favourite was equalled by the favourite's dotage on his mother, so that the Spanish ambassador, in his dispatches home, was able to write facetiously that England was never more favourably disposed for conversion to Roman Catholicism, because more prayers and oblations were offered here to the Mother than to the Son.

It is even possible that the confidence James had in this renowned pair hastened his death, and that through the agency of an Essex doctor. Both the countess—the mother was created Countess of Buckingham in 1618—and the son, dabbled in medical quackery, and when, near the end of his life, the king complained that he felt indisposed, the countess gave him something from her medicine cupboard, and also laid a plaster on his side. James complained that these seemed to have aggravated rather than dispersed his trouble; but the duke assured him that they were approved remedies, supplied by a worthy physician, one Dr. Remington of Dunmow, who had often used them to cure agues and similar distempers. There was great consternation at court about the duke and his mother interfering in so delicate a matter as the medical treatment of the king; but their power was so great that no one could stop them. Three years after the king's death Buckingham was, however, stopped very effectively. He was killed at Portsmouth by an assassin's knife.

So besides the Earl of Suffolk at Audley End, three of the most dazzling figures of the day, Carr, Mountjoy, and Villiers, or, as they became, Somerset, Devonshire, and Buckingham, unrivalled examples of royal favour, and objects of envy, malice, and all uncharitableness to their enemies, disported themselves in the great houses of Essex when their stars were most propitious. They brighten the scene with their insolent splendour; but then as always the real strength of the country was in the men of moderate

standing, whose influence depended more on their own
endeavours than on princes' favours. It was the Barringtons, the Everards, the Mashams, the Maynards, and the
Mildmays, with families of similar rank, who determined
the social and political character of the county. They rarely
became national figures, and only when we study county
and local history do we see how important they were indi-
vidually, and by seeing them multiplied throughout the
land appreciate their value collectively. *Mediocria firma*,
moderate things are most lasting, was the motto of Sir
Nicholas Bacon, and Fuller, in collecting material for his
*Worthies*, came to the same conclusion. Many of the houses
built by the most ambitious, as we saw with Audley End,
were soon beyond the means of either their builders or the
immediate successors of their builders, whereas the houses
built by the moderate men remained occupied, comfortable,
and the homes of honest English families down to the social
revolution of the present century.

The lives of these worthy gentlemen are seldom written.
We find references to them in the records of quarter sessions,
for most of them were magistrates. They conducted the
affairs of their county quietly, and looked for little reward
except the goodwill of their neighbours. The most exciting
public events in their lives were elections, and we are fortunate in having some revealing sidelights on the one for the
first Parliament of the new king.

James, in the first year of his reign, issued a proclamation
forbidding canvassing for votes, which he called 'factious
laboring for the places of knights or burgesses.' But in
spite of this the gentlemen of Essex contrived to make their
elections exciting affairs. The candidates for the two county
seats on this occasion were Sir Francis Barrington, Sir
Gamaliel Capel, and Sir Edward Denny. The court was
behind Sir Edward, which meant that he had the influential
support of the Earl of Suffolk and his toadies, and of many
others who looked to the new king for favours. Sir Francis
had the support of Lord Rich, who did not scruple to call
upon most of the old-established families in the county on

behalf of his 'Cousin Barrington.' Sir Gamaliel, it appears, was not very strongly supported.

One of the most important factors in an election under the old system was the control of the inns in the principal town of the constituency. Any reader of *Pickwick Papers* knows how vital this was in English political life right up to the days of the ballot box. It was probably far more important in Chelmsford than in 'Eatanswill,' which was Sudbury, because the Chelmsford of the seventeenth century was famous for its inns. It was on the main road to the Low Countries, just a comfortable journey of thirty miles from London. The Mildmays controlled it, and Sir Thomas Mildmay could not be persuaded to state publicly which of the candidates he was supporting. This was too delicate a matter to be entrusted to the blustering Lord Rich, so Sir Francis decided to call upon Sir Thomas himself. When the two were together, each regarding the other suspiciously, Sir Francis came to the point by saying that he had heard that Sir Thomas was for Sir Edward Denny and had bespoken most of the inns on his behalf. Sir Thomas promptly replied that he was under no obligation to say which of the candidates he intended to support, that he would be neither led nor driven for any man's pleasure, but would give his voice according to his own liking, indifferent as to whether he should please or offend by so doing. And as to the rumour that he had taken inns in the town, it was true. But who, might he ask, had more right than he to engage inns in his own town? If he were asked on whose behalf he had taken them, he must reply that that was his own business.

Sir Francis had no difficulty in drawing conclusions from this. It was clear enough that Sir Thomas was against him. But the Mildmay control of Chelmsford was not complete. In those days of slow travelling several of the inns were associated by patronage with old Essex families who lived in the north or north-east of the county, and spent a night in Chelmsford when they travelled to or from London. So Lord Rich, on his 'Cousin Barrington's' behalf, was able to secure the New Inn and the 'Dolphin.' He tried to get the 'Lion,' but failed.

Lord Rich was in his element at an election. He was a far better man at canvassing the bailiffs of Colchester, and his cronies at Maldon and Chelmsford markets, on behalf of the worthy Sir Francis, than he was at wooing a lady who had already been won by a poet. We have seen Lord Rich looking rather ridiculous in more exalted circles, so it is good to have a glimpse of him in his own sphere. He worked hard and successfully. Lord Darcy of St. Osyth's Abbey assured him that most of the eastern hundreds of the county were safe for Sir Francis. But that was not the quarter where opposition was to be feared. The Denny lands were at Waltham Abbey in the south-west, and the Earl of Suffolk was in the north-west. The enemy was strong in the west, and the fight would probably be hard. Lord Rich went over to Saffron Walden, into the very camp of the arch-enemy, and boldly canvassed for votes. The earl was furious. He wrote to all his tenants at Audley End and to the townspeople of Saffron Walden saying that he understood they had been 'labored unto' to support Sir Francis Barrington, and pompously expressed indignant surprise that any one should solicit the support of his people without consulting him first, and that his servants, tenants, and townsmen should offer their support without knowing his pleasure. He made it clear that he expected them to give their 'free'—that was his word for it!—consents and voices to his good friend, Sir Edward Denny, and that if they did not pay regard to his wishes he would make the proudest of them repent it.

So much for the 'free' people of Saffron Walden. But the earl did better than that. He had a letter sent from the lords of the council to the high sheriff and justices of the peace of Essex expressing the king's displeasure and their own that the order forbidding 'factious laboring' for votes had been disobeyed. Nowhere in England, they declared, had His Majesty's wishes been so flagrantly disregarded as in Essex, and they asked that the royal displeasure should

be made known.   It was the duty of the sheriff and justices
to see that the people proceeded to a 'free election.'

After receiving this letter the justices loyally met at
Chelmsford, and, being good Englishmen, composed a letter
to be sent to all three candidates, which they hoped would
bring about 'a good concord amongst the gentlemen' and
restore the county to peace.   They suggested, first, that Sir
Gamaliel Capel should withdraw from the contest, leaving
Sir Francis Barrington and Sir Edward Denny in the field
for the two places, and secondly, that those two should meet
before the election and cast lots for precedence.   By this
means Sir Gamaliel would show himself a good patriot, and
fortune would decide between the other two without either
losing honour.   In short, they proposed that like true-born
British sportsmen the favourites should toss for the honours.

Sir Gamaliel agreed.   The other two seemed willing; but
Lord Rich was against it.   He wrote at once to Sir Francis
informing him that on the previous day he had received a
letter from the sheriff, together with a copy of the letter
sent out by the lords of the council.   Were they to agree
to such terms? he asked.   Not if they were of his mind.
Sir Edward Denny was welcome to such faint-hearts as
were frightened by such a move as this.   The letter was
nothing but a confession of weakness, and for his part he
would have been ashamed if his 'Cousin Barrington' had
adopted such a course.   He was still firmly behind Sir
Francis.   'I am,' he concluded with a flourish, 'and will be
firm unto him as the skin of his back, and will never while
I breathe fail my friend of my promise . . . let them be
ashamed that deserve shame.'

Lord Rich was evidently a bonny fighter; but it is doubtful
whether Sir Francis at this stage found his enthusiasm
helpful or embarrassing.

In the meantime the sheriff, Sir Henry Maynard of Little
Easton, pleased with Sir Gamaliel's courteous withdrawal,
invited his good friends, Sir Edward and Sir Francis, to dine
with him the following Sunday and decide in a friendly
manner which should be first.   Both accepted, and thus

Chelmsford in 1591, reproduced from a map of the Manor of
Bishop's Hall, drawn for Sir Thomas Mildmay by John Walker,
' architector ', the most notable of early Essex map makers

High Street, Chelmsford

this very English election, that had begun with so much bold display of force, ended in a quiet little dinner party in the traditional English spirit of honourable compromise.

These two gentlemen, Sir Edward Denny and Sir Francis Barrington, continued to serve their country loyally to the end of their lives. Sir Edward was elevated to the peerage shortly after his election, and in 1626 became the first and only Earl of Norwich of the first creation. Sir Francis Barrington sat in every Parliament of James I and the first three of Charles I. After this long service he opposed the loan which Charles I tried to impose in 1626, and with his son-in-law, Sir William Masham of High Laver, was imprisoned in the Marshalsea. Throughout his imprisonment Lady Barrington, an able and strong-minded woman, stayed with him. It must have been a sad and humiliating experience for one who had served his country so long. His health was so seriously affected by the close confinement that appeals were made for his release. Sir Francis himself wrote to both the king and the lords of the council. With his letter to the lords he enclosed a doctor's certificate reporting his appetite gone, his flesh wasted, and his body weakened by colds caught in the close air of the prison. He was released, but died in 1628 and was buried at Hatfield Broad Oak.

CHAPTER III

## OF GOOD ESTATE

Full many persons of right worthy parts.
Both for report of spotless honesty
And for profession of all learned arts.

SPENSER.

WHAT is left of the old home of the Barringtons is now Little
Barrington Hall, a substantial farmhouse on the eastern edge
of Hatfield Forest. Like most houses of families with roots
in the Middle Ages it was always smaller than those of Tudor
and Stuart favourites. Many of these fine old houses,
which are so much more English than the magnificent places
built later, are now in use as farmhouses. The renewal of
English life and character has always come from sound,
country-bred stocks. If it came from any other source it
would not be true to the English spirit. We are apt to
forget that even our mercantile prosperity was built up in
the seventeenth century by the younger sons of the landed
gentry. Families were large then, and trade was expanding.
The younger sons, especially from the Home Counties, went
into the newly established trading houses, and it might have
been better for both trade and society if the association had
been maintained. But the gentry, unfortunately, withdrew
when they saw that industry was a field that was free for all.

Family pride developed rapidly in the seventeenth century. New homes were built and the old abandoned.
Nowhere can we see better evidence of this rising ambition
than in the church monuments of the period. They were expected to be in accordance with the degree and quality of
the departed. Weever, in *Funerall Monuments*, published
in 1631, says it is expected 'that by the tomb every one
might be discerned of what rank he was living; for monuments answerable to men's births, states, and places, have

always been allowed, and stately sepulchres for base fellows have always lien open to bitter jests.' The Puritans regarded these tombs as products of vanity. They thought the money spent on them should have been used to build churches; but if we may judge by the number that commemorate divines, many learned and devout clerics did not agree!

In spite of the Puritans, these monuments in churches increased in cost and magnificence until well into the next century. Of our Essex memorials, the most elaborate is the great Maynard monument at Little Easton, with the second Lord Maynard in the centre, elegantly leaning upon a marble urn, with busts of his kinsmen arranged round his feet like hats in a milliner's shop window. He was Comptroller of the Household to Charles II, who esteemed him highly. But when James II succeeded, and declared his resolve to have what he called 'the test and sanguinary laws' against Roman Catholics repealed, Lord Maynard dissented. His conscience, he said, would not allow him to consent to the changing of a law made to protect the faith he professed.

'There is no matter of conscience in it,' replied the king.

'No, sir,' asked Maynard boldly, 'is not conscience concerned in defence of religion? I pray, if the test alone be gone, what hinders but you may bring whom you please, and as many as you think fit, into the House of Lords? And so, having the majority, you may make what laws you please, even against the religion established.'

James did not reply, but he bade his lordship think better and speak with him again. Lord Maynard stood firm, with the result that his staff of office was taken from him and given to Lord Waldegrave, who had married the king's natural daughter, Henrietta, the previous year.

This second Lord Maynard died in 1698, and when his will was read it was found to contain the quaint bequest of £4,000 to be devoted in part to 'the marrying of poor virgins . . . as the Vicar, Churchwardens, and Overseers of the Poor of Thaxted shall agree upon and think fit.'

Another magnificent memorial in the same chapel has the

first Lord Maynard, dressed like a Roman commander, with his second wife beside him in the guise of a Roman matron, a common but in this case regrettable conceit, because the second Lady Maynard was such an estimable English lady. She was an Everard of Langleys, Great Waltham, and in a letter, preserved in the Carew Transcripts in the Public Record Office, explaining the cause of her husband's death, she used a phrase that a poet could not have bettered. She described the trouble her husband had had in curbing the 'barbarous soldiers,' who got sadly out of hand in 1640, and added that the worries of these times had 'kurdled all the sommer in his blood.' Shakespeare, it may be recalled, in Act I, scene v of *Hamlet*, makes the ghost say:

> it doth posset
> And curd, like Aygre droppings into Milke,
> The thin and wholsome blood.

The word 'aygre,' which is printed 'eager' in modern editions of Shakespeare, is, of course, the French word from which we get 'vinegar.'

These monuments to the Lords Maynard are masterpieces of their periods. But most men, if they are frank, will prefer Sir Henry Maynard's tomb in the same chapel. He was the first Lord Maynard's father, and a right worthy knight. In the previous chapter we met him as sheriff. He lies upon his tomb in armour; his lady is in the dress of her period, with ruff and farthingale; every detail of their dress is beautifully cut, with the quaintness of the age expressed in the figures of their ten children, especially in those of the boys, who carry skulls in their hands. The inscription daintily informs us that

> Two of the precious ones, a piteous spoile,
> Were erst transplanted to a foreine soile,
> Where the hott sunn, (howe'er it did befall)
> Drew up their juice, to perfume heaven withall:
> When will the heaven such flowers to the earth repay
> As the earth afforded heaven, two in a daye.

The inscription to Sir Henry himself, who was secretary to

the great Cecil, is admirably restrained and dignified. Its Latin is translated:

> Whence, who, and what I was, how held in Court,
> My prince, the peers, my country, can report.
> Ask these of me (good reader) not these stones.
> They knew my life, these do but hold my bones.

Another Maynard tomb, that of Lady Frances Maynard who died in 1613, shows a different kind of costume of the period. She is made to look at ease in her less formal dress and hood, and we can imagine her in this same attire playing her lute, embroidering her samplers and cushions, or carrying simples to the sick tenants on the Easton estate.

The Maynards were well established in other parts of the country at an early date; but they did not come into Essex until Elizabeth's reign. This separates them from the other landed families of the county, whose relationships it would take a lifetime to unravel, and in the reign of Charles I it accounts for their being on the Royalist side when most of the Essex gentry were on the side of Parliament. Blood was as much thicker than water then as it is now, and in studying the political allegiances of these worthy knights it is much more helpful to examine their pedigrees than their principles. The Cromwellian tincture was potent. The Sir Francis Barrington who went to prison rather than pay the money demanded by Charles I married the daughter of Sir Henry Cromwell of Hinchingbrook in Huntingdonshire, aunt to Oliver Cromwell. On 12th September 1653 we find Cromwell at the height of his power writing in characteristic style to Sir John Barrington, Sir Francis's grandson: 'Your person and family are very deere to mee,' and adding, 'if any vexed you causelesslye stop their mouths.' Sir Richard Everard of Langleys, Great Waltham, head of a family that had been settled in Essex since the reign of Henry III, if not earlier, was also a 'cousin.' Cromwell himself married Elizabeth Bourchier, of noble Essex lineage, and he sent his sons to Felsted, an Essex school, where more links were forged. His daughter married a grandson of the second Earl of Warwick. And a Thomas Barrington born in 1643 married Lady Anne Rich, the Earl of Warwick's daughter. This last is too late a connection to matter at the Great Rebellion, but it shows again how interlinked the county families were.

The Great Rebellion, the crucial event of the century and always to be kept in mind, was largely a revolt of individualism against authority. It was that with the people of Essex; but not for reasons of economic necessity, as it was with the tradesmen and workers of the new industrial towns, most of whom were nonconformist in religion. In most counties these were on one side, the gentry on the other. In Essex the gentry, led by the second Earl of Warwick, were for Parliament and many of them even for nonconformity. The development of the nonconformist party in the nation as a whole, under conditions produced by the policy of Charles I and Archbishop Laud, seems natural enough against its social background; but what was an earl doing among the conventicle men? The nation was then evolving a new kind of society, an industrial system centred in towns, while industrial Essex, if we exclude the London corner, was not at the beginning but at the end of its golden age. The progressive middle class, the backbone of the new system, was not and never has been powerful in Essex, which in its essential nature is a county of the land, with all the innate conservatism that goes with it. The wool trade on which it flourished for a few generations, a subject to engage us presently, was a foreign element, superimposed upon its natural economy by refugees from religious persecution on the Continent. The gentlemen of Essex were against the king on constitutional grounds because his policy seemed to be undermining their own power. With them the revolt of individualism against authority was not to liberate new forces but to preserve the privileges of the old.

For this reason the Essex Parliamentarians did not sit comfortably in either camp for long. They were not easy companions for Cromwell, in spite of such tributes as that of the frequently quoted letter of John Hampden to Sir Thomas Barrington, in which he said: 'The power of Essex

is great, a place of most life of religion in the land.' The
Essex country gentlemen had too much character to make
good party men. The names Roundhead and Cavalier suggest distinct and never-to-be-reconciled species: the one
hard and grave, men of iron will and solemn speech; the
other easy-going, gay and sprightly in manner, foppish in
dress. There were, no doubt, both extremes to be found
in their respective parties; but in the majority of men these
characteristics are always engagingly mingled. While they
represent two permanent and conflicting types of character,
both are to be found in every sane individual, for every man
who is not either a fool or a fanatic has both a gay and a
grave side. In some one predominates, in some the other.
Of the best we may say, as Antony said of Brutus, that the
elements

> So mix't in him, that Nature might stand up
> And say to all the world, 'This was a man!'

She might be more precise and say of certain mixtures that
this was an Englishman; but she would be hard put to it to
say with complete conviction of any prominent Essex man
of the period: This was a Roundhead, this a Cavalier. Both,
before all else, were family men and country men.

When we stand in the garden of one of the mellow old
houses built for a seventeenth-century knight and his lady,
or sit in their panelled hall while the logs crackle and glow
on the wide, hospitable hearth, we may imagine their life
as one firmly grounded and free from care. It was far
from being that, though it might have become so for most of
the gentlemen of Essex if it had not occurred to Cromwell that

> 'Tis time to leave the books in dust,
> And oil the unusèd armour's rust;
> Removing from the wall
> The corslet of the hall.

Marvell would have us believe that

> 'Tis madness to resist or blame
> The face of angry Heaven's flame;
> And if we would speak true,
> Much to the man is due,

> Who, from his private gardens, where
> He lived reservèd and austere
> (As if his highest plot
> To plant the bergamot),

> Could by industrious valour climb
> To ruin the great work of time,
> And cast the kingdoms old
> Into another mould.

But for all the eloquence of Marvell, and of Milton his master, there were many good patriots who found it hard to be convinced.

There was Sir Harbottle Grimston, for example. He lived at Bradfield Hall, overlooking the Stour estuary, a moated house still standing, and at Colchester. He was as influential in the north-east of the county as Sir Francis Barrington had been in the north-west. Both represented Essex in Parliament, and both secured the election of their son-in-law. Sir Harbottle's father had gone to prison with Sir Francis Barrington rather than pay the loan demanded by Charles I. But nationally Sir Harbottle was a more important figure than Sir Francis had been. He was prominent in the negotiations with the king in the Isle of Wight, and was a member of the Council of State on the resignation of Richard Cromwell—simple, lovable, Tumble-down Dick, who lived at Cheshunt near Waltham Abbey for more than thirty years. Though a Puritan officially, and unsparing in his attacks on Laud, Sir Harbottle did not take the Solemn League and Covenant—which, incidentally, the reputed author of the *Eikon Basilike*, Dr. John Gauden, did take. There were few in whom the elements were so confusingly mixed. Though nominally with the Parliamentarians, he was said by Clarendon to have 'continued rather than concurred with them,' and if we read his character aright in *A Christian's New Year's Gift*, a small book he wrote for his beloved son and heir, George Grimston, he was a man of quiet spirit and Catholic mind, a true English churchman of the most scholarly type. He was Speaker of the Convention Parliament, and went to Breda to invite Charles II. to return. It was he, too, who delivered the speech of welcome when the new king reached England.

Sir Harbottle was of East Anglian stock, so we may assume that he was bred to Puritanism. Many enterprising men were then filtering into Essex from counties farther north in order to be nearer London. The county's geographical position was a considerable factor at this time. Not only was London at its south-west corner and Cambridge at hand in the north-west, Essex lay along the direct route to Holland, then in the van of political and intellectual progress. These three, London, Cambridge, and the Low Countries, kept the life of the county in a state of ferment. Eventually they were to affect the New World as a result of their vital association in Essex, for so many of the Essex nonconformists crossed the Atlantic that no fewer than thirty-two of the early settlements in New England were given the names of Essex towns and villages.

It is notable that few families of standing from the south or west of England ever settled in Essex. So there was little Royalist infiltration during the early seventeenth century from those quarters. The Petres, who came from Devon, are the most prominent exception. There was also the Honywood family, who promptly took their political colour from their new county. In Essex, that is to say, they were Parliamentarians, while their relations in Kent were Royalists. The Mashams, who came from Yorkshire originally, reached Essex by way of Suffolk, where they were settled for a long time at Badwell Ash. So the Barrington marriage had, perhaps, only to complete what the East Anglian air had begun.

There was yet another important factor that any one not acquainted with the inner workings of Essex history might miss. It was the power of Emmanuel College, Cambridge. To the extent that the modern Englishman tends to take his politics from his newspaper, the seventeenth-century gentleman took his from his college. His tenants, we may note, took theirs from him, for the wealth and power of the lord of the manor was rarely a cause of grievance to the

seventeenth-century cottager. Normally it was the opposite. The poor man regarded a rich master as a guarantee
of security, the only one he could have. The stronger the
lord, the safer the labourer. So far as Essex was concerned, the common people were on the side of Parliament
because their masters were. Their masters, it is suggested,
were there for personal and family reasons primarily. If
other reasons were required, they looked for them to Cambridge, and in particular to Emmanuel College, founded by
Sir Walter Mildmay in 1585. It was the favourite college
of the Essex gentry. Still more important, it was the
college from which the gentry, as patrons of the livings,
drew the most influential clergy.

The Mildmays were a flourishing Essex family whose
relations were to be met in many parts of the county besides
Chelmsford, their stronghold. There were no fewer than
nine branches of them settled in different parts of Essex in
the reign of James I. There were three Sir Henrys, one at
Woodham Walter, one at Wanstead, and one at Graces in
Little Baddow; there were two Sir Thomases, one at Moulsham and one at Springfield Barns; there was Sir Humphrey
at Danbury, Sir Walter at Great Baddow, Sir Robert at
Terling, and Sir Carew Hervey, a rare early instance of two
baptismal names, at Marks, Dagenham. But of all the
Mildmays only three reached the *Dictionary of National
Biography* and only one is found in Fuller's *Worthies*. But
that one is Sir Walter, and Fuller wrote in his most
felicitous vein:

'This knight, sensible of God's blessing on his estate, and
knowing that "omne beneficium requirit officium," cast
about to make his return to God. He began with his bene-
faction to Christ's College, in Cambridge, only to put his
hand into practice; then his bounty embraced the generous
resolution (which the painful piety of St. Paul propounds to
himself, viz.) "not to build on another man's foundation";
but, on his own cost, he erected a new college in Cambridge,
by the name of Emanuel.

'A right godly gentleman he was, though some of his

back-friends suggested to the queen, that he was a better
patriot than subject; and that he was ever popular in parliaments, insomuch that his life did not set *sub nubecula*, under
a cloud of the royal displeasure.'

Fuller does not enlarge on that; but the root of the trouble
was Elizabeth's disapproval of the Puritan bias of his
college.

'I hear, Sir Walter,' she said sternly when he was presented to her, 'that you have been erecting a Puritan
foundation.'

'Madam,' replied Sir Walter, 'far be it from me to
countenance anything contrary to your established laws,
but I have set an acorn, which when it becomes an oak,
God knows what will be the fruit thereof.'

The fruit of Emmanuel was not only to be widely distributed in Essex, but was to be carried into the New World.
It was from Emmanuel that John Harvard went to found
his own university at Cambridge, Massachusetts, and so
extensive became the influence of this Mildmay foundation
in New England that Cotton Mather called it 'Emmanuel's
Land.'

The first Mildmay of note was Thomas, who in 1530 for-
sook the land his ancestors had cultivated to buy Guy
Harlings, Chelmsford, a substantial house that still over-
looks the churchyard, and there set up as a merchant.   In
his will, made seventeen years later, he left to one of his sons
the 'stall in which I used to stand every Wednesday.'   His
son and namesake found a quicker way to fortune than
selling wares in Chelmsford market.   He obtained at the
Dissolution the post of auditor of the Court of Augmentations
of the Royal Revenue.   For this office the essential qualification was the opposite one to that normally required in an
auditor, and this qualification Thomas Mildmay the second
possessed.   It enabled him to maintain himself and eight
clerks on a salary of thirty shillings a day, and at the same
time to acquire the manor of Moulsham and on it to build
for himself and his heirs a noble mansion.   In 1563 he was
able to add to his estate a large part of Chelmsford.

The Mildmays long continued in Essex, and for a short time enjoyed the barony of FitzWalter. That branch, however, died out in the middle of the eighteenth century. They were men of good estate, and excellent landlords. But though they, like the families of ancient descent just mentioned, were to remain prominent in Essex life throughout the seventeenth century, other families had lately risen to power and were now dominant. These were the families whose fortunes were promoted by Henry VIII at the Dissolution. Henry gave little to the old families when he distributed the abbey lands. Most of them were, in fact, supporters of Rome either openly or secretly, and he thought it safer to create his own nobility than to strengthen those with older allegiances who, if provoked, might combine against him. These new families, as we should expect, were far more pretentious than the old, and in assessing rank from church monuments, in spite of what Weever says, we must always allow for the greater ostentation of those but recently exalted. They were much more inclined to spend large sums on commemorating themselves than were the Bourchiers, the de Veres, the Waldegraves, or the Barringtons. It may be these monuments that have led to the popular idea that the English squirearchy began at the Dissolution. To a great extent the families most prominent in the eighteenth and nineteenth centuries came into the public eye then; but the old seignorial families with place-names for their patronymics were the original lords of the land.

There is no reason to be cynical about the costly monuments prepared for the *nouveaux riches*, many of whom were men of great ability, who if they did well for themselves did well for England also. They laid good and solid foundations upon which the mercantile and political greatness of England in later centuries was built. They were the new men of the newly constituted society, and in the villages, though not in the towns, the order they founded lasted for nearly three hundred years. Sir William Petre, who built Ingatestone Hall, to which the present Lord Petre has now

returned, is one outstanding example of the new type of
man who came to power then, though he was in many
respects unique, and another reminder of the danger and
difficulty of generalizing. His power under the Tudors was
immense, and was wielded more effectively in private than
in public. At the Dissolution he acquired, mainly by purchase, vast estates in Devon, his native county, and Essex,
the county of his adoption. His land came from Thoby
Priory, about which we know little, and from six abbeys,
Waltham, Barking, Stratford, Coggeshall, St. John's at
Colchester, and St. Osyth's. Yet whatever this man was
in Henry's reign he was a Roman Catholic in Mary's, and
his family have in the main, whether openly or not, been
Roman Catholics ever since. So astute was Sir William
that he actually obtained from Pope Paul IV a bull con-
firming his title to all the abbey lands he had gained when
they were plundered for the benefit of Protestants. He was
a master of secret diplomacy, and one of the most revealing
stories told of him is of a French official saying at Boulogne
in 1550, at the conclusion of delicate negotiations: 'Ah, we
could have gained the last two hundred thousand crowns
without hostages had it not been for that man who said
nothing.'

Ingatestone Hall must have sheltered many fugitives in
the secret hiding place discovered in 1855. In 1627 'divers
great papists' held a conference there which lasted a fortnight, and there must have been constant coming and going
of priests and prominent members of the old faith in a house
so conveniently situated for escape to the Continent. The
fourth Lord Petre was accused of being privy to the Titus
Oates plot. It was alleged that he had received a commission as lieutenant-general in a Roman Catholic army
about to invade England, and at once he was arrested and
sent to the Tower, where Pepys was his fellow prisoner for
a short while under suspicion of having sold naval information to the French. Towards the end of 1683 Lord Petre
begged the king to release him, or at least to bring him to
trial. 'I have been five years in prison,' he wrote, 'and

what is more grievous to me lain so long under a false, injurious calumny of a horrid plot and design against your Majestie's person and government, and am now by the disposition of God's Providence call'd into another world before I could by a public trial make my innocence appear.' He died in prison the following January.

We do not know what Pepys thought of Lord Petre; but we do know what he thought of his first wife, Elizabeth Savage, a daughter of Earl Rivers. He refers to her in the *Diary*, 3rd April 1664, as 'an impudent jade.' The Chief Justice of Common Pleas had tried to have her arrested for debt, apparently by the advice of Lord Petre's own steward. The whole business seems to have been extremely complicated, for on leaving the House of Lords, to which the Chief Justice of Common Pleas and Lady Petre had been summoned, Pepys saw what he thought a sad sight: Lord Petre 'fall out with his lady (from whom he is parted) about this business, saying that she disgraced him. But she hath been a handsome woman, and is, it seems, not only a lewd woman, but very high-spirited.'

The Chief Justice of Common Pleas was the husband of Pepys's cousin, but whether it was this or Lady Petre's character that made the diarist so interested in the case it would be difficult to say. He made a personal attempt to mollify her, but she was determined to have her revenge which, she said, 'was sweeter to her than milk; and that she would never be satisfied unless he (her accuser) stood in the pillory, and demand pardon there.' She came of tempestuous stock, and seems to have justified all that Pepys said of her. To every one's relief she died the year after this undignified episode.

But the supreme figure of Reformation Essex had been Lord Chancellor Rich, grandfather of the Lord Rich who married Penelope Devereux and became first Earl of Warwick, and great-grandfather of our illustrious second earl. Lord Chancellor Rich built himself a mansion at Leighs, north-east of Chelmsford, on the site of a priory of Augustinian canons. Most of it, by that time in decay, was dismantled in 1753 when it became the property of Guy's Hospital. In 1905, however, restoration began, and in course of time Leighs, or Leez, became the charming country house we see to-day. With the help of Sir William St. John Hope the new owner, Mr. Hughes-Hughes, traced the foundations of both the original priory and the lord chancellor's mansion, and Mrs. Moffat, who succeeded as owner, completed the restoration of the house, tending it devotedly till her death in 1947. In its prime it must have been a glorious place, and we are not surprised to find a gentleman who visited the fourth Earl of Warwick there saying to him: 'My lord, you had better make sure of heaven, or else, when you die, you'll be a great loser.'

The Rich arms and motto, *Garde ta Foy*, are still above the oak doors, and many of the rooms contain the original linenfold panelling. The most splendid fragment of the lord chancellor's house is the three-storeyed gatehouse with its four octagonal turrets, terra-cotta chimneys, and elaborately carved stone window frames. Through the gateway of this eastern tower we pass to what was another courtyard, with a hexagonal fountain in the centre.

Lord Chancellor Rich was a most unpleasant character. He sent many a worthier than himself to the scaffold. As for the way he enriched himself at the suppression, the most charitable way of putting it is Fuller's, who said that at the Dissolution the grants of land passed through his hands, and some of them stuck to his fingers. His monument, the work of an English sculptor, Epiphanius Evesham, is in Felsted church, and was raised by the second Earl of Warwick to instructions in the will of the first earl. In the seventeenth century the house of Rich was again in the ascendant, and as the lord chancellor had been the great man in the county under the Tudors, his great-grandson, the second earl, became the great man under the early Stuarts, though not, of course, as spectacular as the Duke of Buckingham, whom, incidentally, he hated.

The life of Robert Rich, second Earl of Warwick, has never been written. What we know of him comes to us from scattered sources. He was the child of badly mated parents, and all his greatness springs from that strange union. Miss Charlotte Fell Smith, in *Mary Rich, Countess of Warwick*, describes his 'dark lean face' looking out from Van Dyck's canvas 'with all the sincerity of a Puritan, all the spirit of adventure of a great Elizabethan, and all the humour and jollity of an English sailor.' The first characteristic came from his father, the first earl; the second from his mother, the lovely Penelope; and the third from his own triumphant mastery of two conflicting strains. His character is worth studying. We are constantly hearing about the maladjusted children who are the result of broken marriages. But it is only the sick who need a physician. There are no statistics to show how many brilliant and successful children are the offspring of such couples. The number is probably great. Children of easy temperament and constitution seldom accomplish much. The child with a battle in his own breast has a hard time adjusting himself to life. If he fails he becomes the enemy of society; if he succeeds he becomes a man of mark.

When old enough, Robert Rich went to sea. Arthur Wilson, his steward, the man who understood him best, said of him: 'Though he had all those excellent endowments of body and fortune that give splendour to a glorious Court, yet he used it but as his recreation. For his spirit aimed at more public adventure—planting Colonies in the Western World, rather than himself in the King's favour.' He helped to found the colonies of New Plymouth, Massachusetts, Connecticut, and Rhode Island. Land was granted to him both in America and in the Bermudas, which had already been colonized, and we find a reference to him in a poem by Waller describing a fight between two whales left by a tide in a lagoon in the Bermudas:

> Within the bounds of noble Warwick's share:
> Warwick's bold Earl, than which no title bears
> A greater sound among our English peers.

The parts where he held property in the Bermudas were long called by his name, and his plantations there seem to

Robert Rich, 2nd Earl of Warwick

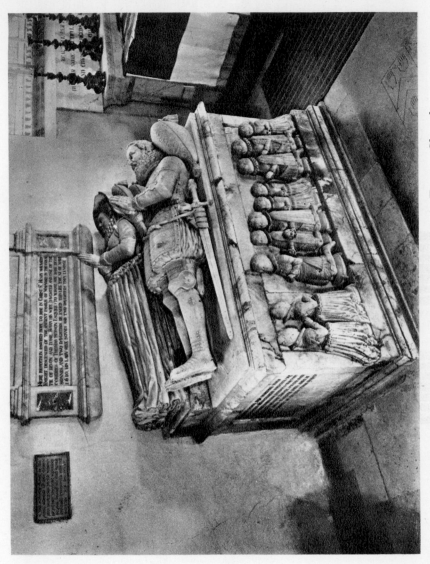

Sir Henry Maynard's Monument in Little Easton Church

have yielded him large profits. He may have gained profit
also from privateering exploits. In 1618 he and a Genoese
merchant of London sent pirate ships to the East Indies,
and in 1627 we again find him engaged in bold, unscrupulous
adventures. He was a virile sea-dog. One who sailed under
his command is reported as speaking with admiration of his
daring spirit. The roughest seas had no effect on him.
When over forty he would climb the rigging to top and
yard as nimbly as any man on board, and in all the fighting he exposed himself to danger with his men, a fearless
commander.

On returning to England and settling on his Essex estates,
he turned his attention to politics and quickly established
himself as leader of the Puritans in the county, though his
mother's blood in his veins saved him from becoming as
grave as some of the brethren. He was, in fact, accused by
less moderate and humorously disposed men of being a
time-server. But Cromwell valued him, and as he was
appointed lord high admiral in 1643, when Northumber-
land's commission was revoked by the king, he was able to
secure the navy for the Parliamentary side. Throughout
the civil wars he played a shrewd and perhaps a crafty
game. His main concern seems to have been to keep the
seas open so that the commerce of the country could continue with the least possible disturbance. With his two
sons-in-law, Robartes and Manchester, he sat among the
twenty-two peers in Parliament and was altogether a man
of great power. In Essex his influence was paramount.
When peace with the king was mooted in 1643, one of the
terms, put forward by the Eastern Association, was that
Warwick should be made a duke.

It is clear that he had both his father's self-righteous
Puritanism and his mother's gay spirit. Clarendon says
that 'he was a man of a pleasant and companionable wit
and conversation, of a universal jollity, and such a licence
in his words and in his actions, that a man of less virtue
could not be found.' It must, however, be remembered
that Clarendon was on the other side, and had no love for

the Puritans. But he probably heard much about Warwick from Sir John Bramston of Skreens, who would know the earl well. Sir John had been one of Clarendon's chamber fellows at the Middle Temple.

At the end of 1643 the Long Parliament made Warwick head of a commission responsible for the government of the colonies, adding to his title of lord high admiral that of governor-in-chief of all the islands and other plantations subject to the English Crown. In March of the following year he and his fellow commissioners granted to Roger Williams, formerly chaplain to the Masham family at High Laver, a patent incorporating three New England towns as Providence Plantation. Warwick, with all his faults, was one of the greatest men the county has known. Two of his sons succeeded as third and fourth earls. The fifth, a cousin of the fourth, did not inherit Leighs. Of the other families mentioned, Sir Harbottle Grimston's line was to be continued not in Essex but in Hertfordshire as earls of Verulam, the descendants of his eldest daughter. The Barringtons were to remain at Hatfield Broad Oak until the middle of the nineteenth century, the Maynards at Little Easton until our own day, when Francis Maynard brought the Warwick title back into the county by marrying a Greville. We should become confused by the number of names if we tried to follow all the families who have continued to hold their estates for centuries without, however, coming into sufficient prominence to make their inclusion essential to our purpose. With each the head of the family's first desire was to see his eldest son secure in possession of the ancestral acres. Many whose names have never been widely known have done that, and have kept their homes and estates so trim that the county is still proud of its fine old manor houses.

## CHAPTER IV

## MY LADY'S BOWER

Give me, O indulgent fate!
Give me yet before I die
A sweet, yet absolute retreat,
'Mongst paths so lost and trees so high
That the world may ne'er invade
Through such windings and such shade
My unshaken liberty.

ANNE, COUNTESS OF WINCHILSEA.

IT is to be expected that by tracing the names of the gentlemen of the county through contemporary records we should
learn something of their worth and character. By the
exercise of imagination we can follow them to their homes
and see them on returning from court discard their yellow
stockings and silk taffety cloaks, to don country clothes
before calling their dogs and inspecting farm-stock. It is
much more surprising, and also more gratifying, to find that
so many of their wives are still personalities to us. We
meet them in different places, so the search for them is not
so simple as the search for their husbands. We learn most
of what we know about one Lady Maynard, for example,
from the sermon preached at her funeral at Little Easton
by Thomas Ken, the good Bishop Ken who wrote the well-
known morning and evening hymns, 'Awake, my soul, and
with the sun,' and 'All praise to Thee, my God, this night.'

Ken was rector of Little Easton from 1663 to 1665, and
on 30th June 1682 he returned to his old parish to preach
at her ladyship's funeral. He had known her first when
she was a religiously disposed young lady of twenty-one,
who had recently become the second wife of Lord Maynard
and the stepmother of his two children. Ken had only
left Oxford a year before becoming rector of Little Easton,
and the youthful lady of the manor and the gifted young

47

man who had become her spiritual adviser found themselves
with much in common. To the end of her life they remained
friends, and it does not require much imagination to re-create
the scene in the Norman nave of the church nineteen years
later. Eight strong woodmen employed on the estate, we
may suppose, carried in the coffin, and after the simple
service Dr. Ken went into the pulpit to remind his congregation of the kindly and gracious lady whose image was in
their minds, and who for nearly twenty years had been part
of their lives. She had lived, he said, in the daily con-
sciousness of God's presence, had served her household,
instructed her sons, been a helpmeet to her husband and a
regular visitor to the cottages of the village folk—all, indeed,
that a virtuous lady of the manor was expected to be. She
had also been a dear friend of the man, for a short time
their priest, who had come into Essex again to honour her
memory.

We meet another lady of the period, Lady Altham of
Mark Hall near Harlow, a lady with royal blood in her
veins, in letters preserved by her descendants. Joan, Lady
Altham, was left a widow by the death in 1632 of her
husband, Sir Edward Altham. When her eldest son married
in 1638 she left her Harlow home and went to live in Norfolk;
but wrote that she still loved Mark Hall more than any other
place. The problems that normally engage the minds of
ladies vary less from one age to another than those that
engage the minds of men, and the usual topics are discussed
in Lady Altham's correspondence. She writes to her son
at Cambridge about her concern at the slow progress her
two younger boys are making with their books. They are
at Mark Hall with her, and their tutor, the vicar of Latton,
is finding their tuition too much for him. He has asked for
a new tutor to be found. Another son causes her great
distress by his extravagance, and yet another because he is
bent on becoming a Roman Catholic. This is perhaps her
greatest grief at the time, and she writes to the Bishop of
Exeter begging him to use his influence to save her boy
from what she regards with such horror.

The grand old lady of the day, Dame Mary Honywood, lived at a house that might be confused with Mark Hall, Harlow. She lived at Marks Hall, near Coggeshall. Dame Mary married when she was sixteen and bore her husband sixteen children in the thirty-three years of their married life. That in itself is not remarkable in the England of that day. What is remarkable is that all except three of them grew up and in turn had families so large that when the old lady died in her ninety-third year she could count three hundred and sixty-seven descendants.

Dame Mary came to Essex in 1605, when her eldest son, who had seventeen children, bought the Essex estate that was to remain in the family for nearly three hundred years. He was then approaching his sixtieth birthday. His mother lived with him for the last fifteen years of her life, and though she was buried with her husband in Kent a marble tablet to her memory was set up at Marks Hall. On it she was shown dressed in her widow's cap, ruff, and mantle, with an inscription below enumerating her descendants at the time of her death. There were sixteen children 'of her owne bodye,' we learn, one hundred and fourteen grandchildren, two hundred and twenty-eight great-grandchildren, and nine great-great-grandchildren.

Her eldest son, Robert, who was born when his mother was only seventeen years old, lived to his eighty-second year. Only seven years after Dame Mary's death he was buried in the parish church, now dismantled, near his own front door. Thus mother and son grew old together.

It is worth noting that when Robert Honywood died he left his wife, herself an old lady, the sole executrix of his will, though his eldest son, the Thomas Honywood who had been knighted in 1625, was an able man and came into possession of the estate only four years later. It was he who after the fall of Colchester was placed in command of the town, with instructions to dismantle the fortifications.

Englishwomen enjoyed considerable freedom in the early years of the seventeenth century. They walked, rode, and played cards. They were honoured in the family circle, and received the daintiest morsels at table. In neighbouring countries England was regarded as the paradise of married women. Some of the letters written in these years show that the ladies of James's court were most capable. Lady Mary Wroth of Loughton Hall, niece of Sir Philip Sidney and author of *Urania*, a pastoral romance somewhat in the manner of her uncle's *Arcadia*, was clearly a highly accomplished lady; but it is nevertheless surprising to find her taking such business-like interest in her husband's negotiations for a new lease from the king of the Loughton estate. Here is the letter she wrote to the queen on his behalf:

'Madame, the infinite favours which from you I have received, although I must confess myself far unworthy of the least of them, besides knowing how willingly the king will hear your majesty, I thus far presume as humbly to beseech you this much: to be [so] pleased as to recommend this petition of Mr. Wroth's to the king. . . . It may be thought to be a matter of profit and so the harder to obtain, yet is it no loss to his majesty at all, Mr. Wroth's suit being but this: that it may please the king to grant him a longer estate in it to avoid all fear of having it taken over his head. . . . Mr. Wroth does not desire it for nothing. As your majesty may perceive from the petition he offers . . . five or six hundred pounds, which he will bestow then upon building. [He] will let the deer feed in his best grounds, to which by his lease he is not bound, but is content to lose a hundred pounds a year rather than trouble them lest it might hinder the king's sports.' The last was a shrewd touch, since the estate was in Epping Forest, the king's favourite hunting-ground. And the final sentence of the letter is a deliciously one-woman-to-another confidence. She humbly beseeches Her Majesty to do her best 'since it will be much for my good, Mr. Wroth having promised to add it to my jointure, all the rest of his land being entailed.'

The appeal was successful, and Lady Mary enjoyed the use of Loughton Hall during her long widowhood of about forty years. Like Sir Philip Sidney she was an extravagant person. Her lavish ways kept her affairs in a state of turmoil, and year after year she was given royal protection 'by reason of her birth and quality, and the earnest intention she expressed of immediately satisfying her numerous creditors.'

The publication of *Urania* in 1621 caused scandal at court, where some of the passages were believed to refer to living persons. Lord Denny of Waltham Abbey, whom we have already met as Sir Edward Denny, was indignant at what appeared to be thinly veiled references to himself, and shortly after the publication of the book he was alleged to have attacked Lady Mary in a set of scurrilous verses. These came into the hands of that spirited lady and amusing letters passed between them:

'My Lord,' wrote her ladyship, 'This day came to my hand some verses under the name of the Lord Denny's, but such vile railing and scandalous things as I could not believe they proceeded from any but some drunken poet; and that rather because they so feelingly speak of that vice and sin. But to think my Lord Denny, who hath professed so much religion, justice, and to be of worth, should fall into so strange a disposition as to slander and revile a woman friend who hath ever honoured him! I was loath to credit it, especially knowing my own innocence, which is as clear and pure as new born, whatever such slanderous conceits have laid upon me. And much I do wonder how nobleness can fall so far as to let such rudeness witness against itself, or rather take that away, and leave bare baseness in place of honour; otherwise before such proceedings had been, truth and worth would have had the matter questioned. But here is no such matter. Violence and falsehood rule. Whereas had I been asked I would have truly and constantly sworn, that I no more meant harm to my Lord Denny or his house than to myself. Nor did I ever intend one word of that book to his lordship's person or disgrace; and this I will yet say to justify myself; but not in way of satisfaction. . . . Now I shall pity your rash folly and wish you amendment of understanding.'

To this Lord Denny haughtily replied:

'Madam, Yesterday, the 25th of this February, I received from you an invective, with an invexion of rhymes enclosed, which you suspect to be mine, but it seems were a Romanza from the father-in-law of Siretius to Pamphilia and so endorsed, which how they can concern either your ladyship or me I cannot conceive.'

He then proceeded through three pages to treat of himself as 'the only chosen fool for a May game before all the world and especially before a wise king and prince with all the nobility.' He swore that many noble witnesses could be brought to aver that her own mouth had published him to be the man whom her 'spiteful and scornful passage concerned,' and wished that she might be like her aunt, Mary, Countess of Pembroke, 'and redeem the time by writing as large a volume of heavenly lays as she has of lascivious tales and amorous toys,' signing himself her 'most well wishing friend, Edward Denny.'

This produced such a fury in Lady Mary that she flew to her pen and wrote:

'My Lord, I never thought on you in my writing. I never meant you. I never meant you. I never spoke any such thing.'

She demanded to be brought face to face with her accusers and spared nothing, as she would certainly not spare him when the time should serve. To which Lord Denny replied that he had no desire to discuss the matter further, that he would be ready to justify what he had said if it became necessary, but would hate to be pressed into being an informer. He thought she knew as much as he did about what had been said, and for the sake of her family, whom he claimed to honour and serve, as well as for her own sake, desired to remain her 'truly well wishing friend if [she] could think so.'

At Gidea Hall, only six or seven miles from Loughton Hall, lived Sir Anthony Cooke and his brilliant daughters. Sir Anthony, himself a scholar, believed that 'sexes as well as souls are equal,' and he educated his daughters in the hope that they 'might have for their husbands complete and perfect men, and that their husbands might be happy in complete women.' In his wisdom he also taught them to regard study as recreation, not labour, and not to neglect to 'place their real business in the needle in the closet, and housewifery in kitchen and hall.' Lady Cooke, a daughter of Sir William FitzWilliam of Gaynes Park, near Epping, supported her husband in these wise motives, and they had the joy of seeing one of their girls the second wife of the great Cecil, Elizabeth's Burghley, and another the wife of Sir Nicholas Bacon and the mother of Francis Bacon, whose greatness, however, they would not live to see. A third, Elizabeth, married Sir Thomas Hoby, and left a diary which gives us a vivid picture of the life of an educated English-woman of her time. Each day began and ended with private prayer and Bible reading, and there were few days when religious works were not studied either in her room or with her chaplain, who often read aloud while she and her maids worked. These chaplains were most useful in the way they took the ladies off their husband's hands, but were apt to make them far too critical of their husband's morals. The country ladies of the day were often much more religious than we might think. The gay ladies of the court are better known to us by name, and the more daring aspects of Elizabethan and Jacobean life tend to be exaggerated. To balance the picture we need to see these quieter country ladies, so much of whose lives—mainly as relief from boredom in bad weather—was spent in study and devotion. They were practical too. Lady Hoby was a careful housewife, and spent much time riding about the estate with her husband, viewing the stock, deciding where to build new cottages, attending to her bees. She worked hard. 'After dinner,' reads one entry, 'I was busy, weighing of wool till almost night.'

Such glimpses as these of the ladies of Elizabethan and Jacobean England give us quick but revealing impressions of their character. To generalize and to particularize about women are equally dangerous pursuits. If there is a cap or

c

a bonnet being bandied about some touchy woman will wear it. But in any kind of survey it becomes obvious directly that their status changed as the seventeenth century proceeded. They had far more spirit at the beginning than they had at the end. If Shakespeare had been born seventy years later he could not have given them so many pert speeches. His boy-heroines would not have been so convincing as the fat, overfed darlings of the Cavaliers, who contributed much to their lord's pleasure, but little to his business. The Elizabethan lady could manage her husband's affairs while he was at court or empire-building—to say nothing of his piratical excursions. The wife of many a soldier in the civil wars kept house valiantly. Lady Harley, it may be recalled, defended Brampton Castle for six weeks when the Royalist forces laid siege to it.

Sir Anthony Cooke's belief in education was justified, but it was long before his views were adopted by parents in general. In 1652 Sir Ralph Verney wrote to his goddaughter, who had informed him that she intended to learn Hebrew, Greek, and Latin: 'Good sweetheart be not so covetous; believe me a Bible (with the Common Prayer) and a good plain Catechism in your mother tongue being well read and practised, is well worth all the rest and much more suitable to your sex.' He did, however, recommend French. Of Essex men, it is Sir Josiah Child of Wanstead House who proves the strongest advocate for the education of daughters. His enlightened attitude is surprising until we discover his reasons. He had noticed how much better educated the Dutch women were than the English, and how well they understood commerce. The great advantage of this understanding of business was that their husbands could continue in business to the end of their lives, knowing that their wives would be able to collect outstanding debts and wind up their affairs afterwards, while in England a merchant was obliged to retire before he became old, because he was afraid that if he died suddenly a large proportion of his wealth would be lost through the inability of his wife to lay claim to it. He found also that a knowledge of arithmetic and mathematics generally not only improved the rational faculties, but inclined the women who possessed them to thrift and economy.

Educated or not, the married women of the first half of the seventeenth century lived both comfortably and usefully. They had servants to do the drudgery if their husbands were well-to-do, and daughters if they were poor. It is particularly noticeable how well the daughters were kept in hand by their mothers. The mothers of the twentieth century are much more in subservience than the mothers of the seventeenth century were. Indeed the emancipation of women in our own day is a pretty comedy. How often they have been liberated from the dominion of men only to come under the dominion of their own daughters! How many of them, after having had a nursemaid to help with their own children, have now become the nursemaids of their children's children!

After studying the lives of women in the seventeenth century, we cannot help feeling that not until our own day have they enjoyed so much active partnership with men as they had under Elizabeth, James, and Charles I. This partnership gave the husband and wife a wide range of interests in common and freed their relationship from the pathetic dependence on sex that marred it after the Restoration. There was real comradeship between man and wife. The wives of the rich hunted and played bowls; the wives of the poor joined whole-heartedly in country games. Both rich and poor baked and brewed and were skilful cooks. The memory of Elizabeth long remained fresh in the national mind and inspired the ladies to resourcefulness and courage.

In one function, alas, they required all too much courage. Child-bearing, with all the crude practices and superstitions that attended it, was not a pretty subject; but Essex has the honour of having been the home for a great part of his life of Dr. Peter Chamberlen, who came of a family of Huguenot refugees and was a pioneer of operative midwifery. He lived at Woodham Mortimer Hall for many years, and died there in 1683 at the age of eighty-two. The use of forceps was in those days considered wicked, and the instruments used by Peter Chamberlen remained hidden under the floor of an upstairs room for a hundred and thirty years after his death. His eldest son, Hugh, continued in his father's practice, but was bitterly opposed by the medical profession, and in 1688 prosecuted for practising without qualification. In spite of this he was entrusted by James II with the birth of an expected heir to the throne. Unfortunately the child was born prematurely and Chamberlen was not in attendance. Late in life he left England and settled in Amsterdam, where he communicated his secret to Hendrik van Roonhuisen. In view of the recent adoption of a state medical service it is interesting to find that in 1694 Hugh Chamberlen published a scheme for paying doctors out of the taxes.

One of the most accomplished guides to the mysteries of housewifery in those days was Mistress Hannah Woolley, the wife of the master of Newport School, near Saffron Walden. Her books include a *Ladies' Directory, Cook's Guide, Gentlewoman's Companion*, and similar works, all of them much in favour during her own generation and more than one that followed it. The titles just given are abbreviated from the long seventeenth-century titles. Perhaps the full title of her most popular book may be given, because in abbreviated form it does not convey the nature of the work: *The Queen-like Closet, or rich Cabinet; stored with all manner of rich receipts for preserving, candying, and cookery.* What a treasure of a schoolmaster's wife she must have been, and what a joy to her husband's boarders, of whom there were often, she tells us, above threescore. She was also in great demand in the neighbourhood in advising both rich and poor, and in nursing them in sickness. *The Queen-like Closet* was reprinted at least four times between 1670 and 1684. Some of her suggestions for curing her neighbours' ailments are more than a little surprising. Snailwater inspired great confidence in the seventeenth century, and the preparation of it was by no means a simple affair:

'Take a peck of snails (with the houses on their backs),

have in readiness a good fire of charcoal well kindled, make
a hole in the midst of the fire, and cast in your snails, and
still renew your fire till the snails be well roasted, then rub
them with a fair cloth till you have rubbed off all the green
that will come off, then put them in a mortar and bruise
them (shells and all), then take Clary, Celondine, Burrage,
Scabeous, Bugloss, five-leaved grass; and if you feel yourself hot, woodsorrel; of every one of these a good handful,
with five tops of Angelica; these herbs being all bruised in a
mortar, put them in a sweet earthen pot, with five quarts
of white wine, and two quarts of ale, let them steep all
night, then put them into a limbeck; let the herbs be in the
bottom of the pot, and the snails upon the herbs, and upon
the snails put a pint of earth worms slit, and clean washed in
white wine; and then put upon them four ounces of cumin
seeds or fennel seeds, which you please, well bruised, and
five great bundles of Rosemary flowers well picked, two or
three races of Turmerick thin sliced, Harts-horn and ivory,
of each four ounces well steeped in a quart of white wine,
till it be like a jelly, then put them all in order into the
limbeck and draw it forth with care.'

But snails were only for milder complaints. For drastic
cures she prescribed woodlice. 'It is the woodlice that doth
the cure,' she tells us in prescribing for cancer of the breast,
sore eyes, scurvy, and drowsiness of the brain. And what
is particularly interesting here is that this belief in woodlice as a cure for cancer is still found in Essex. There is,
or was until recently, a man living in the Colne valley who
claimed to have cured himself of cancer by eating woodlice.

That Mistress Woolley was by no means lacking in
credulity need not surprise us. It is only to be expected.
For example, water to be efficacious must rise in the east,
milk must be from a red cow, chicken from a red cock.
Yet she showed herself sensible and progressive in ridiculing
the idea that it was bad for an invalid to change his linen
often, and in advocating exercise.

On table manners she was superb, and some of her comments are both amusing and revealing. 'I have been invited

to dinner,' she confides, 'at which I have seen the good gentlewoman of the house sweat more in cutting up of a fowl, than the cook maid in roasting it; and when she had soundly beliquor'd her joints, hath suckt her knuckles, and to work with them again in the dish.'

Mrs. Woolley aspired above all things to be useful; but she spared the cook in nothing. The preparation of the simplest dish thought fit to offer to a guest must be a long and strenuous process. It is also sad to note in her recipes how many of our wild birds were sacrificed for food. She has instructions how to boil plovers, quails, blackbirds, rails, thrushes, snipes, wheatears, larks, and sparrows.

If cooking did not keep the ladies of the day fully occupied she had other enthralling pursuits for them. 'The things I pretend greatest skill in,' she says, 'are all works wrought with a needle, all transparent works, shell-work, moss-work, also cutting of prints, and adorning rooms, or cabinets, or stands with them. All kinds of beugle work upon wires or otherwise. All manner of toys for closets. Rocks made with shells or in sweets. Frames for looking-glasses, pictures, or the like. Feathers of crewel for the corners of beds.' A list of things in which she had at least a more than adequate working knowledge would be endless.

One would have thought there was enough to do without making those fantastic picture frames, still to be seen occasionally in old-fashioned country houses, in patterns made up of moss, shells, beads, and curious fragments of glass. These ladies, however, seem to have had endless patience for such work. Sometimes whole rooms were covered with shells worked into patterns and even raised in horrible protuberances like stalagmites. One example, though of later date, is in Hatfield Forest, the property of the National Trust. There is another in a garden on Baldwin's Hill, Loughton.

These grottoes, as they were called, became sentimental retreats to which the more pious ladies of the day could retire for prayer and meditation. The wilderness, a secluded part of a garden designed as fantastically as the walls of the

Easton Lodge, near Dunmow

Leighs Priory

grotto, sometimes to form a maze or labyrinth, was another. There was a famous one at Leighs at the time it was the home—the 'delicious Leez'—of Mary Rich, wife of the fourth Earl of Warwick,

> Whose well-rolled walks,
> With curvature of slow and easy sweep—
> Deception innocent—give ample space
> To narrow bounds.

Mary Rich was a sister of Robert Boyle, the principal founder of the Royal Society. With her lovely curls, parted in the middle to fall about her thoughtful forehead and bright intelligent eyes, she is one of the sweetest women in Essex history, though her piety becomes a little oppressive at times. She was a great friend of the Lady Maynard whose funeral sermon was preached by Ken. Both were favourites with their chaplains. Whether their husbands valued their piety as much is another matter.

When Mary Boyle came to Leighs in the summer of 1641 as the bride of Charles Rich she was a girl of fifteen, and Leighs was still—to the family chaplain at all events—'a secular Elysium, a worldly Paradise.' Whoever laid out the grounds made full use of the plentiful supply of water. The River Ter flows through the garden, so it was a simple matter to produce the lakes and fountains that the taste of the age prescribed. There was so much water about that fanciful admirers have suggested *Les Eaux* as the original form of the name. Dr. Anthony Walker, the favourite chaplain, seems to have held this view, for in a funeral sermon, while describing the deceased fourth earl's imaginary virtues, he indulges in a florid passage: 'O Leez! resume thy name. Melt into waters; turn into a Bochim . . . thy princely gardens put on weeds to mourn in.' This, we know, was all pious humbug. Charles Rich had been a disagreeable, bad-tempered man, and his death must have come as a relief to all who had had to deal with him. Perhaps it was Walker's own relief at his passing that inspired such eloquence. The Wilderness, across the river from the house, was the countess's place of retreat. There she spent two hours each morning in studious solitude. But we must not blame the countess's piety on her husband's gout. Even as a bride of fifteen she was already so devout that her chief source of satisfaction in joining the household at Leighs was that it was a place 'where religion was both practised and encouraged,' and where 'daily many eminent and excellent divines' preached in the chapel. The head of the family at the time was still the second Earl of Warwick, who, as Clarendon told us, patronized the Puritan preachers and gave them shelter at Leighs during the harsher phases of seventeenth-century orthodoxy. Mary would have heard much about her prospective father-in-law's reputation as a supporter of the new nonconformity. She had probably heard less about his privateering exploits.

But the trouble for a young bride rarely came from the father-in-law, who was delighted to welcome a young lady into his household, bringing, as she did, hopes for a new generation. It was the mother-in-law who was the difficulty. Where the lord saw a man to succeed him, his lady saw a woman to supplant her. The position became more difficult still when, as in this case, the countess was a second wife and not the mother of the bridegroom. Charles Rich was the son of the second earl and Frances Hatton, a wealthy heiress who, according to Mary, brought her husband 'the greatest estate any woman had done for many years.' When she died in London in 1623 she was carried into Essex attended by two hundred horsemen bearing torches. Her funeral was long talked about in the Felsted neighbourhood.

The earl's second countess was not on good terms with the wife of her eldest stepson, Robert; so when a second stepson brought home a bride she returned to Bath until she could learn more about her. Mary, she soon discovered, was of milder temperament; but she herself did not live long. So the countess with whom Mary had most to do was the third. This lady, like her new husband the second earl, had already been married twice. By her second marriage she had become Countess of Sussex. She was an exceptionally strong-minded woman who had acquired considerable power in society by her three influential marriages, and this she was later to extend by marrying a fourth time. After the second Earl of Warwick's death she married the second Earl of Manchester, commander of the Parliamentary forces during the civil wars. The relationships of the Warwick household thus became extremely complicated and were an excellent illustration of the complexities of seventeenth-century family life. The Earl of Manchester, whom the Countess of Warwick married as her fourth husband, went one better than his wife by marrying five times. And three of his wives came from the Warwick family. It was one of the jokes of the day that the Earl of Manchester had married Warwick's niece, Warwick's daughter, and Warwick's wife. It was perfectly true. His second wife was the daughter of the Earl of Warwick's sister; his third was Anne Rich, the Earl of Warwick's daughter; his fourth was the Earl of Warwick's widow. It was little wonder that the Church had to restrict the range of marital ambitions.

The eldest son of the second earl died a year, or little more, after his father. But he had lived long enough to have two wives. On the death of his first wife, the Anne Cavendish who had been so unacceptable to her mother-in-law, Waller wrote an ode that was far more complimentary to the lady than to her place of abode. After reading the poetical effusions of prosy parsons on Leighs it is salutary to turn to the prosaic description of a poet. Perhaps, as a Royalist, Waller could not be expected to view the Puritan household of the Warwicks with much favour. But he was very rude about Essex:

> May those already cursed Essexian planes,
> Where hasty death and pining sickness reigns,
> Prove all a desert! and none there make stay,
> But savage beasts, or men as wild as they!

The lamented lady died in her twenty-seventh year, leaving only one son, who was married to Cromwell's youngest daughter.

The generation that saw this marriage of a Rich with a

* C

Cromwell also saw another complication of family relationships by the marriage of another Charles Rich—son of the Charles who on his brother's death became fourth earl and Mary his countess—with another Anne Cavendish, niece of the one whose death was celebrated by Waller. To the unutterable grief of his parents this youngest Charles died of small-pox four months before his twenty-first birthday. When he was buried at Felsted on 24th May 1664 the faithful chaplain, the Rev. Dr. Anthony Walker, was again in attendance with one of those absurd panegyrics so dear to the Puritan heart. On this occasion, however, we may be quite sure that he preached with genuine feeling, because the heir to the earldom was now Hatton Rich, the youngest son of the second earl, a wild young man who may have suffered in youth from an overdose of Puritan piety, for he had promptly announced that if ever he came to Leighs as master he would show the door to all those 'good and holy' ministers who frequented it. Hatton, however, did not succeed. He died less than seven years later, and his death must have been a relief to Mary, though of course she was much too self-controlled to say so. The most she could bring herself to confess was: 'I can truly say I was sorry for him, though, because of his not fearing God, I could not at all delight in his company.'

Poor Hatton! He was the black sheep of the family. He never married and we know very little about him. But there is extant a letter, written by him to Sir Ralph Verney at Blois, from lodgings at Tours which the Verneys had occupied while they were in exile. It contains, surely, more humanity than most of the pious utterances of the Warwicks and their Puritan chaplains:

'Your friend Antoinette, and all the rest here, kiss your hands, but if they should know that you will not allow them to be belles, I believe it would breed ill blood betwixt you. I have formerly commended the Hay [Hague] for good people, but indeed, these are so far before them, as there's no comparison, and for the good old man here, he doth so confound me with civilities, both by words and actions, that if he were an old woman, I think verily I should marry him. Now I come to tell you particulars: first, for outward ceremony, he will hardly put on his hat without I use my rhetorick with him, hardly eat a bit of meat without I face him to it, then if he sees that I do not eat, he is always chiding his daughters that they do not get me that I like, so that I am forced to eat till I burst again, although I have no appetite; and always laugh though I am melancholy, lest they should think something displeased me. He hath heard that I borrowed money sometimes at the Hay: he hath asked my man forty times already, whether I want any, and that all he hath is at my service, so that I think I must be fain to borrow money from him lest he should take it ill of me (but pray let not my Lord Willoughby know that, lest he should again dun me) for frolic apart, they are the best people in the world.'

Mary Rich was only fifty-three when she died in 1678, five years after her husband. A selection of her devotional writings and an autobiographical work have been published. Her diaries are in the British Museum.

# CHAPTER V

## A PRIDE OF PARSONS

What makes all doctrines plain and clear?
'About two hundred pounds a year.'
And that which was proved true before
Prove false again? 'Two hundred more.'

*Hudibras.*

ANTHONY WALKER spoke for all his kind when he described
Leighs as a 'Worldly Paradise.' For parsons it undoubtedly
was. None of them appear to have been in the least troubled
by the shade of the sinister lord chancellor who built it,
though he had on his hands the blood of Sir Thomas More and
many of the Marian martyrs. They, good virtuous men,
could not be expected to sympathize with Penelope Devereux,
sold in marriage to the father of their patron, our noble
second Earl of Warwick. Nor for that matter were they
perturbed by rumours that their patron himself, so pleasant
in address and so gracious to the displaced clergy, had been
a bold and devil-may-care pirate.

Leighs was a lovely place; but it may not have been
particularly healthy. It lies on low ground, and there was
then far too much water about the gardens in winter, however
attractive this might be in summer. Stephen Marshall, the
famous vicar of Finchingfield, is said to have gone there to
recover from a cold. He is much more likely to have caught
one. But these people were always so good at turning things
their own way and hiding shady corners with fine tapestries,
both actual and metaphorical. Why, Stephen Marshall's
common cold had to be refined into a 'deepe distillation of
my heade upon my lungs.' No wonder Mary Rich, who was
so young and romantic when she arrived at Leighs, came under
the spell of these learned ministers. And it may have been
for the best, in view of all she was to suffer later from her

64

husband's tiresome moods, that they instructed her so dili-
gently in 'sanctified affliction,' and warned her against the
'tinsell glories of this deluding world.'

In most households the chaplain was only a superior kind
of domestic, but at Leighs he was an honoured guest. If the
Rev. Dr. Anthony Walker had any worries at all they must
have been concerned with the propriety of a Puritan being
so comfortable. On quitting Leighs he was installed in the
commodious rectory at Fyfield, near Ongar, where he spent
the last thirty years of his life in ease and tranquillity, with
occasional excursions into print. In 1690 he wrote a memoir
of his wife, Elizabeth Walker, which has a charming personal
note on cider making. The doctor confides that when friends
dined with him at Fyfield rectory they would commend his
cider, saying it was the best they had ever tasted, whereupon
Mrs. Walker, between jest and earnest, would exclaim: '*His*
cider! 'tis *my* cider. I had all the pains and care, and he
hath all the praise who never meddles with it.' He then tells
us the story of the last cider Mrs. Walker ever made. They
had good orchards of both the Herefordshire redstreaks and
the Worcestershire jennet-moyles, two cider apples that make
drink of different body, gust, and flavour, and Walker wished
them to be ground and pressed separately. Mrs. Walker
objected.

'My dear,' she said, 'thou knowest not the trouble of
drawing off so many vessels; I 'll make an hogshead of them,
putting them both together.'

That was what she did, and the result was so successful
that it was judged the best cider she had ever made.

It is pleasant to think of a Puritan parson enjoying his
cider like a jovial monk or an honest farmer; but Walker's
title of remembrance rests upon his association with the
learned Dean of Bocking, Dr. John Gauden, who was born at
Mayland in Essex, and was the high-stepping horse among the
clergy of seventeenth-century Essex. He returned to his
native county as chaplain to the second Earl of Warwick, an
office he filled before the arrival of Dr. Anthony Walker, who
had formerly been Gauden's curate. When he left to become

rector of Bocking, Gauden was still in the neighbourhood and continued to be in regular attendance at Leighs, where the company was doubtless more to his liking than any he could find among the weavers of his own parish.  Walker says that he lived in his deanery 'at a rate of a thousand a year, and made the greatest figure of any clergyman in Essex, or perhaps in England at that time.'   So he and his patron must have been an imposing pair—the earl a gallant and commanding seaman, the dean a proud and haughty cleric.

The title of dean is enjoyed by the rectors of Bocking by special privilege.   The parishes of Bocking in Essex and Hadleigh in Suffolk were 'peculiars.'   Until 1838, when all such were abolished, they were free from diocesan control and subject only to the authority of the Archbishop of Canterbury.   From the thirteenth century to 1572 the title of dean was held only by rectors of Bocking; but at that date it was transferred to the rectors of Hadleigh and held by them alone until Gauden assumed it again in 1650.   Since then it has been held by the rectors of both Bocking and Hadleigh, 'conjointly and severally,' as a co-title.   Gauden's gabled rectory is still in use, and near it is a dovecote with a hundred and thirty-five nests, which was built during his incumbency.

Gauden will always be remembered as the reputed author of the *Eikon Basilike*, which for ten years was accepted everywhere as the work of Charles I.   There are still some who argue in favour of the royal authorship; but there is little doubt that it was the dean's, though the whole story is full of baffling inconsistencies.   How did this chaplain to the Puritan earl come to write a defence of the king, we may ask; and having written it, why did he not claim the authorship until ten years later?

The *Eikon Basilike* appeared within a few hours of the king's death, just when Royalist feeling was most impassioned. And as a rumour was immediately circulated that the king had written it, the book became the bible of the Cavaliers. It contributed more than anything else to what critics have called the 'myth' of the 'royal martyr.' Cromwell's ascendancy was said to be due to his religious character. If the king could be similarly sanctified, it was argued, his cause would be promoted. So the public were persuaded that His Majesty had written these pious reflections and left them as a testament to his people. Gauden appears to have been at all stages a party to this deception. He may have invented it. The tone of the book is a mixture of royal pride and Christian humility. Its every sentiment was calculated to go straight to the hearts of the king's devoted followers and persuade them that he was a saint no less than a king. Whether or not the king connived in the deception we shall never know. It is not even certain that he ever saw the manuscript.

The sales of the book were enormous. When the Parliamentarians saw how affected the nation was by its arguments they engaged Milton to reply. His counterblast was the *Eikonoclastes*, which though written as in reply to a royal apologia suggests that the hand of a clergyman was suspected. Milton probaby believed that one of the bishops had either written or edited it.

When we reflect that so many of those who argued about the authorship knew Gauden intimately the conflict in the evidence seems incredible until we remember that they were all writing late in life, and long after the original publication. Gauden's own claim to authorship was made in a letter to Clarendon in 1661, and it is to be noted that Clarendon in reply said that he already knew who had written the book and wished he did not. The belated claim was, as we can readily imagine, as embarrassing as the publication had been timely. But why was it made at all after this long delay? Gauden said that his sole object had been to 'vindicate the king's wisdom, honour, and piety,' which had been done more effectively by allowing the public to believe in the royal authorship, but that he could see no reason for the deception to be continued after the Restoration.

We need not question the dean's sincerity in wishing to present the king in the best light. He may even have satisfied himself that he was justified in allowing the wrong person to be accepted as author when the deception was so beneficial to the cause. He would certainly think it prudent to remain in obscurity until he saw how the Commonwealth prospered. In judging him we must remember that there were many others in the county as well as in the country who began as good Parliamentarians and changed their course when they saw how revolutionary the New Order threatened to be. It was largely because his policy had appeared to them revolutionary that they had first rebelled against Charles. Few of the Essex gentry had ever been fanatical in their allegiance to the New Order. It was parliamentary government they supported. They were never easy about the Parliamentary army. In 1649 Gauden himself had addressed to Fairfax *A Religious and Loyal Protestation* against the proceedings in Parliament.

When Gauden claimed to be the sole author of the *Eikon Basilike* he had recently been made Bishop of Exeter, a see that had turned out to be less remunerative than expected. He wished to be translated to Winchester, and produced the authorship as a secret service to the Stuart cause which might be counted in his favour. It was undoubtedly acknowledged, for though he was not given Winchester he was translated to Worcester, and died as its bishop. But to allow the claim privately and to announce it publicly were two widely differing propositions. Here was a middle-aged bishop claiming for himself all the honour and sanctity that for a decade had been so devoutly accorded to the martyred king. If he had still been at Bocking it might have looked like a case of mental derangement such as was not, after all, uncommon among rural clergy. It was not so easy to dismiss the claim of one who had only a few weeks before been elevated to a bishopric. A glance at the work—no one could be expected to read it now—will show how impossible it was for Clarendon or any other responsible person to make full avowal of the deception. The author had even gone so far as to produce the prayers the king had 'used' in committing his soul to God in his last confinement,

to say nothing of the alleged royal arguments against the
pretended jurisdiction of the High Court. No wonder
Clarendon said he wished himself ignorant of the secret. And
no wonder Hume, Bishop Christopher Wordsworth, and
others of like stature have found it hard to believe that any
one should have had the presumption to claim such familiarity with the innermost thoughts and aspirations of His
Sacred Majesty.

In the controversy that raged over the Gauden claim of
authorship three Essex clergymen figured prominently.
They were Dr. Richard Hollingworth, vicar of West Ham
and afterwards of Chigwell, Edward Symmons, sequestered
vicar of Rayne, and Dr. Anthony Walker, Gauden's curate
and loyal friend throughout both their lives. Hollingworth
and Symmons were for the king, Walker for Gauden.
Walker's evidence is weighty, especially as much of it was
confirmed by Gauden's widow, though obviously we cannot
know to what extent the two of them put their heads together
over it. An annoying feature of Walker's story is that it
provokes one or two questions which he did not live to answer.
Though he had told the story previously for publication by
others, his own published account did not appear until after
his death in 1692, more than forty years after the appearance
of the *Eikon Basilike*. The advertisement of the Walker
account disarmed criticism to some extent by its announcement that 'the reverend author, Dr. Anthony Walker,
coming to London to publish this treatise, it pleased God
before it was produced at the press to take him to Himself.'

Dr. Hollingworth's view rested on the testimony of Symmons, whose parish of Rayne adjoined Bocking. Symmons
was an ardent Royalist, a scholar and also a writer. He
said that the work had been sent to him before publication
by the king with a request that he should peruse and correct
it. The manuscript moved him so deeply that he could not
contain his transport, and sent for Gauden in order to share
it with his distinguished neighbour. Gauden, said Symmons, begged to be allowed to take the manuscript home and
keep it for a few days while he studied it. Symmons

allowed this. And while he had the work in his keeping, the Symmons account continues, the cunning dean, with the help of a secretary, transcribed the whole, ostensibly for his own edification. Symmons was told that this had been done, and when the two met again it occurred to them that it might be prudent to substitute the Gauden transcript for the original in sending the work to the printer, in case the handwriting should be recognized and the manuscript seized by the Parliamentarians. Thus Symmons explained Gauden's handwriting in the copy used by the printer, which was carried to the press by Walker.

To this story Walker replied: first, that any one who knew Gauden and Symmons would ridicule the idea of the obscure parson of Rayne sending for the great Dr. Gauden. We cannot assess the value of this point, but it seems a weak one when we reflect that Symmons was sending for Gauden not on his own business but on the king's. Walker's next point is not much stronger. He says that some of the events mentioned in the book happened after Symmons had left Rayne, and could not have been described in time for him to read of them before his own sequestration in February 1643. This is undoubtedly true. But it has never been uncommon for a manuscript to be altered after apparent completion. The real strength of Walker's testimony is in his account of discussions he had with Gauden about the manuscript; his indication of the use in it of a number of characteristic turns of expression that Gauden was given to repeating in his sermons, prayers, and writings; and similar small things that in the aggregate carry considerable weight. But the entire story is full of curious complexities. The oddest is that if Symmons was in fact the rascal the Gauden side would have us believe him, those neighbours of his did not discover it sooner. If they did see through him, then why did they entrust him with the manuscript at any stage? All the accounts agree that he did prepare the *Eikon Basilike* for the press. And here again we have an almost incredible story, even as Walker tells it.

While Symmons was staying with a friend in Hertfordshire,

a troop of horse from the regiment of Colonel Rich, the eldest son of the Earl of Warwick, came to quarter in the neighbourhood under the command of a Lieutenant Arwaker. The lieutenant himself stayed in the same house as Symmons, and the two quarrelled while discussing the army's treatment of the king. Arwaker went so far as to threaten revenge in a way that made Symmons take to his heels and fly to London, where he had lodgings in Carter Lane. Not long afterwards, while correcting the proof sheets of the *Eikon Basilike*, he discovered that Arwaker was also staying in Carter Lane—that he was, in fact, quartered at the 'Bell.' A few days later the two met, and, though no word passed between them, they recognized each other. Arwaker swung round at once and dogged Symmons to his house, which he had no sooner entered than a brace of bullets was discharged at the door from the lieutenant's gun, apparently to mark it. Six troopers were then called out by Arwaker and the house was promptly and thoroughly searched. Symmons, however, had escaped through a window by the time the troopers reached his room. His papers were carried away; but not the proof sheets of the *Eikon Basilike*. These were lying on the table. But they were evidently thought of no account, for they were merely dashed off and scattered about the floor. Some blew out into the street, where they were picked up after the troopers had left.

Walker was staying at Warwick House, the Riches' London home, at the time, and there he heard the story from Symmons himself, who begged Walker to speak to Colonel Rich about his lost papers, and try to persuade him to order the lieutenant to return them. So between prayers and dinner that evening Walker took Charles Rich, afterwards fourth Earl of Warwick, aside, and asked him if he would be kind enough to intimate to his brother, the colonel, that Dr. Walker had a favour to ask. This was done, and the colonel called the chaplain to him, assuring him of his entire goodwill towards so faithful a friend of the family, and asking what he desired. Walker asked the colonel if he had not a Lieutenant Arwaker in his regiment. The colonel said that he had. Walker then explained that in a pique this lieutenant had broken into a poor minister's closet and had stolen his sermon notes, adding jocularly: 'He hath undone a poor parson in robbing him of his tools.'

The colonel at once saw what was required. He called for pen and paper and ordered the lieutenant to return all that he had taken.

Such were the mishaps and complications that attended the printing of the *Eikon Basilike: the Portraiture of His Sacred Majesty in His Solitudes and Sufferings*. Or at all events, that was the kind of gossip that went round the Essex parsonages about the great Dean of Bocking, the parson of Rayne, and old Dr. Walker, who lived so long at Leighs and Fyfield, and was known to every one in those parts.

There was other gossip. Parsons get far more involved in affairs of the heart than the laity ever hear about. Indeed it is doubtful whether any class endures more than the clergy from the indiscreet affections of ardent young ladies. One of the young clergymen who suffered in this way during the period under review was Roger Williams, founder of Rhode Island, which the Earl of Warwick helped to settle, and to which many Essex families emigrated. It was while he was chaplain to Sir William Masham of Otes, High Laver. Sir William, it will be recalled, was the son-in-law of Sir Francis Barrington, and his fellow prisoner in the Marshalsea after refusing to pay the tax levied by Charles in 1626. Roger Williams seems to have joined the Masham household early in 1629, or perhaps in 1628, and to have attracted the attention of Lady Barrington's niece, who would, presumably, be the cousin of his mistress, Lady Masham. When old Lady Barrington, who, as we have seen, was Cromwell's aunt, heard that her niece's name was being coupled with that of her daughter's chaplain she was extremely angry. But this remained unknown to Mr. Williams until stated in unambiguous terms in a reply to a letter he wrote to the old lady, more or less asking for her blessing. Evidently Lady Barrington did not foresee the illustrious future awaiting Roger Williams in the New World, and it is equally evident that, for all his greatness as a pioneer, Roger Williams was a vain and opinionated young man, with no real feeling for the young lady, but who was not averse to marrying her if her family would accept him. If he had, in fact, married her he might have become an Essex country parson, perhaps another Dean of Bocking. As it was, a little over seven months after the Barrington episode he married a Mary Barnard at High Laver, and in 1631 took her with him to New England.

Williams wrote two letters to Lady Barrington. Both are in the British Museum (Egerton MS. 2643), and are most entertaining documents. They must, however, be given in abridged form because these seventeenth-century preachers were more garrulous in their hour-glasses than topers in a tap-room.

'Madame,' wrote Williams, 'Your ladyship may wonder at this unwonted absence! And also ask what means this Paper dignity! Give me leave, dear Madame, to say with David, to his brother in the field: Is there not a cause? A just, haply a known and open cause. I am sure to your ladyship, who as an Angel of God discerneth wisely, a known and open cause. Many and often speeches have long fluttered or flown abroad concerning your Ladyship's near kinswoman and my unworthy self. What little ear I have given that way, further than I have hearkened after your ladyship's mind, all that know me do know. Yet like a rolling snowball or some flowing stream the report extends and gathers stronger and stronger. Which causes me this day to stand behind the hangings and not be seen any way countenancing so great a business, which haply may want strength to bring it forth to see the light. It is the command of the God of Wisdom by that wise King Solomon, Establish thy thoughts by counsel. I presume therefore to consult, as most of right I acknowledge I ought, at the soonest with your ladyship, especially considering her loving and strong affection, together with the report as strong abroad.

'Good Madame, may it please you then to take notice: I acknowledge myself altogether unworthy and unmeet for such a proposition. The nearness of her blood to your ladyship and godly flourishing branches hath forced me to confess her portion in that regard to be beyond compare invaluable. Yet many fears have much possessed me. Longed I have to discover that sincerity and godliness which makes the Lord himself to like his creature, and must make me if ever I have received some good testimonials from my own experience, more from others, not the least from your good ladyship's self.

'Objections have come in about her spirit, much accused for passionate and hasty, rash and inconstant; other fears about her present condition, it being some indecorum for her to condescend to my low ebb. There I something stick, but were all this cleared, there is one bar not likely to be broken, and that is the present estate of us both. That portion it hath pleased God to allot her, as I hear, is not for present and haply, as things now stand in England, shall never be by us enjoyed.

'For my own part, it is well known, though I would gladly conceal myself, how a gracious God and tender conscience, as Balak said to Balaam, have kept me back from honour and preferment. Beside my former offers and that late New England call, I have had since two several livings offered me, each of them a hundred pounds per annum, but as things yet stand among us I see not how any . . . [MS. faded]. Nor do I seek, nor shall I be drawn on any terms to part, even to my last farthing, from Otes so long as any competency can be raised or liberty afforded. I shall impart the utmost to your ladyship, more punctually than ever yet to any. Besides the means I now from hence enjoy little is there that I can call mine. After the death of an aged loving mother, amongst some children I may expect, though for the present she is close and will not promise, some twenty pounds or so per annum. . . .

'I have been bold to open to your ladyship the whole anatomy of the business. To wrong your precious niece and answer her kind love with want would be like gall to all the song of my life and mar my marriage joys. The kind affection of your dear ladyship and worthy niece is of better

merit and desert. . . . The Lord that hath carried you from
the womb to grey hairs crown those grey hairs by making
your last days, like the close of some sweet harmony, your
best: fruitful like Sara's in old age, outshining all those
stars that shine about you, going down in grace, rising in
glory in the arms of your dearest Saviour, to which ever-
lasting arms he often commits your soul.

'Yours, who is,

'Your unworthiest, though faithful, of all that
truly serve and honour you,

'ROGER WILLIAMS.'

Lady Barrington remained unmoved by all these blandish-
ments, and replied in terms that brought a second and very
different letter from the lover who only desired to serve her
ladyship, whom he had described as an angel of God in his
first letter. She had now become a fallen angel. On 2nd
May 1629 he wrote:

'MADAME,

'I doubt not but that your good wisdom and love have
fairly interpreted my carriage in the late treaty, and I
also trust quieted and stilled the loving affections of your
worthy niece. We hope to live together in the Heavens
though the Lord hath denied that union on Earth. Dear
Madame, let me beg your Christian pardon if I shall acquaint
your ladyship with a business of more weight and consequence and much nearer concerning yourself. . . . Good
Madame, it is not for nothing the God of heaven hath sent
such thunderclaps of late and made such great offers at the
door of your ladyship's heart—distractions about children
and their affections, deprival of a dear and tender yoke-fellow.
Weaknesses in the outward and troubles in the inward man,
what are they but loud alarums to awaken you?

'The Father of Lights himself be pleased to show you the
interpretation of these dreams. Certainly, Madame, the
Lord hath a quarrel against you. Woe unto me, if I hold my
peace, or hide that from you which may seem bitter at present,
but it may be sweeter than honey in the latter end. I know

not one professor among all I know, whose truth and faith-fulness to Jesus Christ is more suspected, doubted, feared by all or most of those that know the Lord.   Woe to me if I shall conceal what great thoughts of heart the Lord suffers yet to be and break forth in his dearest saints about you. And yet no hand is with me.   The God of heaven and your dear self only know these secret lines.   It hath almost astonished me, and I trust will deeply affect your ladyship, that not only inferior Christians, but ministers, eagle-eyed, faithful and observant to your ladyship, after so many years of God's patience towards you, so long profession, such helps, and means, incomparable, should yet be driven to sigh, to say little, to suspend their judgments, to hope, but to fear and doubt. . . .'

'Remember, I beseech you, your candle is twinkling and glass near run.   The Lord only knows how few minutes are left behind.

'Your ladyship's most faithful and obedient,
'ROGER WILLIAMS.'

After that we are not surprised to learn that Lady Barrington refused to have any further communication with him.

We may laugh at these priggish and self-righteous Puritans now that more than three centuries separate us from their arrogant bluster.   There was little laughter to be enjoyed when they were near.   But there were exceptions.   Stephen Marshall, for example, though an influential Puritan divine, chaplain to the Earl of Essex's regiment, member of the Westminster Assembly, and, according to Clarendon, as great a power among the Parliamentarians as Laud was among the Royalists, was as human as we could wish a country parson to be.

When Edward Symmons was driven from Rayne for preaching against the Parliament that Stephen Marshall supported, by a band of hooligans and agitators who threat-ened to murder him, it was the same Stephen Marshall who came to his rescue.   When Symmons was tried for his alleged offences it was again Stephen Marshall whose 'testimony and friendship' saved him from imprisonment, and who stood bail for him.

Stephen Marshall's private life was quite different from his public life, if we are to trust the accounts of those who knew him best, and much more attractive. But then he had the advantage of being written about by Giles Firmin, author of *The Real Christian*, one of the most engaging country parsons in the Essex of his day, a gentle creature and the devoted friend of Marshall to the end. Instead of putting down gloom and despondency to such causes as those so nauseatingly recited by the stricter brethren, Firmin, who was ejected from his living at Shalford in 1662, quietly suggested that as likely as not it was due to having to live with 'an unequal yoke-fellow, with unhandsome carriage,' or to having a partner whom 'the house will not hold,' or one whom 'the dumb devils seize.' Calamy described Firmin as 'a man of peace, not rigid or morose, but of great moderation,' one who 'went about doing good, and therein was his chief delight.'

Before settling in Essex as a parson, and marrying the daughter of the parson of Stondon Massey, Firmin was a physician in New England. Few Puritans enjoy the advantage of having such a man as this to write their biographies.

In Firmin's account of Stephen Marshall we see a thick-shouldered man with 'shackling gait' and large fierce eyes standing in the pulpit at Wethersfield or Finchingfield, of which he was vicar for twenty-six years. There are numerous accounts of Stephen Marshall as the great man. Here we may glance at him from another angle, and try to see him, not as Roger Williams tried to see Lady Barrington—as reflected in 'the great Taskmaster's eye'—but as reflected in the eyes and hearts of his own people. Physically he was a rough-hewn, clumsy man, untidy in dress and awkward in manner; but strangely attractive, particularly to the ladies in his congregation. It is the same story. His fierce, impassioned oratory and the emotional depth of his character held them spell-bound throughout his sermons and made him the favourite topic of conversation in their cottages. The men were sometimes inclined to be amused. 'Look, look, he shakes his shoulders,' Firmin reports hearing a Mr. Wiltshire say to his neighbour as they sat listening to him, 'we shall have something anon.' Firmin, watching the performance with the eye of the professional, summed it up by saying that 'whatever good his preaching does upon men's souls, it works mightily upon women's affections.'

Again, as with Williams, a young lady of gentle birth came along and fell a victim to the preacher's zeal. Marshall was only the son of a poor glover of Grantchester, but when Susanna Castell, 'a gentlewomen of considerable fortune,' came over from Woodham Walter to stay in the neighbourhood of Wethersfield, there was no Lady Barrington to keep the lady and the preacher apart. They married and had three daughters while at Wethersfield. Then they moved to the valuable living of Finchingfield, at that time worth two hundred pounds a year and an important parish. The patron of the living was the eccentric William Kempe of Spains Hall, a violent, morose person who one day in a fit of passion accused his wife of unfaithfulness, and was afterwards so distressed that he vowed never to speak again. For seven years he kept silence, and a local tradition has it that he died at the end of that time while struggling to regain the use of his tongue. Giles Firmin's story, which is probably the correct one, is that Kempe did in fact talk again after seven years of complete silence, and that the man who persuaded him to do so was Stephen Marshall. When Kempe first took part in public worship after his long silence the entire village turned out to witness it. His wife, Philippa, did not accompany him. She had been dead two years when Stephen Marshall came to Finchingfield.

Four more children were born to the Marshalls in Essex, and Stephen was regarded by his neighbours as a foolishly indulgent father. Indeed it was the one thing about him that the villagers strongly criticized. Instead of the austere fare that Puritan children ought to have had to give them a proper view of the miseries of this mortal state, the Marshall children lived well and went to parties. Their education,

Spains Hall, Finchingfield

Marks Hall, Coggeshall

one person said, consisted in 'going from one good house to another to eat cheese-cakes and custards.' As for their dress, it was sinful. They followed the London fashions, wore silks and taffetas and had their frocks cut far too low at the neck, 'insomuch that the Godly party were sorely scandalized,' for at that time the good were expected to have

> Religion in their garments, and their hair
> Cut shorter than their eyebrows,

as Ben Jonson has it in *Every Man out of his Humour*. And, incidentally, the frivolity of his family is not the only curious feature about Stephen Marshall's brand of nonconformity. He preached like a Puritan, and Parliament honoured him as one; but many features that no strict Puritan should have allowed to remain are still to be seen in Finchingfield church. The Pelican of Piety is carved on the door, and just above the handle is a crucifix. He even allowed a figure of the Virgin Mary to remain on an altar tomb, though that has been removed since his day.

Whether the upbringing of his children was as much in their father's hands as it should have been is open to question. Stephen Marshall would never touch his wife's fortune. In this he may have shown his enlightenment; but the money did his daughters no good. If the head of the household had controlled it, less might have gone in pandering to their vanity. We do not know. He was an indulgent father, and perhaps they would have got what they wanted even if he had asserted the rights that the law of his day gave him over the fortune his wife brought with her. What we do know is that vanity got the better of his children, and that later the wise old folk of Finchingfield were able to wag their heads and say they knew no good would come of allowing young people to have so much freedom. Only one of his daughters was any comfort to him in his old age. Two of them were a sad embarrassment and may be said to have disgraced his memory. They became actresses. And if you would know what else you must refer to Pepys, who had a fancy for Beck. He admired her acting, her pretty hands, and thought her 'mighty fine and pretty, and noble.' She was noted also for the laxity of her morals. The *Diary* entry for 26th October 1667 has: 'Mrs. Pierce tells me that the two Marshalls at the King's house are Stephen Marshall's the great Presbyterian's daughters: and that Nelly [1] and Beck Marshall falling out the other day, the latter called the other my Lord Buckhurst's [2] mistress. Nell answered her, "I was but one man's mistress, though I was brought up in a brothel to fill strong water to the gentlemen; and you are a mistress to three or four, though a Presbyter's praying daughter."'

When the old man lay dying his five unnatural daughters thought only of the money they might get by his passing. They went so far as to persuade the husband of the one faithful daughter to advance them one hundred pounds each, giving him in exchange an illegally drawn-up document conveying to him 'all their estate and interest in Waies in Finchingfield.' Stephen Marshall heard of this, and though near the end he pulled himself together, called for his will, and added a codicil. Each should repay to Peter Smith the hundred pounds she had received, and Peter Smith on his part should give up all claim to the estate they had illegally conveyed to him. Failing this, Peter Smith should retain five hundred pounds of the legacies. Not a single word of reproach did he add.

That was not the last injury that great man was to suffer. He was buried in Westminster Abbey; but at the Restoration his body was dug up along with nineteen others and cast into a pit dug behind one of two prebendal houses that stood at that time between the Abbey and St. Margaret's.

[1] Nell Gwyn.
[2] Of Copt Hall, near Epping.

## CHAPTER VI

## THE COUNTRY HOUSEHOLD

Provide for thy husband, to make him good cheere,
Make merrie togither, what time ye be here.
At bed and at boord, howsoever befall,
Whatever God sendeth, be merrie withall.

TUSSER.

NOWHERE in Essex do we need to travel far to find an old
farm or manor house where the household scenes of three hundred years ago can be imagined with ease. But if those who
first occupied these houses returned, they would be puzzled.
The differences would be more apparent to them than they
are to us. Yet in essentials these knights and their ladies
were not so remote from us as they appear in portraits
painted by Van Dyck, or clad in armour on their marble tombs.
They were no better than we are. Some, we may feel, were
worse, though we are certainly not entitled to feel superior
to our ancestors. On the contrary, we should think of them
as kindly as we can if only to encourage our descendants to
be generous in remembering us. There is no need to hide
their faults; there is every reason for remembering the fun
they had. And they did have fun. They dressed gallantly,
told far too many naughty stories, and were in the habit of
kissing their maids. They were also decorous enough to
disapprove of other people doing these things. Even in
Henry VIII's household the regulations stipulated that officers
of the bedchamber should 'not caress the maids on the
stairs, as many household utensils are apt to be broken as a
result. Such pages as seduce the maids of the King's Household, so that they become mothers,' the same order proceeds,
'shall pay a fine of two marks, for the benefit of His Majesty,
and shall go without beer for a month.' It was also laid
down that the cook should 'not engage ragged assistants,
who run about naked, and who sleep on the floor, or before

the kitchen fire.' As these things were forbidden we may be quite sure they were done.

Kissing, we find, was much more widely practised in England then than it is now. Erasmus, it may be recalled, wrote in glowing terms of this happy state of things: 'Wherever you go every one welcomes you with a kiss,' he said, 'and the same on bidding farewell. You call again, when there is more kissing . . . you meet an acquaintance anywhere and you are kissed till you are tired. In short, turn where you will, there are kisses, kisses everywhere. And if you were once to taste them, and find how delicate and fragrant they are, you would certainly desire, not for ten years only, like Solon, but to death, to be a sojourner in England.'

We do not sufficiently appreciate the gallantry and zeal of Samuel Pepys, Esquire, in trying to revive this civilizing custom after the Restoration.

Erasmus also said some rather unpleasant things about English hygiene, but we need not repeat them. It is probable that the dirt has been a little overdone in descriptions of medieval life. As G. B. Harrison has said: 'Even in Elizabethan England the majority of men were reasonably honest and genuinely charitable. They paid their debts, they were faithful to their wives, fond of their children, and they died as peacefully in their beds as the physician would allow them.' It is curious that so many disparaging things should have been said about our forefathers. But then worship of ancestors has never been indulged in very extensively by the English.

There is no better account of life in Elizabeth's England than that of our worthy topographer and chronologer, William Harrison of Radwinter. From him we learn of improvements in the standard of living that followed the Reformation, though he was by no means complacent about them. 'When our houses were builded of willow,' he writes, 'then we had oaken men; but now that our houses are come to be made of oak, our men are not only becoming willow, but a great many, through Persian delicacy crept in among us, altogether of straw.' It is reassuring to find that even the Elizabethans were accused of being decadent.

Harrison tells us how both rich and poor furnished their houses, what they ate, and what they drank. He explains how for twenty shillings his wife and her maid brewed more than a hundred and fifty gallons of beer, which he thought reasonable for the drink of a poor parson. He boasts about his garden, 'the whole area thereof little above three hundred foot of ground,' in which he grew nearly three hundred different simples. He deplored the get-rich-quick spirit of the age, but found 'the artificer and husbandman . . . liberal, and very friendly at their tables,' and so merry that it did a man good to be in their company. We had no one so racy in the seventeenth century; but such families as the Petres and the Barringtons kept their accounts carefully, and from their day-to-day entries we can construct a picture of the life that centred in the great house.

The Petre records enable us to trace the progress of this old Essex family from their first home at Ingatestone, to which they have returned, to their most prosperous days at Thorndon Hall, where they maintained a large establishment in keeping with the income of the owner, which about the middle of the seventeenth century appears to have been about ten thousand pounds a year. The estate books make an interesting study. Farm and kitchen were closely linked until the eighteenth century. Neither can be dissociated from the other, though besides supplying household needs Lord Petre's farm was run to substantial profits. The accounts for the year 1683 show receipts of £634 4s. 8d., against payments of £380 13s. 2d., so that there remains in his hands,' as the steward puts it, £253 11s. 6d. His stock at this date was 145 runts, or young cows, 80 cows, 3 bulls, 121 ewes, 93 lambs, with 52 ewes and 33 lambs on other land. The profits continued steady over a number of years, and the farm was evidently well conducted. In the early sixteen-eighties Lord Petre's cows, which we may be sure were good animals, sold at Romford market at £3 to £3 10s. each. In 1684 he sold forty lambs for £15 10s. Twenty oxen sold in

1682 for £135, and four in the same year for £26 10s. Straw sold at 5s. a load, hay at 20s. a load, and in 1681 eighty-eight pounds of wool were sold for £2 11s.

The life of domestics in such a household as Lord Petre's must have been livelier then than it was in later years, when there were fewer to do the work, which itself had less variety. Such an estate as Thorndon was a little kingdom, a self-contained and self-supporting community, ruled over by the owner with absolute power, though never with the tyrannical power of continental landowners. Wages for those who lived in the house were low, but were fixed at quarter sessions, not by the employer. In addition, there was casual employment of people living in their own cottages, paid for at the rate of approximately a shilling a day. Sometimes an old woman came to help in the kitchen at Thorndon for sixpence a day, and a certain Robin Lanman got the same for 'going to market,' which probably means going into Brentwood to do what little shopping was necessary—perhaps to buy a new ink-horn for her ladyship.

We can imagine how these servants would watch the progress of the family. The old people who had worked on the estate all their lives would tell their grandchildren of the different state of affairs under a former lord at Ingatestone, for it is obvious that the establishment at Thorndon Park in 1650 was very different from that at Ingatestone in the previous century.

There had been great advance in domestic comfort between the middle of the sixteenth and the middle of the seventeenth century. Furnishings had become more elaborate. By 1650 tapestries would be hanging in all the principal rooms and perhaps the new printed wall-papers would adorn the bedrooms. Brightly coloured carpets would be flung over tables and chairs, and cushions would have been introduced for the use of the ladies, who had gained more leisure. They would now have fine linen on their beds, and probably as much as two thousand pounds' worth of plate for their tables. Contemporary accounts show that even farmers by this time had their cupboards of plate, tapestry hangings to their beds, and fine napery on their tables. Pewter platters and metal spoons had replaced the old wooden spoons, still used in the kitchen.

The ladies would spend more time in their drawing-rooms, and do delicate needlework. Fifty years earlier they had been kept busy in their kitchens most of the time. But they were still far from elegant at the table. There were as yet no finger bowls and few forks. Hands were washed after a greedy and greasy meal in a basinful of water, which served the whole company, for water was scarce and precious, particularly in so dry a county as Essex. Sometimes, indeed, a diner would only be allowed to dip the corner of his napkin into a beaker of water and with that clean his finger tips— and often his teeth at the same time. Incidentally, a man's rank could be discovered by learning at what time he had his meals. Gentlefolk dined at 11 a.m. and supped at 5 p.m.; merchants at 12 and 6; husbandmen at 12 and 7 or 8; scholars, it is said, dined at 10—if they could afford a meal.

Perhaps the fullest accounts we have of an Essex household in the seventeenth century are those of the Barringtons. They cover a period of forty-five years between 1622 and 1667, with a few short breaks. Canon Galpin, while vicar of Hatfield Broad Oak, examined them with great care and contributed summaries to the *Transactions of the Essex Archaeological Society*. The first appeared in the twelfth volume, the second thirty-two years later in part two of the twenty-third volume. Both aroused great interest, particularly in America.

To sit down and open an account book that someone used three hundred years ago is to pass out of one life into another. The unfamiliar handwriting, in a way that print cannot do, conveys subtle and indefinable differences of value even in an everyday item of expenditure. But we are soon at ease with the writers. They are of our world, though whether they will be of our children's world we cannot say. Men are nearer to other races than they were, but farther from their own grandparents. Before the First World War there was at least one family in almost every village to whom the past

D

three hundred years were all in one piece, as it were. In expansive moments they could open a cupboard or safe and take out a few faded documents that preserved for them the traditions of their ancestors. It is much better for students to have so many of these documents indexed and labelled for reference in large record offices; but what were once intimate possessions, as personal as a ring or a precious stone, or perhaps a piece of plate kept in a family for generations, may tend to become museum pieces. It is not enough merely to preserve our archives; it is vital that we should preserve also the memory of those who owned them, and thus be able to see documents in relation to living persons. So with these old account books of the Barringtons; it is interesting to the student of social history to see how much it cost to repair shoes or buy new ones, but to re-create the life of the period we need to know the persons named—the Mr. Barrington whose stockings cost sixpence to refoot, the Mr. Gobert for whom a new pair of shoes cost two shillings. Some, alas, we have no means of knowing—such persons as Joe Clayden, still a common name in Essex, who helped in the kitchen or did carting and got only fourpence a day for it in 1634, or Goody Lamberte and Goody Longe, who got a shilling a pound for spinning flax.

Who then was the clever lady whose quick fingers wrote the entries in *My Ladies Booke*? She was the second wife of Sir Thomas Barrington and the daughter-in-law of Sir Francis. What is more to the point is that she was a daughter of Sir Rowland Lytton of Knebworth, and therefore a member of an accomplished family. We are not surprised to find her a most capable woman with an artistic bent—nor for that matter to find that she was a tremendous talker. It seems probable that she practically ran her husband's affairs. She had no children of her own, but Sir Thomas had sons and one daughter, Lucy, by an earlier marriage. Miss Lucy seems to have been brought up by her grandmother, old Lady Barrington, and in the family accounts there are numerous references to her education. Her tutor, Mr. Harrison, was paid £30 a year. A musician, who taught her to sing, had £2 10s. a month. A dancing master was paid £13, but for how long is not stated.

The most exciting items relating to Miss Lucy appear at the close of 1639, when she was married to Mr. Cheyne of Chesham Bois. Her trousseau cost £108 18s., and the festivities in honour of that event extended over several days, with musicians in attendance on at least two. Cooks were kept busy preparing partridges, woodcocks, capons, beef, mutton, veal, tongues, ducks, geese, teal, plovers, larks, snipe, smelts, flounders, whiting, pike, salmon, as well as tarts, barberries, pears, and sundry vegetables—not potatoes, however. Potatoes were introduced into England at the same time as tobacco, but nearly two centuries were to pass before they became popular. Mutton in this particular list meant a whole sheep, salmon a whole salmon, which cost 16s., and pike a great pike costing 12s. 6d. There was neither champagne nor port. Both came into fashion later in the century. Champagne, in fact, came in most fittingly at the Restoration. When Miss Lucy married the list was white wine, sack, claret, muscadine, and twenty-two barrels of beer. The wine merchant's name does not appear, but it is not unlikely that it was Mr. Houblon, the merchant adventurer whose ships brought up the Thames such costly merchandise that they might well have inspired verses as gay as the first two stanzas of John Masefield's poem *Cargoes*. The Houblons were later to be near neighbours of the Barringtons in Essex, for they lived at Great Hallingbury Hall, on the opposite side of the forest, for several generations.

A funeral in those non-austerity days was as costly as a wedding. When Sir Thomas himself died in 1664 the mourning for his family and dependants cost £257. In the present fluctuating state of money values it is impossible to say how much that would be in present-day currency, but it would be a very great sum. The funeral of any person of rank in those days was a great occasion. It was attended by banners charged with the badges and coats of arms of the departed and his connections by birth and marriage, borne in brave display of rank and wealth. Oxen, sheep, and calves were killed for the feasting at Sir Thomas's funeral, as well as cranes, swans, and most of the other things already recited for the wedding. Larders were not mere cupboards in the kitchen in those days, and there were no death duties.

It is said that the Spaniards who came to England in Mary Tudor's reign were astonished to see the English living in such poor houses, as they considered our half-timbered dwellings to be; but no less astonished to see how well we fared at table. We fed, they said, like kings.

Among the things that have always interested civilized peoples, clothes take a high place. The fine clothes of gentlefolk were expensive even in the seventeenth century. Here in 1633 we find: 'Garters Roses & poynts for Mr. Rowlands £2. 1s.'; and later: '2 purle bandes & cuffs, 2 playne bandes and cuffs, and 8 prs. of Boot hose for a gentleman £1. 6s.' Then comes an item: 'For one silver pott £3. 18s.; spoons etc. £9. 9s. 11d.' The pot was probably a porringer. It was not a coffee pot, for even John Evelyn did not see any one drinking coffee until 1636, and it took thirty years for the public to get accustomed to the new drink. There would be no coffee drunk by the Barringtons in 1633, nor tea either, which was at least thirty shillings a pound in 1680, and at the end of the century as much as three guineas a pound, the duty was so high.

Long strings of prices may be dull; but a few items should be interesting. About 1640, according to the Barrington accounts, beef was 2½d. to 3½d. a pound; a leg of mutton 1s. 10d.; a shoulder 1s. 8d.; bacon 6d. a pound; butter 5d. to 7d. a pound; milk 2½d. a pint; strong beer 2d. a pint; ale 1d. a pint. Such provisions as these were only bought in London. At Hatfield they were all produced at home. The year 1640 was a fairly normal sort of year. There was a bad epidemic of smallpox in London in the following year, but nothing extraordinary to affect prices in 1640. It is, of course, interesting to see how the condition of the country does affect the food markets. In both the plague year of 1665 and the following year, the year of the Great Fire, prices were exceptionally low, in London, because there were few people left to buy the produce brought in. Parish registers may also be useful guides to local conditions if we take the trouble to read between the lines. In the register of Woodham Walter, for example, against the date 1622, we read 'There were none marry<sup>d</sup>—it was a deare yeare, exceptinge Ed. Maut and Annie Smith.' [1] Another point we notice in going through old Essex account books is the quantities of bacon produced by ancestors of our familiar Essex saddlebacks. Pigs were always plentiful in Essex, largely because it was a county of forests, and the pigs could feed on the acorns and beech mast.

The Barringtons were obviously rich before the civil wars. Their total disbursements in 1641 amounted to £3,379 7s. 11d. But if we follow various items through the steward's accounts we can trace the growing unrest in the county until at last war broke out. Men were drilled in readiness for the expected disorders. There were payments for pikeheads, and the seriousness becomes plain when we find the family plate being turned into money—five hundred pounds' worth one year, two hundred pounds' worth the next.

Tobacco first appears in 1630 at the reasonable price of 1s. 6d. an ounce and 2s. 4d. for tobacco stalks. The first tobacco smokers must have looked odd to their neighbours. Harrison of Radwinter, that estimable country parson who called foreigners 'comelings' and natives 'homelings' in his *Description of England*, describes the process as 'the taking in of smoke . . . by an instrument formed like a little ladel, whereby it passeth from the mouth into the head and stomach.' It is a perfectly accurate description of smoking; but somehow it reads strangely to us in the twentieth century. In the seventeenth it must have seemed even stranger that any one should indulge in such a practice. To justify themselves in such apparent folly the first smokers explained that they did it, not out of public-spirited zeal for the revenues of the Chancellor of the Exchequer, but because they found it a sovereign remedy for rheums and respiratory disorders,

[1] *Essex Review*, vol. i., p. 99.

which were by no means uncommon in Essex before it was
properly drained.　Others had more gloomy views on the new
practice.　Long-faced physicians told of corpses dissected
to reveal sooty brains and black lungs caused by smoking
this vile weed.

As the century progressed, innocent indulgences were
increasingly frowned upon. The poor especially were
watched.

Here is a representative report, bearing the signatures of
Sir Thomas Barrington and Sir William Masham:

> '*The Information of John Plaile of Morton in the said
> Countie, Carpenter, taken on oath before Sir William
> Masham Bart. etc.　March 11th*, 1635.

'He sayeth about three weeks or a month since he and
some others were at play at cards in George Burrells house
of Moreton, and stayed there from one of the clock till three
of the clock in the afternoon, and sayeth he thinketh there
was about twenty persons.

> '*The Information of Margrett the wife of George Burrell
> of Morton, Tannar, taken as aforesaid.*

'She confesseth that upon Candlemas Eve last there was
four strangers came into her house and played there at cards
and dice; and on Candlemas day that there was divers that
played at cards, and that then there was fiddling and dancing
in the house, and further sayeth that since Christmas last
there hath been playing at slideboard.

> '*The Examination of George Burrell of Morton, Tannar,
> taken before Sir Thomas Barrington Kt. & Bart. and
> Sir William Masham Bart. etc. the 12th of March 1635.*

'He confesseth that on Candlemas Eve last there was 3 or
4 strangers came into his house and played there at cards,
and also that on Candlemas day last there was much company
in his house, but knoweth of no play nor drinking; and about
a month since he sayeth there came to his house a boy with
a hobbyhorse and two other men with him that shewed

Ingatestone Hall

Chelmsford

Barrington Hall

Danbury Place

tricks and drew much company to his house. He further sayeth that sometimes his Neighbours come in and play a game or two at slidegroat for a jug of beer, but sayeth he knoweth of no money played for at it.' [1]

The seasons with their appointed festivals had kept life far more varied than it is for most people to-day, but these were censored by the Puritans, who came to predominate in Essex. Christmas, however, seems to have been kept up, and some of the stricter rules were then relaxed for a few days. Cards, for example, might be brought out by the Puritans at this time of the year; but many of the old customs associated with the great festival were discouraged. John Aubrey, in a manuscript dated 1678, preserved in the Ashmolean Museum at Oxford, says: 'Before the last Civil Wars in Gentlemen's houses at Christmas the first diet that was brought to table was a Boar's Head with a Lemon in his mouth.' This custom was, we may be sure, continued by some of the more genially conservative in spite of the official prejudice against it. Morant, in writing of Hornchurch, informs us that 'the inhabitants pay the great tithes on Christmas Day, and are treated with a Bull and Brawn. The Boar's Head is wrestled for. The poor have the scraps.' There was no special work to be done on the farms for a few days after Christmas, so the people had time for a little mirth and mischief. Entries in the Barrington account books provide ample material for the imagination to convert into lively scenes in hall and kitchen. The festivities continued until Twelfth Night, and a few of the items will serve to suggest the character of the jollifications:

| | |
|---|---|
| To my Lady for Wassellers and the Morris dauncers | 5s. 0d. |
| Given to the fellow that daunced with the Hobby horse | 1s. 0d. |
| To my Lord Illrule [Lord of Misrule] | 5s. 0d. |
| To the boys that showed tricks at Christmas | 1s. 6d. |
| Given to the fidlers on Christmas Day | 1s. 0d. |

Such landowners as the Earl of Suffolk and Sir Thomas Barrington, we find, still kept their own jesters.

[1] Essex Record Office, Q/SBa, 2/24.

So now is come our joyful'st feast;
 Let every man be jolly.
Each room with ivy leaves is dressed,
 And every post with holly.
Though some churls at our mirth repine
Round your foreheads garlands twine,
Drown sorrow in a cup of wine,
 And let us all be merry,

wrote Wither.

In all these accounts musicians figure prominently. As Dr. Percy Scholes has frequently pointed out, music was an art still honoured under Puritan rule. It was a great part of life all through the century and seems to have been appreciated by every one. Money was given by the Barrington steward to the musicians from Takeley and Epping, to the fiddlers from Sawbridgeworth, to Lord Morley's musicians from Hallingbury Place, and many other companies. Small bands of wind instrumentalists were maintained by towns and cities at the expense of the corporation, in addition to the bands of singers and fiddlers who went round the streets at Christmas singing carols. These also visited the houses of the country gentry, and gratuities were given by the Barringtons to the waits from as far away as Colchester, Newmarket, and Cambridge. Each year there must have been such music at every great house in the country as would have gladdened the heart of Hardy or Kilvert. There was also bell-ringing everywhere. At the beginning of the century Queen Elizabeth's birthday was always celebrated on the village bells, which were rung on the slightest excuse. Not only were they rung when the lord of the manor returned from service overseas, but even when he returned from the assizes at Chelmsford.

These were all pleasant interludes in lives that were strenuous enough most of the time. The general impression is of hard work, but of far greater sociability than now.

It is true that the picture was obviously two-sided. Such an item as 'Given to y<sup>e</sup> poore this Christmas £3 9s. 10d.' does credit to the baronet and his lady; but the contrast between conditions in the cottage and conditions in the great house cannot be lost sight of. Winters were hard for the poor, though it seems unlikely that many went short of food at the beginning of the seventeenth century, except in the towns. The servants still dined at the same table as the family. They dined, of course, below the salt, and the Barrington accounts have an entry: 'For mending the armes of the great Salt Candlesticke £1 8s.' This was the candlestick placed to divide the two.

On the subject of servants there is an amusing set of entries relating to the engaging and dismissing of a maid from Hertfordshire:

*October* 1631,

| | |
|---|---:|
| Paid to the man that brought the Maide out of Hartfordshire for his journey | 3s. 6d. |
| Paid for his horse hyer | 1s. 4d. |
| ffor his bayting by the way | 1s. 2d. |
| ffor his goeing back | 9d. |

But the maid was not satisfactory, and the following month we find:

| | |
|---|---:|
| Pd. the Maide that come out of Hartfordshire her wages for a month's troubling the Howse | 4s. 0d. |
| Pd. the charge of the horse and man that carried her back again | 3s. 0d. |

Such an entry may be some consolation to those who think the servant problem came with the twentieth century.

The maid from Hertfordshire's wages were evidently a shilling a week, and as it cost 9s. 9d. to fetch and return her she was rather expensive. A shilling a week may not seem much to us now; but it was good pay for 1631, and she must have been expected to take up responsible duties to get it. An ordinary maid could be had for about thirty shillings a year still. Her clothes were found, and it is curious to note how little they changed in style right through to the Victorian age. In 1631 indoor and outdoor work would still be mixed, and the mistress would often work with her maids much as the farmer's wife of to-day does—except that the modern

*D

farmer's wife would never dare to cuff her maids for being foolish or lazy.

Essex wages were, in fact, high. When Essex labourers were getting a shilling a day those in the midlands were getting eightpence, and those in the north sixpence or even less. Only in Kent could the poor command higher wages. But they rose considerably as the century progressed. The civil wars practically doubled them. At the beginning of the century 33s. 4d. with a livery, or 6s. 8d. more if the livery was not found, was a good rate of pay. In the middle of the century it had risen to approximately £3, and was still higher at the end. The average for Essex about the middle of the century seems to have been sixpence a day with meat and drink in winter, a shilling without; eightpence a day with meat and drink in summer, fourteen pence without. In 1665 the housekeeper of the Barringtons had £10 a year; Lady Barrington's maid £4; the cook maid £3; four under maids £2 10s. each.

Wage rates, as we have seen, were fixed at quarter sessions, and here, to give an idea of the number of house-holders in a medium-sized market-town and its satellite villages who employed maids early in the century, is a repre-sentative list for Waltham Abbey. It was authorized at the sessions held at Chelmsford on 4th January 1611:

'Servants in Waltham Town. Servants to William Cooke sen., gent.—3 menservants, one at £3, the other at 50s. apiece; 2 maidservants at 26s. 8d. each. With Roger Cook —2 menservants, one at £3, the other at 54s. 8d. Nicholas Vavasor gent.—2 menservants each 40s.; 2 maidservants each 26s. Robert Bridge gent.—one manservant 40s.; one maidservant 30s. John Standish—one manservant £3 6s. 8d.; one maidservant 30s. Widow Golding—one maidservant 30s. William Dane—one manservant £3. Thomas Thorne—4 menservants, 2 at 53s. 4d. each., 2 at 40s. each.

'Servants in Upshire. With Mr. Fox—2 men, one at 53s. 4d. the other at 40s.; 2 maids, one at 30s., the other at 26s. 8d. Mr. Cantforth—one man 53s. 4d.; one maid 20s.

John Greene—one man 33s. 4d.; one maid 26s. 8d.; Edward Bradley—one man 40s.; one maid 26s. 8d. John Sumner jun.—one man £3; one maid 30s. John Shelly—one man £3; 2 maids, one 30s., the other 26s. 8d.

'Servants in Sewardstone. Mr. Smith—one man, £3 6s. 8d; 2 maids 30s. each. Mr. Blincoe—one man £4; 3 maids 50s. 45s., 25s. Thomas Sock—his chief man 53s. 4d., one other 32s.; 2 maids 30s. each.

'Servants in Nazeing. Martin Trott, gent.—one man 40s.; 2 maids 26s. 8d each. John Shelley—one man 40s.; one maid 28s. John Nicholes—2 men 40s. each. Thomas Beck —one man 50s. Robert Gibs—one man 50s. Giles Paison —one man 40s. Nicholas Campeone 50s.

'Servants in Roydon hamlet. Mr. Vaughan—2 men, £3, 40s.; 2 maids 26s. 8d. each. John Wailet—2 men, 53s. 4d., 40s.; one maid 28s. Edward Campe—2 men, 28s., 26s. 8d. George Smith—one man 50s.

'Servants in Epping. Andrew Benton—2 men, £3, 40s.; 2 maids 30s. each. William Stracy—2 men, £3, 40s.; one maid 26s. 8d. Richard Searle—one man £3; one maid 30s. Edward Searle—4 men, £3, 53s., 2 at 40s.; 4 maids, 2 at 20s., 2 at 17s. William Benton—2 men 53s. 4d. each; 2 maids 20s each. George Campion—2 men and 2 maids all at 20s. Francis Archer—one man 26s. 8d., one maid 30s. John Black—one man 53s. 4d.; one maid 30s. Mr. Noades—one man £3; one maid 30s. Mr. Boothby—one man £3; one maid 30s. John Butterfield—one maid 30s. Robert Puttney— one maid 30s.

'Servants to tradesmen in Waltham Town. John Allison glover—3 apprentices bound by indenture according to law. John Brasier baker—2 apprentices bound according to the law, and one journeyman by the year at 50s. George Bridges butcher—one apprentice bound by indenture according to the law.'

Poor relations were often found working in a household as servants, and there was certainly less class distinction than later. The steward was probably an educated man and well connected. The Barringtons' steward, for example, was

John Hawkins, a kinsman of the Elizabethan seaman. He felt no dishonour in being the servant of a baronet, and indeed sons of noblemen often went into service, either at court or with other noblemen, in order to learn their business as heads of families, just as the sons of tradesmen to-day often spend a few years with other tradesmen before going into their own family business. Large households, such as there were in those days, required skilful management. We can imagine something of the trouble there must have been with so many relations under one roof. Fortunately women in that age were trained to be obedient not only to their husbands but also to their mothers-in-law, with whom they often had to live for twenty or thirty years before coming to authority themselves. As they usually married in their teens we may say that they were obliged to spend the best years of their lives dancing attendance on their husband's mother. The curious thing is that after their long years of subservience they so often blossomed out as strong-minded dames as soon as they had the opportunity. The young Lady Judith Barrington, for example, had to submit for years to the will of Lady Joan, Cromwell's aunt, but she became an autocratic old lady herself, and caused no end of trouble for her stepson, Sir John, the third baronet, though his wife was her own niece.

The best means of diverting elderly widows from interference in their children's affairs was to keep them as busy as possible with charitable work. The multifarious committees of our own day were unknown then, but private charity was widely practised, and often in their wills these ladies provided for their benevolent work to be continued by endowing almshouses and other charities.

It was a full and fairly rich life for the gentry. They were domesticated, though not so homely as the Dutch; they were proud, but not so proud as the French. Above all they were intensely individualistic, as we see from the number of family portraits painted at the time. Indeed, there were few pictures on their walls that were not family portraits. As most of the county families were related, their lives were similar, and to look into one household is to look into all. We have dealt with only the Petres and the Barringtons, but there was hardly a village in the county that had not a family living a similar household life.

There seems to be no limit to the interesting possibilities of a bundle of musty account books. We never know what precious thing may be discovered on the next page we open, tucked away between such commonplace items as payment for a day's work in the kitchen and an ordinary shopping item. The very disparity between the items for luxuries and the items for labour may be material for a political satire or an indignant sermon; but we are not concerned with politics at the moment, and there were so many dull sermons preached in the seventeenth century that no man in his senses would ask for more. So we turn instead to what is to such a snapper-up of unconsidered trifles as myself the most entertaining of these Barrington account books, that in which the extraordinary expenses were entered. Here, for example, is a letter to Sir John Sedley, one-and-sixpence to a man who brought oysters from Colchester, sixpence for gathering poppies, and the same to a madwoman at the door. Insignificant items, yet each producing a picture and a speculation. In scanning these pages we have all the thrill of peeping through a keyhole without the danger of being found out or of losing self-respect. We are reading other people's private letters, diaries, and ledgers—a thing all intelligent men long to do, and all women whether intelligent or not. The instinct is as old as creation. Even the Creator Himself punished Adam for doing this very thing, and tried in vain to prevent Eve doing it. And when we raise our eyes from the fading parchment we see in fancy one of these Stuart ladies in silk or velvet, sitting in her high-backed chair slowly writing, or standing by her casement to look out upon a garden designed as formally as the carpet she stands on, softly singing to herself such an air as that of Master Constable:

> Diaphenia, like the daffadowndilly,
> White as the sun, fair as the lily,
> Heigh-ho, how I do love thee!

## CHAPTER VII

## MAIDS ARE SIMPLE

'Maids are simple,' some men say,
'They, forsooth, will trust no men.'
But should they men's wills obey,
Maids are very simple then.

CAMPION.

No matter how much pleasure historians may derive from contemplating the vices and follies of our ancestors, they must often regret that so little is known of their virtues. The records of the various courts where presumably immaculate justices mete out punishment to their erring and imprudent fellow mortals are valuable sources of information; but there are few records of courts where virtue and happiness are rewarded. There are, of course, few such courts. Essex has one, and as sad tales that were told in other courts must be noticed presently, we may fortify ourselves against depression by attending the happier one first. Virtue, a friend of mine is fond of saying, has no box-office appeal. It is too dull. But in this particular Essex court it was far from dull. It was, in fact, a joke. Yet the court was instituted, according to tradition, by Robert FitzWalter, who led the barons against King John, and had little cause to be merry. It was the court that awarded the Dunmow flitch of bacon to the couple who could swear on oath that they had been married for a year and a day and had not once regretted it.

Robert FitzWalter was the father of the 'Fair Matilda' of Dunmow, who is said to have been poisoned because she rejected the amorous addresses of King John. An alabaster figure in Little Dunmow church, which is part of the old priory church, is sometimes said to be hers; but its date makes this impossible.

Whoever founded the 'flitch' in Essex seems to have taken

the idea from a similiar award offered at the abbey of Saint Melaine, near Rennes in Brittany. The Dunmow court was held at the priory at Little Dunmow with the prior as judge, and its fame spread far. It was mentioned in Langland's *Piers Plowman*, and Chaucer's Wife of Bath says of three of her husbands:

> The bacoun was nat fet for hem, I trowe,
> That som men han in Essex at Dunmowe.

On presenting themselves at the priory, the happy couple were required to take an oath solemnly chanted to them by the monks. In the modernized form used later it ran:

> You shall swear by Custom of Confession
> That you ne'er made Nuptial Transgression;
> Nor since you were married Man and Wife,
> By Household Brawls or Contentious Strife,
> Or otherwise in Bed or at Board,
> Offended each other in deed or word;
> Or in a Twelve month time and a day,
> Repented not in Thought anyway;
> Or since the Church clerk said Amen,
> Wish'd yourselves unmarried again,
> But continued true, and in desire,
> As when you join'd hands in holy Choir.

When the oath had been taken and the bacon brought out, the prior awarded it to the couple with these words:

> Since to these Conditions without any fear,
> Of your own accords you do truly swear;
> A whole Gammon of Bacon you do receive,
> And bear it away with love and good leave;
> For this is the Custom at Dunmow well known.
> Though the Pleasure be ours, the Bacon 's your own.

At the conclusion of the ceremony the claimants, who were called pilgrims, were carried through the village in a chair, shoulder high, with the monks, brethren, and villagers following in jovial procession. The bacon was carried on poles at the head, and the couple were well feasted before they returned to their home. The earliest award of which the record survives is dated 1445, when a Norfolk yeoman came from Badbury, near Norwich, was sworn before John Cannon, the prior, and received the flitch. In 1510 Thomas le Fuller of Coggeshall received it from John Tylor, who was then prior. Another early claimant was Stephen Samuel of Little Easton, husbandman.

Though the priory was suppressed by Henry VIII, the bacon was saved, and, instead of the prior, the steward of the manor presided at the trial, supported by a jury of maidens and bachelors. The court was held at Priory Place, and an account of the ceremony written in 1737 claims that it was instituted 'in ye year 1111 and continued to this day.' Roll 25 of the Lansdowne Collection of manuscripts in the British Museum has a record of the proceedings at the manor court at Dunmow in 1701, at which two gammons of bacon were awarded, one to John Reynolds, steward to Sir Charles Barrington of Hatfield Broad Oak, and his wife, who had been married ten years; the other to William Parsley, a butcher of Great Easton, who had been married three years:

'At a Court Baron of the Right Worshipful Sir Thomas May, Knight, there holden upon Friday, the 7th day of June, in the 13th year of the reign of our sovereign Lord William III, by the grace of God, &c., and in the year of our Lord 1701, before Thomas Wheeler, Gent., Steward of the said Manor. It is thus enrolled:

|         | Elizabeth Beaumont, spinster. | |
|---------|-------------------------------|-------|
|         | Henrietta Beaumont, spinster. | |
| Homage  | Annabella Beaumont, spinster. | Jurat |
|         | Jane Beaumont, spinster.      | |
|         | Mary Wheeler, spinster.       | |

'Be it remembered, that at this court, in full and open court, it is found and presented by the homage aforesaid, that William Parsley, of Much Easton, in the county of Essex, butcher, and Jane his wife, have been married for the space of three years last past, and upward; and it is likewise found, presented, and adjudged by the homage aforesaid, that the said William Parsley and Jane his wife, by means of their

quiet, peaceable, tender, and loving cohabitation for the space
of time aforesaid (as appears by the said homage), are fit and
qualified persons to be admitted by the court to receive the
ancient and accustomed oath, whereby to entitle themselves
to have the bacon of Dunmow delivered unto them, according
to the custom of the Manor.

'Whereupon, at this court, in full and open court, came
the said William Parsley, and Jane his wife, in their proper
persons, and humbly prayed they might be admitted to take
the oath aforesaid. Whereupon the said Steward with the
jury, suitors, and other officers of the court, proceeded with
the usual solemnity to the ancient and accustomed place for
the administration of the oath, and receiving the gammon
aforesaid, (that is to say) the two great stones lying near the
church door, within the said Manor, when the said William
Parsley and Jane his wife, kneeling down on the said two
stones, the said Steward did administer unto them the
above mentioned oath, in these words, or to the effect
following . . .'

The old rhyming oath was then taken and the bacon
awarded. Other claims followed. Half a century later, John
Shakeshaft of Wethersfield and his lady went through the
court successfully and were borne through the town in the
chair, with the bacon carried like a banner before them.
But John proved worthy of his name by improving on the
ceremony to his own advantage. Five thousand people
had assembled for the occasion, and John took out his knife,
cut up the bacon there and then, and sold it in slices as
souvenirs.

That was the last award of the bacon at Little Dunmow.
When in 1772 John Gilder and his wife put in a claim, the
gates of the priory were locked against them. The lord of
the manor, for reasons of his own, was not favourably disposed towards loving couples, so the ancient custom that a
high-hearted peasantry and generous manorial officials had
carried forward so gaily from the pre-Reformation church
was abandoned. It was not revived until 1855, when Harrison Ainsworth, the novelist, became interested, and was so

successful in rousing interest in others that its popularity still survives,   But as the lord of the manor of Little Dunmow would have no part in it, the court was transferred to Great Dunmow, two miles away.   On 19th July 1855 it was held in the town hall with Mr Ainsworth as judge, supported by a jury of bachelors and spinsters.   The two couples who presented themselves had to undergo an examination lasting two and a half hours, but the exacting jury was at length satisfied and the oath administered in Windmill Field before seven thousand spectators.

Another old Essex custom connected with marriage was the holding of a dog-hanging feast, a profitable kind of wedding banquet, to which Tag, Rag, and all who would come were invited.   The meal consumed and the company merry, one of the musicians got up and 'set forth his voice like a town-crier.'   At this summons a table was put in readiness, and the bridegroom, dressed in a white sheet as though doing penance for his folly, was set at one end, with the bride simpering at his side.   The company then came forward with their wedding gifts, the last of which was always an embroidered pair of gloves, hung with ribbons. This was put up for auction, and went to the highest bidder, who had the privilege of kissing the bride.   There is an account of one of these dog-hangings in a jolly parody of *Don Quixote* called *The History of Sir Billy of Billericay and his Squire Ricardo*, published in 1687.   A pair of these gloves is still to be seen in the church at Theydon Mount, near Epping.

As labourers' cottages were not large enough to hold all the guests invited to a wedding, there was often a large room in the parish, conveniently near the church, kept for the purpose.   Only one of these is left.   It is the fifteenth-century 'Marriage Feast Room' at Matching, near Harlow.

It was always the custom at village jollifications, and particularly at wedding banquets, to bring food as well as gifts for the home, so that 'the more the merrier' was a fact. No labourer in the old days could have borne the expense of providing for so many as usually came.   It was therefore understood that he should only be at the charge of bread and beer.

There was, of course, a certain amount of rowdyism. Already in the seventeenth century the difference was marked between the quiet, restrained conduct of the gentle, and the noisy talk, conviviality, and buffoonery of the labouring poor. This vigorous enjoyment of the coarser pleasures of life has always served to compensate the poor in some small measure for the hardness of their lives. Seen in its proper light there is something heroic in it. Robert Bridges appreciated this in the third book of his *Testament of Beauty*. Such brave display of spirit may turn the clown into a philosopher and the beggar into a king. No one could have glorified it more than did Shakespeare. Without convivial fun no picture of English life on a large canvas would be complete. But as disapproval of mirth is as constant as enjoyment of it, we must have this curious report of a dog-hanging feast in the spring of 1646. It comes from the parish where Lawrence Washington, the President's great-great-grandfather, had been parson until the Puritans turned him out in 1643. The Isaac Aleyn who sat in judgment was a strict and somewhat officious magistrate. He lived at Hazeleigh Hall, near Maldon, and whatever we may think of his fondness for meddling, those of us who dabble in Essex records must bless him for his beautiful handwriting. Here, then, is the dog-hanging record:

> '*The information of Thomas Read of Purlie, husbandman, taken upon his oath this twelfth day of March, 1646, before Isaac Aleyn Esq., one of the king's majesty's justices of peace of this county, against Robert Bigges of Purlie, husbandman, for the misdemeanour of the said Robert Bigges.*

'The said Thomas Read upon his oath saith that on a Saturday at night he heard William Came of Coldnorton say that the next day being the sabbath day he was to go to a dog-hanging feast to Robert Bigges's house in Purlie.

'ISAAC ALEYN.

'*The information of Lewis Martin of Purlie, husbandman, upon his oath the day and yeare aforesaid taken
before the said Isaac Aleyn concerning the said misdemeanour of the said Isaac Bigges.*

'The said Informant upon his oath saith that his master
Mr. Andrews, Parson of Purlie, hearing from Thomas Read
of Woodham Ferrers, husbandman, that there had been a
drunken dog-hanging feast at the said Robert Bigges's house
in Purlie on the Sabbath day, very shortly after the said
Mr. Andrews did send this said Informant to the goodwife
Turnedge to inquire of it.  And the goodwife Turnedge did
then name goodman Knott of Woodham Walter and Jona-
than Jollie, who they said were at the same dog-hanging
feast, and that John Martin, the goodman Fen's man, did so
inform the goodwife Turnedge.  And further she, the said
goodwife Turnedge, told the said informant that he, Robert
Bigges, came laughing to her house and told her how that
Parson Andrews had a warrant for him, but if he did not
serve it the sooner he would have a warrant for the Parson.

'And in the hearing of this Informant Robert Bigges used
these words to the said Mr. Andrews: Do tell me no lies.

'ISAAC ALEYN.

'And the said Robert Bigges in the hearing of Richard
Pake, Constable of Purlie, and of divers others then present,
did the day and year aforesaid before the said Isaac Aleyn
use these words that he would give ten shillings to have Mr.
Andrews gone out of Purlie, and that they were fewe in Purlie
but would give something for that purpose.'

The people of Purleigh, it appears, would have been glad
to see Parson Washington among them again.

We need not doubt that this dog-hanging feast was a shocking affair.  But without occasional lapses from virtue we
should be cut off from a great deal of delectable human experience.  Man must be a little lower than the angels or he
would never realize how high the angels are!  He might also
come to think more highly of himself than is right and proper.
But if he desires the pleasures of sin he must be prepared to

pay for them. We have it on the best authority that debts are to be settled elsewhere; but it has long been the custom to demand something on account, as it were, in this present world, and for that praiseworthy purpose courts of justice are set up. Their records yield pleasure and profit in full measure. They are full of the liveliest stories, each concluding in the most satisfactory manner with suitable rewards and punishments. The proceedings of archdeacons' courts are the most gratifying, but often need censoring before being offered to the public. An archdeacon, with his stronger moral stamina, could bear much cruder presentations of life that could be served up to a mere justice of the peace. Chaucer's archdeacon, we may recall, took this part of his duties seriously:

> Whilom ther was dwellinge in my contree
> An erchedeken, a man of high degree,
> That boldely dide execucioun
> In punisshinge of fornicacioun,
> Of wicchecraft, and eek of bauderye,
> Of diffamacioun and avoutrye.

Here we can only venture into the records of quarter sessions, and from a very big pie extract a few plums. Each man would turn to his own village first, so I searched for Loughton and was rewarded with the tale of John Rich, a tailor, who was examined at the Easter sessions in 1609.

John Rich, though a Loughton man, had a tailor's shop at Abridge, which, as the principal road in the district ran through Abridge and not through Loughton, was more conveniently situated for his customers. Like every able-bodied person in the village of his day he went into the fields at harvest time, and there he met a certain young lady named Grace, who, along with her sister, helped him to pitch hay and afterwards to tread the haymow. He also went into the barn with Grace and kissed her 'too often,' as he sadly confessed. These fair maids of Abridge made a great fuss of him. They frequently sent for him to give him a 'mess of cream.' And he had to confess that while with Grace he had 'tumbled her up and down.' But he had done nothing, he protested, 'to get her with child.' The child, however, was there, and John Rich was ordered to pay sixpence a week until it was nine years old.

It is the old, old story, told in every generation and in every village. John Rich got off lightly at sixpence a week. Sometimes double that sum was required, and if the child had to be brought up by a person found by the court the mother also might be asked to contribute twopence weekly, or a similar small sum, towards its upkeep. If the father could not be found, the mother of an illegitimate child might be sent to the house of correction at Chelmsford or Colchester, and there she would have to earn her keep by spinning or carding wool or flax until she could be bound with sufficient sureties to discharge the parish of the cost of the child's keep.

Here, in the record of the same sessions, is a darker, sadder story, and of another tailor, curiously enough, one John Banson, of Widdington. Banson confessed that he was the father of a child born at the 'White Horse' at St. Neots in Huntingdonshire. The mother Frances Barker, alias Lacey, of Black Notley in Essex. She told a tragic story of Banson's passionate and brutal wooing. 'Oftentimes when she was about her business,' she said, 'he would draw his dagger and set it to her chest' and vow 'that he would kill her if she would not do as he would have her. And that about Christmas last he did meet her at Dunmow, he being on horseback and she on foot, and did earnestly desire her to go with him to Ireland.' He would have carried her off then, but 'a man coming by did prevent him, and chiding on the highway she departed with as much speed as she could, otherwise she was persuaded that he would have offered violence unto her. And further that he being committed to the Fleet, presently on his enlargement came to her and she said she was great with child by him, who answered that if he had known that he would have taken such order with her that she would never have come unto that, and therewithal gave her a pinch upon her belly, after which she was never well until she was brought in bed, which was seven weeks before her time.'

Knowledge of Frances's condition came to John Lacey,

her brother, a husbandman of Widdington, who, according
to Banson's report, told him that he must take Frances out
of the county to hide the disgrace.   According to Lacey,
Banson offered him forty shillings to take the girl to Barley
in Hertfordshire, where he promised to join her.   Frances
only wished to hang herself, and said she would send her
clothes home by one Bucke, a tanner of Newport.

Brother and sister set out one Wednesday morning and
were joined by Banson at the alehouse at Barley as arranged.
The brother then returned to Widdington, while the miserable
couple went on to Royston.   The next day they travelled to
St. Neots, 'where on Sunday she was brought in bed of a boy
at the sign of the "White Horse," and the next day the child
was baptized in the chamber where she was brought in bed.'
The minister's wife of the town, and six or eight women,
came in to help the hostess of the inn to take care of Frances
and the unwanted child, and at the christening the hostess's
daughter was godmother, while 'the Bellfounder of Cambridge' and one of his workmen, who were lodging at the inn,
were godfathers.   A day or two later, according to both
parents, the child died and was buried at St. Neots; but there
seems to be some doubt about this.   Frances herself must
have been very ill.   She could not be moved from the
'White Horse' until three weeks and two days had passed.
She was churched there, and it is clear that the minister of
St. Neots took a kindly interest in the case.   Banson 'was
carried upon a warrant procured by one Clapton, being constable of St. Neots, before Mr. Cromwell, one of the justices
of the peace within the county of Huntingdon, the which
Mr. Cromwell did discharge this examinant, and that the
minister of St. Neots did take this examinant's bond with a
surety for the saving harmless of the minister.'

The only one of the girl's own family who seems to have
shown any humanity towards her was her grandfather, 'Old
Lacey,' who 'willingly received her' into his own home when
she was able to return to Widdington.

Another tale from the north-west corner of Essex came to
the notice of the justices at Chelmsford at the sessions

held on 5th October 1615. It should, I think, be given exactly as the clerk recorded it, but with the spelling modernized except where the original seems preferable.

*'Sessions held at Chelmsford of the 5th October 1615*

'4 July 1615. ORDER by Geoffrey Nightingale and Thomas Adams esqs., justices nearest the parish of Newport, upon complaints of the inhabitants of the parish, where a bastard child is left by its mother, Mary Whitby, who has run away to places unknown and left the child there, to discharge the parish for keeping the child being born there of Mary Whitby servant to Peter Weekes gent., about 14 May last. Whereupon according to the Act of 18 Elizabeth Mary came to Geoffrey Nightingale about 17 Jan. 1615 before she was delivered, and being examined did charge Mr. Weekes her master to be the father, whom she also charged with it at its birth, as was specially verified upon the oaths of Ellen Nightingale, the midwife, and by divers other very honest women who held her very straitly to it for the father of her child, and would have had to have laid the begetting of it to one Richard Harvye of Newport, who was in love with her before that time, and intended to have married her but that he found her to be with child, and she at that time confidently affirmed that the child was her master's, and none of Harvye's. And being in her great extremity said Mr. Weekes would be glad that it was a man child, for he had none of his own. And upon her examination first before Mr. Nightingale, then before the midwife and the other honest women then and there assembled, and before some other women privately and sworn before them, they affirmed out of her mouth that Mr. Weekes gave her "a gowne cloth of kersey which he bought at Stortford, a payre of stockings, a drawne worke coyfe, a silken tiffony to weare over it, and money towardes the buying of a lawne ruffe and some money towards the buying of a smock and a petticoate cloth" and some money towards the buying of some malt which should have been for brewing drink for her wedding, and that since that time he gave her money, as Elizabeth

Whitby widow affirmed upon her oath that her daughter Mary told her that Mr. Weekes offered her £5 to lay it to Richard Harvye, and said he would make it up £20 if she would do so.

'And Lucy, wife of Simon Colebeck, upon her oath affirmed as much, and further saith that Martin Cartar was in hand with her to take her oath that she did see Harvye naughty with Mary Whitby and would have her to go to Walden to affirm so much before the justices there, and if she would do so she should not lose her labour, which she utterly refused; and that Martin Cartar being distressed for money his wife said to him,

'"Yf Mr. Weekes will give me tenn poundes I will cleare him of this childe,"

'and thereupon they went to Mr. Weekes and after that to Walden before the justices and there did swear for Mr. Weekes; and further saith that Mr. Weekes and Mr. Howland his son-in-law after that sitting brought Cartar home to his house on the backside thereof 20s. [sic] as Cartar's wife confessed to Lucy Coleback, saying also to her,

'"Yf you had gone with us to Walden you had spedd as well as we have,"

'which said 20s. Cartar paid presently for his wood; and Simon Coleback coming out of Suffolk said to Cartar,

'"Thou hast gott good store of wood into thy warde."

'"Yeae," quoth he, "I gott this by my goinge to Walden."

'And Mr. Weekes wished Carter to come to London to go before the Lord Chief Justice to swear as much before him as he swore at Walden. And forasmuch as Mr. Weekes was at two several meetings of the justices with his counsel and examined, and brought many witnesses both men and women who seemed to be of no credit, and finding in the end that he would not say anything material to move them to the contrary opinion, they therefore take Peter Weekes to be the father of the child, and order that he shall become bound with good sureties to the overseers to discharge the parish from being at any further charges for the keeping of the child, and shall pay from 14 May last 16d. weekly, and Mary 4d. weekly towards the bringing up of the child for the space of

twelve years, and to pay to the townsmen all the money that
they have disbursed about this business.   And they further
order that Mr. Weekes (being discharged of all other punishments) shall pay to the overseers for the use of the poor 20s.
within one week after notice given him of this order.'

To this there was added in a different hand: 'This order
annihilated and quashed by all the justices, and Mr. Weekes
discharged of being the reputed father and also all suspicion.
And Richard Harvy charged to be the reputed father in all
respect according to this order.'

The concern of the Laceys to avoid the disgrace of having
an illegitimate child in the family, and the careful examination of Peter Weekes when accused of being the father of his
servant-girl's child, are both typical.   In the late eighteenth
century, and the first half of the nineteenth, illegitimacy was
so common that it was regarded almost with indifference.
In the seventeenth century it was rare.   When Dr. J. C.
Cox made a detailed examination of the registers of Lether-
ingham, Suffolk, he found only one child born out of wedlock
among the one hundred and forty-four baptized between 1601
and 1650.   Among the one hundred and forty-seven born between 1751 and 1800 he found seven, or one in twenty-one,
and between 1801 and 1812 one child in ten was illegitimate.

The reason for this increase is not necessarily a moral one.
The living standards of the labouring poor degenerated after
the commons had been enclosed.   Overcrowding became
common.   The well-to-do kept more servants, and young
people were thrown together as they had not been formerly.
Often, particularly under the Puritans, these unwanted
children were given names that branded them with their
parents' sin.   Occasionally, however, the parson was a man
of charity.   There was such a parson at Wolstanton, Stafford-
shire, at the end of the century.   On 12th June 1689, Mr.
W. E. Tate tells us in *The Parish Chest*, he entered in his
register:

'Baptized Providence, an infant whom her father and
mother abandoned; but God will take care of her.'

Thomas and Ann Shakeshaft claiming the Dunmow Flitch

The Old Sun Inn, Saffron Walden

# CHAPTER VIII

## VILLAGE LIFE

The shepherd upon a hill he sat;
He had on him his tabard and his hat,
His tarbox, his pipe and his flagat.
His name was called jolly, jolly Wat,
   For he was a good herd's boy,
      With hoy,
For in his pipe he made so much joy.

In all aspects of old-time village life we have two contrasting pictures. In one we see carefree country folk enjoying a life of simple pleasures; in the other dull and brutish peasants crowded in wretched hovels. There is truth in both. There was no less merriment then than now; there was more misery. I have been haunted for several days by an entry in the parish register of Boreham, near Chelmsford:

'1646. 20 Jan^y. A woman that was passed from Cunstable to Cunstable died at the Anker.'

This dying woman was probably passed from constable to constable not because she had committed some crime but because she was no longer able to support herself. Such persons were sent back to the place of their birth. No other parish would be responsible for their maintenance. Often they died on the way. Another instance is recorded at Little Chesterford:

'1623. 4th September. Buryed a poore man brought by the Little Chesterford constables to be examined by the justice; the justice being a hunting the poore man died before his coming home from hunting.'

The parish authorities were obliged to provide a 'convenient habitation' for homeless persons. These were usually built on commons, and the poor who lived in them were seldom popular with their more thrifty or fortunate neighbours. James I, in a speech in the Star Chamber in 1616, condemned these cottages on commons, and he probably had places like Sewardstone and other hamlets on the border of Epping Forest in mind. He said they were as bad as alehouses, and accused those who lived in them of stealing deer, conies, sheep, oxen, horses, as well as of house-breaking and 'all manner of villanies.' He was thinking, no doubt, of his own sport; but he was expressing an opinion widely held. Roger North, in *A Discourse of the Poor*, written in the seventeenth century but not published until 1753, wrote:

'Gentlemen of late years have taken up an Humour of Destroying their Tenements and Cottages. . . . This is done sometimes bare faced, because they harbour the Poor that are a charge to the Parish.'

With the capital on the west, and the coast on the east, Essex magistrates were more guarded than those of most counties in dealing with wanderers.

But even such melancholy chronicles as these can yield amusing tales. There is a delightful case from 1606 of a cottage being provided for a woman who turned out to be a doubtful advantage to the local society. The overseers of Faulkbourne sent a petition to the justices at Chelmsford asking for a cottage to be allowed to stand, though it had not the required four acres of land attached to it. They explained 'that they were charged, upon the complaint of a poor lame woman, Susan Froste, born in their parish, to provide her and her two children with a dwelling-house, by warrant from the Lord Suffragan, and were constrained to make suit to the Lord of the Manor for a piece of waste, and having obtained his licence they erected a cottage.' Five months later, on 30th September 1606, a letter signed by Richard, Bishop of London, John, suffragan Bishop of Colchester, and others was addressed to the same justices complaining 'that they are informed by Mr. Harris, minister of Faulkbourne, that Susan Froste, a very incontinent woman having had sundry base-born children and not leaving her incontinent life notwithstanding she has undergone ecclesiastical censures, is now placed in a new erected house of purpose

built for her in the king's highway very near the minister's
house, to the annoyance of the said Mr. Harris and all the
king's liege people passengers that way, and by her sole
habitation she shall have fit opportunity to continue her bad
course of life to the high displeasure of Almighty God; and
they are also informed that this proceeding against the quiet
of the said Mr. Harris is chiefly moved by one Oliver, an
obstinate recusant and enemy to the gospel; therefore they
request that the said house may be removed and the woman
punished for her incontinent life, and the placers of her
there, contrary to warrants directed against them, be duly
censured.'

As the overseers, in petitioning for the cottage to be
allowed to stand, had stated that it had been erected on the
strength of a warrant from the lord suffragan, it would be
interesting to know which 'placers of her there' were
censured.

Susan Frost may have felt honoured in having been
thought worthy of these episcopal, let alone ecclesiastical,
censures. Usually, virtuous neighbours had their own
methods of dealing with offenders, and often for much less
serious offences than those of the shameless Susan. Tales
of Chaucerian ribaldry are to be found in the records of every
parish. At Little Baddow, for example, an over-industrious
cobbler was presented to the archdeacon's court for mending
shoes on the sabbath. He was evidently one of the gay
young men of the village, for he complained when tried that
two women, Elizabeth Turnishe and Frances Silvester, had
come into his bedroom, pulled him out of bed, and had done
their best to sew him up in a sheet. One of these women
was alleged to have been immorally associated with him.

There were, of course, many unfortunate people who had
fallen on evil times through sickness, and there were many
hard cases of the all-too-familiar kinds—hard masters,
wastrel sons, heartless daughters. But there is nothing to
be gained by dwelling on them. When their passions were
not roused most people were as charitable as they knew how
to be. The great Poor Law of 1601, prolonged in 1604 and

made permanent in 1640, was the foundation of poor law administration for over two hundred years. It provided among other things for the churchwardens, one elected, the other nominated by the parson, and four, three, or two substantial householders to be nominated each year, to serve as overseers for relieving the poor. The minutes of a meeting at Finchingfield while Stephen Marshall was vicar will give an idea of the way one small Essex village carried out its duties to the unfortunate:

'At the meetinge at Gyles Wolfes this 24th of February, 1630.

'Imprimis it is agreed that goodman Chaplyn, goodman Wolfe, and goodman Chote shal goe to Waldone to bye some Corne for the poore.

'It is agreed that Edward Johnsone shall have somethinge allowed him for a while vntill it please God his wife recouer her health.

'It is agreed that Murgan should Carry a letter to Mr. Wallis about some Corne. He is to be allowed xvi *d.* for his Jurnye.

'It is agreed that Watsone should kepe Garrettes child a while should be allowed 20*d.* by the week for kepinge of it, afterwarde that it should be putt out a Sume of monye is to be given with it.

'It is agreed that Mr. Brouen, Mr. Sparrow, Mr. Tyme, Richard Harrington, Thomas Whithead, Will Moswell and Simond Wyborowe should be spoken to for to Joyne with us in our Monthly Meetinge.' [1]

There were fourteen signatories, the vicar among them.

One of the points to be noticed in this document is the large number of different surnames. It is a matter of constant surprise to those who study Essex records. In some parts of the country we find villages with only two or three names in each. We find this only in extremely isolated parts of Essex, though it is also noticeable that the same names continue through the centuries.

The amount allowed for a child's keep is interesting, and

[1] *Essex Review*, vol. viii, p. 128.

also that a sum of money was to be given with it when it became an apprentice. It is also to be noted in these minutes that a man was to be allowed something to compensate him for the loss of his wife's earnings, though so far as we know he himself was working. And finally we see that corn rather than money was to be given to the poor.

The price of corn was then the vital factor in village economy. When wages were fixed by the magistrates at quarter sessions they were supposed to be regulated by it, and in a rough way they probably were. But wages were not expected to be adequate. Chief Justice Hale, in *A Discourse touching Provision for the Poor*, published in 1683 but apparently written earlier, gave ten shillings a week as the lowest income upon which a man could provide for himself, his wife, and four children, in meat, drink, clothing, and rent. The average weekly earnings of an agricultural worker might then be three shillings a week, and his wife might earn a shilling. It was never thought to be enough to keep them in food and clothes, as well as pay their rent and buy their fuel. The labouring poor had in fact few money payments to provide for. Their rent was merely nominal. Every cottage had its plot of ground where much of the family food could be grown, where a pig could be fattened for the winter, and where domestic fowl could be kept. There were rabbits to be snared and ample food to be picked up by an able-bodied man who had his wits about him.

Throughout the century, and indeed until 1775, it was against the law to build a cottage without four acres of land attached to it, which is the origin of the adage about 'Four acres and a cow,' long regarded as a guarantee of security. A similar adage, offered as a recipe for good health, 'Sixpence a day and earn it,' comes from the same age. That both should have been kept alive by people for so long is an indication that they were regarded by many as sound. When they first became popular, the old village weavers were beginning to suffer from the competition of capitalized industry in towns, and the agricultural workers congratulated themselves on having stuck to the land. The idea behind the four acres to a cottage law was that it was against the national interest to allow a wage-earning class to be created in the rural areas. The husbandman was believed to be the 'body and stay' of the realm. This law did not operate in towns, which were regarded as the proper place for industries, nor did it operate within a mile of the sea, where other means of gaining a livelihood had been provided by nature. Elsewhere it was enforced, except in cases of hardship, when appeal could be made against it. So town and country planning and direction of labour are not, as some people suppose, inventions of the twentieth century.

Another modern innovation, that of regulating wages by reference to a cost of living index, is, after all, only a development of the old method of regulating them by the price of corn. And the importance of controlling the price of the corn itself was fully grasped by both rich and poor. Many serious and more than a few humorous references to the buying and selling of corn are to be found in official records. Here are two complaints that were dealt with at the quarter sessions held on 9th and 10th January 1606. The first was 'that there is no market bushel cheyned up at the crosse in Chelmsford that thereby the byeres and sellers of corne maye mesure and try mesures by.' The other that 'Richard Aylet, one Makin, Turner, Graves, and Banister, loaders, keep bushels in Chelmsford to buy their corn by in the market that are greater than the standard.'

But while some people were trading in corn to the disadvantage of the poor, there was one rare soul, a Mr. French of East Tilbury, who was in trouble from 'the cavilling complaints of some of very turbulent spirits' because he cut his prices. It would be useful to know whether he was as disinterested in doing this as the vicar and curate of his parish believed. Price-cutters have not always been public benefactors. However that may be, Mr. French persuaded these two clergymen, 'eye-witnesses of his life and honest conversation,' to plead for him against those who were putting out what his friends alleged to be unjust accusations. He had, they said, been kind to the poor and had performed a work of great charity in selling his corn at such low prices. He had also, they submitted quite irrelevantly, shown praiseworthy zeal towards the Church of God and the preachers of His word.

Other important laws designed to protect prices were the one making it illegal to buy produce 'off the ground,' that is to say, acres of wheat, barley, oats, and so forth, and also the one which made it illegal to buy and sell cattle without keeping them at least five weeks. Those who broke this latter law were fined twice the value of the animals they sold, but in spite of this heavy penalty many took the risk. Black market activities, then, as well as town and country planning, direction of labour, and, we may add, snooping and informing, are by no means modern innovations. Snooping, indeed, was a profitable calling, for when a fine was imposed the informant received half.

Even a cursory glance at the operation of justice in the courts of the day is enough to show that all statutes were not held in equal favour. Perhaps the greatest liberty was taken with the Statute of Apprentices, which came into force in 1563. It required each man practising a 'trade or mystery' to serve a seven years' apprenticeship. In administering this law it is clear that the justices took local conditions into account; but in Essex it was held in greater favour than in most counties. There were two movements undermining the efficacy of the statute during the century, and both were resisted by the Essex weavers. The first began in 1619, when James I hit upon the dubious plan of selling pardons to those who practised a trade to which they had not been apprenticed. He saw, no doubt, that the English were given to interpreting the law according to the spirit rather than according to the letter, so he thought that it would be a simple matter to make money out of this national peculiarity. The plan was naturally unpopular among those who had served their apprenticeship in the normal way, and in Essex feeling ran high, particularly among the wool-combers of Coggeshall. Songs in the streets were then an effective means of protesting against injustices, and they

E

had the advantage of remaining in the memory.   One verse of the wool-combers' song ran:

> From such as would our rights invade,
> Or would intrude into our trade,
> And break the law Queen Betty made,
> *Libera nos Domine.*

The verses were again heard in 1654, when an ordinance of the Commonwealth gave all ex-service men the privilege of engaging in any handicraft or trade 'in any city or town corporate or in any other place whatsoever.'   This ordinance was the only way of dealing with the problem of those who had been called to take up arms before serving their apprenticeship, and were now too old to give the required seven years.   It was a just measure for them, but it made the enforcement of the Statute of Apprentices virtually impossible.

There is another side to the apprenticeship problem. There were wicked apprentices as well as wicked masters, and as this is often forgotten, a petition from the Billericay barber and painter about his unruly appentice may be mentioned.[1]   This unhappy man, William Noone, surely related to the woman in the nursery rhyme called Nothing-at-all, complained that four years earlier the parishioners of Hutton had given him Stephen Thorpe, then nine years of age, to be trained in the mysteries of painting and barbering. Since then he had fed and clothed him, 'tendering him,' he said, as his own child; and 'not anywise abusing him with hard usage or unreasonable correction.'   But Stephen had shown himself, 'though young in years, of a most wicked and thievish disposition.'   He had done many robberies and had broken more than twenty walls.   Three times he had been sent to the house of correction at Chelmsford and once to the jail at Colchester.   'But wickedness,' said the suffering Mr. Noone, 'is so rooted in him that there is no hope of amendment, for that he groweth from evil to worse, and threateneth to do more mischief than ever he hath done.   And for so much

[1] Essex Record Office, Q/SBa.

as by means of the said wicked boy your poor orator is utterly undone for ever.' Mr. Noone then begged to be 'quite released of the said boy,' adding devoutly: 'And as God, no doubt, will be pleased with so charitable an act, so shall I and mine be bound, according to duty, continually to pray to Almighty God to bless your Honours and Worships with all earthly content and heavenly happiness.'

Along with so much that is variable and subject to speculation, what cannot be doubted is that for better or worse the old English village was a planned community, with the squire and the parson at the centre, and that towards the end of the century the squire was not only master of the village, but was also on thoroughly good terms with his farmers, drinking with them in the village inn, and joining with them in country sports.

> When masters made them merry with their men,
> When all the coats alike were russet brown,
> And his rude speech was vulgar as their own.
>
> CLARE.

There were many exceptions, as we know; but the average English squire, as he came to be known about the middle of the century, was a sportsman, a gentleman, and a good fellow. He was not, as a rule, a snob. Feudalism by this time had mellowed. The lord of the manor had become paternal, and had not yet become dandified. Here, however, Essex is not well represented, and it seems likely that the untidiness of the general run of villages in south Essex, their shapelessness and lack of pride, which makes them so different from those in the north of the county, is due to the failure of the landed gentry to form themselves into a squirearchy.

The explanation of this is to be found in what has already been discovered about Essex, namely, the fact that the leading gentlemen in the south of the county were national figures spending much of their time in London. Chelmsford, though the administrative centre, was not a provincial capital in the way so many county towns were. London was too near. Village life, therefore, tended to have less of the family and purely local character than it had in the

north and west of England.    And it was not only the gentry
who always had London in mind.    The farmers kept an eye
that way.    London was the market for south and central
Essex.    It is true that the produce of the villages was sold
in such markets as those of Chelmsford and Romford; but
the London buyers already dominated them.

In planned communities, fear of the Law must always be
more potent than fear of the Lord, so we need not be
surprised to find that the importance of the parson, who
shared with the squire the control of the seventeenth-century
village, was due quite as much to his legal as to his spiritual
authority.    The Poor Law was administered by the parish
vestry, over which he presided.    He was even required to
stand by while rogues were whipped by the constable, because
he had to certify to the justices that those stalwart officers
had done their duty.    In many villages the names of the
parish officers have been preserved with the church records,
and show how great the civil authority of the parson was.
At Great Dunmow these records from 1679 to 1768 are in the
churchwardens' account book.

As an illustration of the various duties of parish officers,
and of the close relationship between civil and ecclesiastical
affairs, take these consecutive items from the presentments
to justices at the midsummer sessions in 1612:

'Jury list and presentment for the Hundreds of Harlow,
Waltham and Ongar.

'That the Church Bybles and books of common prayer
within our severall hundreds are conformable and agreable
unto the honour and worshipp of Almightie God.

'We doe knowe neyther of any treason or felonie to have
bene committed within our severall hundreds.

'Chrystopher Byrde and wife and Widow Hookes of
Stondon Massey, for wilfully refusing to go to church for the
space of 7 years.

'Richard Smith of Sheering for keeping a common alehouse
without licence.

'William Sollie of Great Parndon who keeps a common
alehouse, for being a drunkard.

'John Hylles of Stondon Massey for being a drunkard.

'A lane in Theydon Garnon called "Lynnetts lane," being very noisome and dangerous, to be amended by the parishioners, in repect of their lands on both sides of it.'

The Chrystopher Byrd referred to was the son of William Byrd, the composer; other members of whose family to be presented as recusants were Thomas, a son, Rachel (Hooke) and Mary (Hauckes), daughters.

Village life, sacred and secular, grave and frivolous, was all of a piece, grey threads and scarlet all woven into the one cloth. Under a good parson the system could be entirely beneficent. At the end of a volume in the library of Trinity College, Cambridge, an interesting claim is made by an Essex parson of the period, Godfrey Goodman, who became Bishop of Gloucester and bequeathed his books to his old college. Hoping that the record would be preserved with the book the old man wrote:

'I was parson of Stapleford Abbots, in Essex, Anno Domini 1607, where I continued near 13 years; then I was parson of West Ildersley, in Berks, where I continued near 30 years, and in neither of my parishes (I prayse God for it) I had—

 1st, Not a beggar;
 2,  Not an alehouse;
 3,  Not a suite in law;
 4,  Not a quarrell;
 5,  Not an unthrift;
 6,  In the weeke days no labouring man ever wanted a dayes work;
 7,  On the Sunday noe poore man dined at his owne howse but was ever invited;
 8,  Noe man was ever presented for fornication or any great crime;
 9,  Noe murder, robbery, or felonie ever committed in the parish;
 10,  Noe man ever came to a violent end;
 11,  I never had any howses burnt in my parish;

12, I never had 2 men that died of the plague in my parishes until Mr. Nubery had his sequestration, and then a plague came, and a fire burnt all my parish in effect, and when I gave him orders there, he brought the small pox there. God make me thankful for all his blessings.

GODFR. GOODMAN, Gloucr.'

Goodman is an interesting figure. He has the distinction of being the only bishop of an English see since the Reformation to turn Roman Catholic. In his will, which was dated 1655, he declared that he had lived and would die 'in the doctrine of God's Holy Catholic and Apostolic Church, whereof I doe acknowledge the Church of Rome to be the Mother Church.' No other Church, he declared, had any salvation in it except so far as it concurred with the faith of the Church of Rome.

But the parson and his deputies were not always blameless themselves before the law, even in matters of common honesty. Here is a curious case from High Ongar, brought before the justices in 1610:

'26 March. Richard Stanes of High Ongar, Deputy Commissary of Robert Tye, Doctor of Theology, for extortionately, corruptly and unjustly taking at Hatfield Broad Oak, by colour of his office, of John Garrard of the same, yeoman, 13s. 2d.

'10 Jan., discharged because insufficient in law.

'Endorsed: Garrard saith that he being cited to appear before Stanes for divers offences which he saith were unjustly laid to his charge, viz., being away from church on 8 Oct. last, for carrying corn on St. Matthew's Day last, for sitting with his hat on his head in church in time of divine service, which offences he denieth to be true, notwithstanding his being judged to pay for his citing 16d., for his excommunication 18d., and for other charges which he knoweth not 10s., before he could be discharged of the court—this we find to be the evidence of Garrard.

'Further subscribed: "They find the monie taken but not in the place where it is alleged."'

Farm-house and yard at Dunmow

The Silent Woman, Widford

The obligation to attend church, which gave the parson great power over his people, remained statutory long after it had ceased to be enforced; but at one time it was strictly, even rigorously compelled. We have ample evidence of it in Essex. Here, as an example, is a case from the record of the Epiphany sessions, 1642:

> '*The information of Jane Earle, widow, taken upon Oath before Sir Benjamin Ayloffe Baronet, Sir Thomas Wiseman Knight, and Henry Nevill Esq. This 27th day of November Anno Domini 1641:*

'She saith that on Sunday was sennight she was laid on her Bed (she being then weary of a journey, having come on foot fifteen miles the day before) and about three of the Clock in the afternoon Robert Garrard, Philemon Pledger, John Freborne, and Nathaniell Garrard came to her house, and knocked at her door, whereupon she arose from her Bed, and let them in, and they requiring a reason why she was absent from Church, she told them that she came fifteen miles the day before, and was very weary and sick, yet they not being satisfied, but by force carried her to the cage, where they imprisoned her about a quarter, or half an hour.

'(Signed) BENJAMIN AYLOFFE. THOMAS WYSEMAN.'

Even diet was in a measure controlled by the parson. Everybody ate fish during Lent. It was an ancient custom of the Church, and a very useful one—there was not much meat about at that time of year. If, however, meat was essential, the parson was asked for a licence, and if he thought it necessary, or in some way desirable, he granted one; if not, he withheld it. One instance of the granting of such a licence is found in the charity accounts of Little Burstead. It is dated 10th March 1632, and allows 'Mistress Anne Walton, the wife of Mr. William Walton, Esq., and her two small children to eat flesh during eight days of the time of this lent, wherein the eating of flesh is to others prohibited, in regard of the weakness and infirmity of her body, and her children's weakness and smallness.' The licence was granted for only eight days at a time, though it was renewed four times to cover the period of denial.[1]

On the south side of Rivenhall church lie buried two sisters who left a legacy of £4 a year for herrings to be given to the poor every Friday in Lent. Similar bequests were not uncommon. One of the Mildmays left £3 6s. 8d. to buy three barrels of white herrings and four cades of red herrings to be distributed among the poor of Chelmsford and Moulsham in the first and second week of 'clean Lent.'

The labouring poor were certainly bound hand and foot, though there were stirrings of revolt—as there always had been—and a petition from Theydon Mount in 1612 shows that even in rural areas they could, if sufficiently united, appeal successfully against the will of the lord of the manor. In this case, Sir William Smythe of Hill Hall had appointed George Mott parish constable seven years previously without the consent of the parishioners, and had not provided an opportunity for another constable to be elected, though George Mott was 'one of the poorest men in all the parish, and a man of evil disposition and very bad qualities, who had wronged the parishioners very much, and made great strife amongst them.'

Sir William Smith, the petitioners stated, would not allow another constable to be appointed because George Mott 'serveth his turn.' They asked the justices to appoint instead 'an honest man, Thomas Field, a subsidy man and very sufficient for that office.' Thomas Field was duly sworn after an investigation which revealed that no court leet had been held in Theydon Mount for more than twenty years.

The constables of the neighbouring parish, Theydon Garnon, were stout fellows, which may have made the parishioners of Theydon Mount look to their own appointments. The Garnon constables in 1609 were so bold as to indict the king's own commissioners. On 15th October 1609 we find in the sessions rolls: 'Thomas Ives of London, gent.,

---

[1] 'Singular as it may appear in the present day, an office for granting licences to eat flesh in any part of England, was opened in St. Paul's Church Yard, and advertised in the public papers, anno 1663.'
WILSON, Life and Times of De Foe, i. 43.

being deputy of Henry Jenyngs, for feloniously and deceit-
fully cutting down at Theydon Garnon in a place called
"Burchen coppye," by virtue of his commission, for purvey-
ance for the king's use, ten timber oaks worth £7 10s.
belonging to John FitzWilliam, Esq., without making an
appointment with the constables of Theydon Garnon and
four discreet men of that parish, and without sealing
tallies.'

There is much amusing and interesting material to be
found on this subject of parish constables.  Theirs was a
thankless job.  They were elected to arrange for watch and
ward to be kept in the parish, to arrest vagrants and bring
them before the justices, and to perform other corrective
duties, some of which might all too easily make them unpopular with their fellow villagers.  They were also expected
to see that the stocks, whipping-post, and pillory were kept in
repair, and in connection with this there is a petition of 1645
which shows that Walthamstow, then a straggling village on
the southern border of Epping Forest, was in the happy but
unsatisfactory state of having neither whipping-post nor
stocks.  It also shows how the officers of that parish were
elected:

    '*The humble petition of the constables and other of
    the inhabitants of the parish of Walthamstow in the said
    County:*

'humbly shewing that in the parish of Walthamstow there
is at this present neither a pair of stocks nor a whipping
post, which by the Law ought to be in every parish in this
kingdom, the very sight whereof might be a means to keep
some from offending the Law, a means for the execution of
the Law upon others, for want whereof the said constables
cannot punish offenders according to the Law, and therefore
desire an Order from this honourable Court that there may be
a pair of stocks and a whipping post provided within the said
parish.  And whereas within the said parish of Walthamstow,
formerly and customarily there hath been a Court Leet
holden within the Manor of Walthamstow Tony, alias high
hall in Walthamstow aforesaid, once in every yeare, yearly

  *E

at which said Court Leet there were yearly chosen Officers
commonly called ale cunners, for the looking to the Assize
of bread and beer; Officers so necessary that for want thereof
many do suffer, the poor especially.  And for these two years
last past there hath been no Court Leet kept in the said
manor at the time accustomed, and consequently now no
such Officers in the said parish, and therefore do desire this
honourable Court to grant an order for the choosing of such
said Officers.'

We dare not be so romantic as to speculate whether the
stocks had been removed from Walthamstow as a tribute to
the poet who had lately lived there, Nicholas Breton, who, in
*An Invective against the Wicked of the World*, wrote:

> Look but on beggars going to the stocks,
> How master constable can march before them,
> And while the beadle maketh fast the locks
> How bravely he can knave them and be-whore them,
> And not afford one word of pity for them,
> When it may be poor honest silly people
> Must make the church make curtsy to the steeple.

In the same year a petition came to the justices from the
constable of Henham: 'The humble petition of John Wood of
Henham in the Countie of Essex, yeoman.'   John Wood had
been constable for more than a year, and had carried out his
duties 'to his great charge and hindrance, being a man unfit
to travel, and having none fit to follow his business in his
absence.'   He thought it was time for another man to be
appointed; but there had not been a court leet held in Henham for a long time, nor could he see any likelihood of one
being held.   He was therefore obliged to appeal to the justices
to choose and swear a successor.   If they would do so, he
added feelingly, he would be 'ever the more bounden to pray
to God for to give [them] long lyves, health, happinesse and
prosperitie.'   The justices could not resist an appeal which
carried with it the prayers for their comfort of a faithful
yeoman, so they appointed another constable.

John Wood expressed himself like a stout-hearted East
Saxon.   Affairs were not always conducted with such good

spirit on both sides. The Scots, as we have suggested, caused trouble enough in various parts of the county; but a more alarming invasion came to Epping. An Irishman, one Darbie Flanagan—may his soul have peace—came to this growing town on the Newmarket road as an innkeeper, and in 1646 the innocent people of Epping actually conceived the idea of setting him up as custodian of English liberties and dispenser of justice in the town: in other words, 'at a court leet holden for the manor of Epping bury' the jury elected Darbie Flanagan and George Pricklove their constables for the ensuing year. But Darbie Flanagan, true to the ancient traditions of his race, 'peremptorily refused and still doth refuse to be sworne,' which George Pricklove thought unfair, 'the said town being a market town' and in 'need of able officers in these times of trouble.' The justices had evidently had very little experience of the Irish, for they made an order for Flanagan to be sworn by the nearest justice, and, if he still refused, for him to be bound for a period of two years.

It would be unfair to suggest that Essex folk themselves never kicked against authority for the sake of mirth and merriment. Happily they did. Though less inclined that way than the Irish, the English usually tend to sympathize with the man who rebels against authority, however much they recognize its necessity. Most of us have a tender regard for poachers, moochers, and other vagrants. Even the constables seem to have been glad to chase offenders out of their own parishes rather than drag them before the courts. It is all very wrong; but we are made that way. I remember asking a constable in Newmarket even in our own law-abiding days about the difficulties of the county boundary of Cambridgeshire and West Suffolk running down the main street of that cheerful town. He thought there were far more advantages than disadvantages to it, and with a twinkle in his eye told me of the fun they had after a race meeting in chasing drunks across the road to be dealt with by the police of the other county. Perhaps one of his ancestors hundreds of years before had laughed as light-heartedly in doing precisely the same thing. When lives were so laborious the villagers were entitled to all the fun they could get.

It is impossible to say how much suffering and how much pleasure there is in life at any given time. Both depend far more upon temperament and the grace of God than upon circumstances. There was always sorrow and there was always joy:

> It is right it should be so;
> Man was made for joy and woe;
> And when this we rightly know,
> Thro' the world we safely go.

What we can see is that the instinct for happiness, which every healthy creature has, expressed itself in a rich variety of lusty sports and recreations. Fynes Moryson, in his *Itinerary* of 1617, said: 'The English are naturally inclined to pleasure, as there is no country wherein the gentlemen and lords have so many and large parks only reserved for the pleasure of hunting, and where all sorts of men allot so much ground about their houses for pleasure of gardens and orchards.' As a race we were at this time fond of display— more so indeed than at any other time in our history, and never have buildings been designed to provide so colourful a setting as they were under the Tudors and early Stuarts. Under Elizabeth especially our new gentry had made this gallant little island a proud and hearty place. Our ruling class was as yet unsoured by the Puritans and their wits had not yet been dulled in the courts of the early Georges. They rode about attended by their retinue of servants, mounted and wearing their master's badge on their sleeves. They ate much, drank much, then stimulated their overworked livers on horseback in hunting and hawking, and whatever they did was done as noisily as possible. If they had no other means of making a noise they went up into the nearest belfry and rang the bells—the parson permitting.

Henry VIII had been a man of great physical prowess and it had been in his reign that outdoor sports had been revived. The prestige of games was such as to reduce learning in popular esteem to an exercise suitable only for weaklings and men of the lower orders, a mistaken view still not eliminated from the English mind. In his *Poesye of Princelye Practice* Sir William Forest had written:

> In featis of maistries bestowe some diligence.
> Too ryde, runne, lepe, or caste by violence
> Stone, barre or plummett, or such other thinge,
> It not refuseth any prince or kynge.

Even when the weather made outdoor exercise impossible, weight-lifting and other strenuous games rather than reading occupied the leisure hours of young gentlemen.

In those days the hunting was not with county packs as it is now. Each man hunted on his own estate. Because hunting and hawking were the sports of kings they were accounted 'honest recreations.' Bowling also was accounted proper exercise for a gentleman and approved by those who sat in judgment on other people's morals. In Essex, football was universally popular because so many pigs were kept, and in November, when the poor man killed his pig, the bladder was blown up to make a football. It was by this sport that the young people kept themselves warm in winter. The game was not played by teams until much later.

There was also universal pleasure in native music. Foreigners particularly noticed how common it was for the English to sing their folk songs and ballads as they went about their work. Even in the smallest villages there were such companies of musicians as would have rejoiced the heart of Hardy. They attended all the village functions and played for a small fee at private celebrations. There were wandering minstrels who collected their livelihood from the ale-houses on their route and were usually welcomed at farm and manor houses. There were bull-baiting, bear-baiting, cock-fighting, and other cruel sports, but also the civilizing round of Church festivals, made popular by wakes, fairs, and feasts.

Control was always necessary. One of Charles I's official duties when he became king was to sanction the Act of 1625 framed to secure a more reverent and seemly observance

of Sunday. The baiting of bulls and bears and the performance of interludes or common plays on Sunday were
forbidden. It was also illegal for the people to leave their
parishes for purposes of sport or recreation. Two men of
Ilford, I find that I have noted, were in trouble 'for suffringe
stage players uppon the Saboth daie . . . in tyme of
Eveninge prayer.' Offenders were liable to a fine of three
shillings and fourpence, or three hours in the stocks. The
Puritans were in the ascendant.

But in 1633 Archbishop Laud prevailed upon the king to
re-issue the declaration now familiarly known as the *Book of
Sports*. The clergy were ordered to read it from their
pulpits. Many of them, we find, refused to do so, and were
suspended from their livings; others left the country, fearing
that the land would now be given over to revelry and ungodly
junketings. They remembered the scenes when the *Book
of Sports* was first issued—how morris dancers would come
into church in their linen blouses, gaily coloured scarves and
dresses, and the jangle of bells that was heard until they had
settled in their places. All the things, in fact, that returned
to Thaxted when Conrad Noel was vicar. Such goings-on
were in the spirit of the ancient English Church, but were out
of keeping with a three hours' sermon on the nature of the
Trinity from the Rev. Obadiah Drybones. So incensed were
the Puritans by this mirthful declaration, designed to keep
the nation sane, healthy, and contented, that when Cromwell
succeeded Charles the *Book of Sports* was burned by the
common hangman.

We have the names of two of the gay company of fiddlers
and minstrels against whom this new restriction was directed.
They are preserved for us, curiously enough, in Warton's
*History of English Poetry*. They were Outroaring Dick and
Wat Wimbas, and they made, we are told, as much as twenty
shillings a day by singing ballads at Braintree Fair.

When we think of these brighter aspects of old-time
village life it is gratifying to reflect that the man who wrote
the standard work on *English Sports and Pastimes*, Joseph
Strutt, was an Essex man, born at Springfield Mill, near

Chelmsford, and of the family that produced the Lords Rayleigh.

Other pleasant old customs were more closely connected with everyday toil. The liveliest was the Horkey at the end of harvest. It is obsolete in the country now; but was continued until well into last century at Manuden, near Bishop's Stortford. When the last load of harvest, which was called the horkey load, had been led into the barn the labourers, led by the 'lord of the harvest,' went round the parish to collect what they called largesse. Then came the feast itself, with the harvest men, their wives and families, making merry over bacon or boiled beef, followed by apple pie with lashings of rich cream. If labours were hard, pleasures were hearty.

# CHAPTER IX

## BAYS AND SAYS

I will buy my true love yellow say,
    For Sundays, for Sundays,
To wear about her middle small.

ANON.

THERE is a statute of Queen Elizabeth's reign which refers
to the 'fair large' towns of Essex, 'inhabited of a long time
with cloth makers, which have made and daily do make good
and true cloth to the great commonweal of the country there,
and nothing prejudicial to or for the commonwealth of
this realm.'

It seems strange that it should have been thought desirable
to state officially that the manufacture of cloth did no harm
to the nation. No government of the last hundred and fifty
years would have thought such an assurance necessary.
But, as we have seen in reviewing our village life, the
Tudors were afraid of creating a wage-earning class, without
land or stock, depending on their craft alone for support.
At first, cloth-working had been a spare-time job, welcome
especially to the women. Their wages in farmhouse kitchens
were small, and spinning was the employment they turned to
when they had nothing else on hand. It was not hard work.
It could be followed at any odd moment and therefore did not
interfere with the care of the family in the home. For the
men, it was useful employment when the weather or the season
made outdoor work impossible. As a secondary occupation
it was useful to every one. But as a sole employment its
advantages long seemed doubtful. By Elizabeth's reign,
however, it was already becoming apparent that the trend of
industrial development was in that direction, and progressive
economists were beginning to accept it.

Unfortunately, progressive economists—such as there were —had little say in the fixing of wages. The justices of the peace, who fixed them at quarter sessions, were worthy and public-spirited country gentlemen who did their best for the weavers; but the land was their chief interest. They thought of wages in terms of agricultural rates, which, as we have seen in the previous chapter, were only to supplement what the labourers could produce in their own holdings. Consequently the wages they fixed were inadequate to maintain spinners and weavers in the new landless cottages being built along the village streets. Professor Thorold Rogers showed that employers often paid more than the minimum prescribed at quarter sessions, but it was a long time before any one—including the workers themselves— understood how much more was needed when either all or most of the food had to be bought. Six shillings a week might seem generous pay to those who had only earned three shillings a week on the land. It was not realized that at least ten shillings a week would be needed to support a family, especially as the cost of living was constantly rising. This is not the place to go into the question in detail, but professional economists will agree that by the time the price of provisions had risen 100 per cent, wages had risen less than 50 per cent. The correct proportion is more depressing than that, but a hundred against fifty is near enough to show how little those in authority understood what was happening. In 1614, for example, the weavers of Wiltshire complained that they received 'no more than what was accustomed to be paid forty years past, notwithstanding that the prices of all kinds of victual are almost doubled from what they were.'

One way of bridging the gap was to increase the number of looms for each weaver. The Weavers' Act of 1555 limited weavers in villages to two looms each, but the restriction was not observed. Many had five or six. The same expedient was tried in Lancashire in the cotton trade depression between the two wars of the present century, and I happened to witness some of the disturbances that followed attempts to increase the number of looms per person from four to six or eight.  In the early seventeenth century the old system of village weaving was breaking down, just as the nineteenth-century system was breaking down in the nineteen-twenties.

There is a seventeenth-century ballad called *The Clothier's Delight*, which goes:

> We will make [them] to work hard for sixpence a day,
> Though a shilling they deserve if they had their just pay.

The two cloths on which the workers starved and a few clothiers grew rich in Essex were bays and says.  Bay was a kind of blanket cloth or coarse baize; say, an earlier form of serge.  In the middle of the seventeenth century the industry had reached its peak in Colchester, its principal centre, and in a few other towns, notably in Coggeshall, where Thomas Guyon, a baymaker 'scarcely to be matched in England,' flourished.  When he died in 1664 he left nearly a hundred thousand pounds.[1]  A Colchester baymaker of the day employed 'four hundred households of spinners, fifty-two of weavers, and thirty-three of others.'[2]  It is sad to reflect that this great industry, which brought so much wealth to the eastern counties in the Middle Ages, enriched so many proud families, built Paycocke's House at Coggeshall and others like it, and contributed so handsomely to the building and adorning of some of the noblest churches in the land, was shadowed in its last days by the poverty of its workpeople.

One of the worst depressions in English trade history came in the sixteen-twenties, when the export of cloth fell to two-thirds its previous figure.  The first royal commission ever set up to inquire into the cause of unemployment was formed in 1622.  Trade did not improve, and seven years later, in April 1629, two hundred weavers of Bocking and Braintree attended the quarter sessions at Chelmsford to present a petition.  They complained of 'extreme necessity and disability to maintain and relieve themselves and their families.'  If some speedy remedy were not found, they

[1] *Victoria County History, Essex*, ii. 396.
[2] *State Papers, Domestic*, 1673, pp. 88, 115.

declared, thirty thousand persons would be reduced to miserable poverty. The justices, including Lord Maynard, Sir Henry Mildmay, Sir William Masham, and eighteen other gentlemen of standing in the county, heard their plea with sympathy, but were powerless to relieve them. At once they sent a letter to the lords of the council, setting out the grounds of complaint and their own fear that 'persuasions to settle them in quiet and order could not prevail long unless something should be enacted which may remove the true cause of their complaint.'

The inadequate nature of the reply is to be divined in a second letter sent by the Essex justices, with the Earl of Warwick and Lord Maynard as principal signatories. They said that the justices of Essex had met to consider how they could carry out the directions of the lords of the council; but, they continued, 'when we fall into the examination of the abilities of those parishes within the hundreds where the clockworkers dwell, we find all so equally interested in that trade as that we know not any one parish within those hundreds which are able to set their own poor on work, and if we should now go about to force the neighbouring parishes to contribute to those towns, instead of appeasing the disorders now on foot, in some few of the great clothing towns, we should thereby infinitely increase the complaints in all the parishes within those hundreds, which by the Statute (whereto your lordships are pleased to refer us) are only liable to any taxation which we have power to make out of the general Quarter Sessions. And whereas your lordships are pleased to require us to make diligent inquiry to find out such disorderly persons as sort themselves amongst the clothiers though they be not of the trade, nor would apply themselves to labour if they should be set on work, and severely to punish all their misdemeanours, we are very careful to inform ourselves of them, and as we shall find them out, and have just proofs of their offences, which as yet do not fully appear unto us, we shall be ready to punish them according to their demerits.'

The same month the weavers themselves appealed to the

king, and their letter is so important a document that it must be reproduced in full:

*'To the King's Most Excellent Majesty*
*'The humble petition of the Weavers of Bocking and Braintree in the County of Essex and the neighbouring towns thereabouts to the number of One Hundred Thousand with them which doe depend upon them.*

8th May, 1629.

'Humbly shewing that the trade hath been decaying for this seven years or thereabouts to their utter undoing, Now they have no work at all, by reason whereof they are grown into that extremity, that for themselves and families and are fain to lie in straw, all which many worthy gentlemen of that country can testify, and if there may not be some certain course taken for them they, their wives and children, are like to perish, for in this declining time they are not able to subsist any longer by reason of the abatement of their wages, which is at the least seven shillings in the pound, which they are unable to bear, their wages being but small in the best times, yet their Masters are unable to help them by reason their trading is taken from them, for the Merchants will not to buy their Bayes so that these stocks lying dead in their hands are hardly able to help themselves. So in this extremity your Petitions did petition to your Majesty's justices of peace which sat at Chelmsford, not doubting of their cares, hoping that they would make your Majesty acquainted with their miseries, which is insufferable, which they did. And having gracious answer from your Majesty which put your suppliants in great hope and comfort that their wants and necessities should be supplied, they have rested satisfied, and in hope have sustained themselves and families with so small a portion of bread as is hardly to keep life and soul together, which finding nothing done, they think their miseries are not credited, which they beseech your Majesty to consider that they may not starve in time of plenty.

'And had it not been that the right honourable the Earl of Warwick, the Lord Maynard and others, worthy gentlemen, had appeased them many wretched people would have gathered together in a Mutiny and have been with your Majesty before this time to have made their miseries known unto your Majesty, for they said words would not fill the belly nor clothe the back. So the Earl of Warwick did appease them by mild persuasions and told them that the wardens should come to your Majesty to entreat your gracious favour, which they humbly beseech your Majesty graciously to grant for Christ Jesus sake, that they may not perish, but live to do your Majesty's service according to their duties,

> 'And continually pray for your Majesty's
> Long and prosperous Reign.'

After this it is not surprising to find that on the 22nd of the same month there was a disorderly rising of the Braintree and Bocking men. Three hundred of them marched to Heybridge Basin at Maldon and raided a ship belonging to two north-country merchants, which was carrying corn to Hull. The chief merchant himself was captured and robbed of £20; the weavers gained possession of the ship for a short time, and stole as much grain as they could carry away with them. Four of their number were caught, and after being tried by the Earl of Warwick and other justices, three of them were hanged. The fourth was reprieved. A Maldon woman, Agnes Carke, who described herself as their captain and had been touring the distressed areas stirring up insurrection, was hanged with them. The people of Maldon were 'much pleased with the Justices, being before that time much dismayed with the insolence of these people.'

With the continued decline of the trade and the poverty it brought, petitions and riots became common. The intensification of competition brought irregular trade practices, which in turn provoked stricter enforcement of restrictive laws. At the Easter sessions held at Chelmsford in 1637 the justices publicly stated their belief that the taking of apprentices in ways contrary to the law was 'a great cause that so many poor do abound and daily increase in divers parts of this county and especially in clothing towns.' The truth was that the trade had outgrown the villages and that in consequence the old system of control was obsolete.

All this is much more depressing than Herrick's pretty rhyme for St. Distaff's Day, the day after Twelfth Night:

> If the maids a-spinning go,
> Burn the flax and fire the tow.

It is equally remote from the scenes described by travellers through the villages of East Anglia on summer days, with cheerful women sitting at their cottage doors spinning and gossiping, though there were certainly many cheerful episodes in the lives of the village weavers.   One of the most delightful pictures that comes to my own mind in thinking of them is of the great log that was tied to one end of the loom, on which the children used to sit in order to weigh it down and so tighten the threads.   This is pleasantly described in the lines:

> A huge oaken log that to one end was tied,
> While on it some half-dozen urchins would ride;
> Thus increasing its weight we kept tight every thread,
> And the warp round the beam was most evenly laid.

Fuller, as we should expect, put the best face on things.   He said of Essex: 'This county is charactered like the good wife described by Bathsheba, "She layeth her hand to the spindle, and her hands hold the distaff."'   The distaff had been displaced by the spinning-wheel in most homes; but there were still, and long afterwards, some who preferred its finer thread:

> There are, to speed their labor, who prefer
> Wheels double spol'd, which yield to either hand
> A sev'ral line; and many yet adhere
> To th' ancient distaff, at the bosom fix'd,
> Casting the whirling spindle as they walk.

One amusing circumstance that no one seems to have pointed out, is that in those days of fanatical religious sectarianism a great proportion of the cloth produced in this industry sponsored by Protestant refugees was used to clothe Roman Catholic monks, particularly those in Spain, Portugal, and Italy.   But perhaps the weavers of Braintree and Bocking cared little who bought their cloth so long as they were paid for it.

The question of who started the work in Essex is not easily answered. There had been woollen manufacture in the county since the time of Richard II, if not earlier. The trade probably dates from the Norman Conquest. Bay-making, however, was not ancient, An old rhyme tells us that:

> Hops, Reformation, Bays, and Beer,
> Came into England all in a year.

Its development into a large and prosperous industry was the work of foreign settlers. Since the earliest days of Protestantism the eastern counties have benefited from the settlement in their towns of skilled workers driven from their own countries by religious persecution. That may be what the rhymer had in mind when he said that bays and Reformation came together.

One of the most important of these waves of immigrants, exiled from Flanders by fear of the tyrannical Duke of Alva, settled at Sandwich in 1570 and formed a Flemish community there. Soon there were more of them than the town would hold, and Colchester, already a town known for its strong Protestant sympathies, received about fifty. At the time of their arrival the trade of Colchester was depressed, and the authorities rightly thought that these honest, God-fearing people, hard-working and skilled in crafts that were then unknown in the town, would instruct others and bring prosperity. Their trust was not misplaced. Colchester soon had a promising new industry.

These early settlers lived in a separate community, organizing their own religious, commercial, and social life in the manner of their own country. At first they were given the use of St. Giles's Church, afterwards of All Saints', until they were able to build a chapel of their own in St. Mary's Lane. At the top of High Street they built their guildhall, of which the ground floor was an open market, the upper floor the Dutch Bay Hall. Here officials of the trade examined every piece of cloth made in the town, then graded and fixed their seals on them to denote the class they should be placed in. Several of these seals are to be seen in the museum at

Colchester Castle.   When a cloth was below standard a fine
called rawbote was imposed.   These fines were duly collected
and handed to the town authorities for the relief of the poor
—the fines from the English clothiers to the English poor,
those from the Dutch clothiers to the Dutch poor.   Between
1680 and 1695 the yield from rawbote in Colchester averaged
£200 a year.   The highest amount, £243 5s. 3d., was
collected in 1683.

The fifteen-seventies brought several communities of
Flemish settlers into Essex.   One came to Harwich, the port
for the Low Countries, while forty families settled at Halstead
in 1577.   And all the time Colchester continued to receive
new weavers until the bailiffs issued an order forbidding any
more to settle in the town except by special permission,
because, they said, the town was in danger of becoming
nothing more than a colony of Flemings.   For all that, others
appear to have got in, and in 1590 we find the baymakers of
Halstead leaving that town and settling in Colchester.   They
prospered to such an extent that towards the end of the
seventeenth century they were bringing £30,000 a week
into Colchester alone.

Of the value of these refugees as citizens there can be
no question.   They never became a burden on the parishes
where they settled, and they contributed handsomely towards
equipping the forces that went to meet the Armada in 1588.
But in spite of this there was strong prejudice against them.
James I had political reasons for not viewing them with the
favour they deserved.   Religious jealousy crept in.   The
Bishop of London in 1615 complained that some of them
attended communion in English churches instead of keeping
to their own chapels.   There were ugly scenes.   James, in
need of money, brought what appear to have been unjust
charges against them in order to impose heavy fines.   One
very unfair case, that of Thomas Reignolds, a Colchester
baymaker employing five hundred hands, belongs to the next
reign.   In 1637 he was charged with having paid some of his
workpeople in kind instead of in money.   Though ninety-six
persons came forward to testify that the statements made

against him were 'malicious calumnies, and that he had ever
dealt honestly' with his workpeople, he was ordered to pay
double the wages he was alleged to have kept back.  For a
week he was imprisoned in the Fleet, and while he was there
his works were burned down.

On the religious question, Archbishop Laud took a different
line of action.  He disliked the separate congregations and
tried, though without much success, to persuade the children
of the second descent born in England to attend worship in
the parish church.  After Laud's death an Act of Parliament
was passed giving full freedom of worship to the Dutch
churches, and it is notable that even the Act of Uniformity
contained a clause in their favour.  As so often has happened
in Church history, kindness reduced their separatist fervour,
and we find many of the descendants of the original settlers
taking advantage of the Naturalization Act of 1672.  In
1782, a hundred and fifty-eight years after its formation,
the Colchester congregation was dissolved.

The different workers engaged in the fully organized
village wool trade so often appear in local records that it may
be useful to name them, and explain at which point they
came into the process.  After the farmer, then, came the
wool-sorter, who took the fleece and did with it what his
name implies.  The wool-comber came next.  His job was to
comb that part of the wool set aside to be warp for the
spinner, while the gigger prepared the part that was to be used
as weft.  The seamer oiled the wool prepared by the gigger,
and the spinner made the prepared wool into yarn.  The
scourer cleaned the grease out of the spun yarn.  The winder
wound the wool prepared by the wool-comber on to bobbins;
the warper took the wool from the bobbins and put it into
chains; the papper dipped the chains into size.  The weaver
produced the cloth.  After him, the fuller came along to
thicken it, the rougher to give it a nap by scratching it with
teasels, and finally the drier or stretcher to hang it out on the
tenters in the fields.  It was from this hanging of the cloth
on tenters that we got the expression 'being on tenterhooks.'
A field at Dedham is still called Tenterfield.  Some of the

most expressive words in the English language have come to us from the village wool trade. Even the word spinster is derived from its being the usual occupation of unmarried women. Phrases such as 'spinning a yarn,' 'a tangled skein,' 'dyed in the wool,' all come from this medieval trade, once so widely distributed.

It had a great effect, too, on the shape and appearance of the Essex villages. The larger windows in the cottages were introduced to provide more light for the looms; the open space by the water was left for the fullers to wash their cloths; the rows of weather-boarded cottages were built for the weavers and spinners. It might be an exaggeration to say that they owe their origin in Essex to the wool trade; but it is worthy of remark that they belong to the weaving districts rather than to the purely agricultural areas where half-timbered cottages with wattle-and-daub panels seem to have been usual. The memory of this lost craft is preserved in innumerable small ways, but most effectively in two well-known buildings, each now unique of its kind in Essex. One is Southfields, Dedham, often said to be an old bay and say factory, though there are no signs of the characteristic weavers' windows in the walls. It may have been a clothier's dwelling-house and warehouse only. The other is Paycocke's House, the home of a wealthy clothier in Coggeshall.

Southfields, in Constable's favourite village on the Stour, is a late fifteenth- or early sixteenth-century house built on a courtyard plan, which was later converted into a group of cottages. Its massive corner posts with their moulded capitals, its stout old timber frame, fluted beams, original door and window frames—most of them blocked now—and its towering chimney stack, make it one of the grandest monuments of Tudor England to be found in Essex. The south-west wing was the master's house, and the upper storey of the east range may have been the weaving room, unless, as seems possible, it was a warehouse. No other building in Essex brings us so close to the character of the medieval wool trade, though many similar buildings are to be found in Suffolk, particularly in Lavenham.

Dedham, near Colchester

Coggeshall

Paycocke's House, so carefully restored by Lord Buxton, then Mr. Noel Buxton, who bought it in 1905, is an early sixteenth-century timber-framed house built in the elaborate style of the day by a rich merchant of Coggeshall. Most of it seems to date from about 1500. When Lord Buxton bought it the front was plastered and had sash windows; but when the plaster was removed the beautiful ornamental work and the timber framing were found to be in sound condition. The oriel window had gone, and the doors had been altered; but sufficient of the original remained to enable the replacement to be done correctly. It was also a happy circumstance that the restoration was done by a local craftsman.

Along the beam that supports the upper storey runs a carved stem with leaves and flowers springing from it. Intertwined with these are figures which include a king and queen clasping hands, intended to symbolize the union of the houses of Lancaster and York by the marriage of Henry Tudor and Elizabeth, daughter of Edward IV. Three lozenges bear the initials T. P. and the middle one has Thomas Paycocke's badge, an ermine tail. The double doors in the archway have linen-fold panels and foliage carving in the spandrels of the arch. On moulded pedestals that stand out from the side posts are two figures, one a jester, with ass-eared cap and baton, the other a mummer carrying a shield. The woodwork indoors is no less rich in its mouldings, and the whole is a most eloquent expression of the spirit of an age that looked towards the future with gaiety and unrestrained optimism.

We can hardly look at such a house, remembering that it was a merchant's dwelling, without feeling that the dry facts of industrial history are inadequate for the expression of medieval clothmaking. We have the same sense of a different world in the town, for Coggeshall is still a place of the Middle Ages in its looks. A large proportion of its houses date from the sixteenth century. Two of its inns, the 'Fleece' and the 'Woolpack,' still have names that came from the trade they flourished on. The 'Fleece' is seventeenth century, with a sixteenth-century south-west wing.

These old houses tell a better tale than figures. It is the tale of Bottom the weaver, hobnobbing with Snout the tinker, Starveling the tailor, Flute the bellows-minder, Quince the carpenter, and Snug the joiner. And when we look at the houses such men built we see that they were far better carpenters and joiners than many who succeeded them. The great breastsummer at Paycocke's House, with a fierce-looking dragon at the east end, with a stem ending not in a flower but in a bird's head, with a female bust protruding from one open flower and a boy diving into another, is better evidence than learned authorities can produce from books of Shakespeare's understanding of the minds of common people. He was nearer the spirit of those working men than we might have supposed when he put them into a play along with Peaseblossom, Cobweb, Moth, and Mustardseed. His father, we may remember, traded in just such a town, and Shakespeare grew up among such buildings as we see here. These places are valuable records, providing we have a little imagination to serve as a candle to read them by. Let us drink our pints, or what we will, at the 'Woolpack' with the memory of these good people of *A Midsummer Night's Dream* fresh in our minds, and with Robin Goodfellow at our elbow.

It might so well have been a weaver from one of these cottages who offered to roar, as he said, 'that I will do any man's heart good to hear me. I will roar, that I will make the Duke say, let him roar again, let him roar again.' It might equally well have been in the fields behind Paycocke's House that the same merry company met to discuss how they should bring the moonlight into a chamber so that Pyramus and Thisby might meet in the right setting:

*Snug.* Doth the moon shine that night we play our play?

*Bottom.* A Kalendar, a Kalendar! look in the almanack; find out moon-shine, find out moon-shine.

*Quince.* Yes, it doth shine that night.

*Bottom.* Why then may you leave a casement of the great chamber window, where we play, open, and the moon may shine in at the casement.

They played in such great chambers as we see in these houses, and the two figures on the posts at Paycocke's House, the jester and the mummer, bear witness to the spirit of their revels.

Such buildings remind us again that there was a genuine love of beauty in Tudor and Stuart England, shared by every class of society. Objects in common use in the homes were made in pleasing designs. Furniture was plain, perhaps, in the seventeenth-century homes of artisans, but even there it was of good proportions and sound workmanship. England had not yet become Disraeli's two nations. It was not until the eighteenth century that good taste became the prerogative of the well-educated rich.

Whatever the weaknesses that caused the breakdown of village industries may have been, there were many things to be said in their favour. They did enable different classes to know each other as they mingled in each small community. Industrial life no less than household life was more personal before the factory system developed. Often the good apprentice married his master's daughter and inherited the business. With a good master it was a sound system, though with a bad it was slavery—as it still was when Dickens was writing. It is when we think of the women and children in industry that we see the hardest side. The cloth-makers always looked to them for their thread and yarn. As trade grew, the men could gradually withdraw from other employment, such as farm work or gardening. But the women still had to carry their burden of cleaning, cooking, and child-bearing. Their work was badly paid, and in consequence the children had to be taught to help as soon as they were able. Many children were actually spinning when they were seven or eight years old. So the work had both light and shade, colour and gloom. As a phase of social history it is a fascinating study. But it had to pass. Essex returned to the land, and Coggeshall, where Thomas Guyon became rich and Thomas Paycocke built his beautiful house, became a seed-growing centre with fields full of flowers on every side.

## CHAPTER X

## THE FRIENDLY INN

To tell a merry or a wondrous tale
Over a chearful glass of nappy ale.

PUBS and paradoxes were so dear to the genial heart of
G. K. Chesterton that it seems likely that somewhere in his
voluminous writings he must have dilated on the sobering
influence of the English inn.   I do not remember such an
occasion, but in view of the apparent probability I should be
a bold man if I were to try my hand at exploring the implica-
tions of this curious contrariety.   Perhaps it will be enough
to point out that while the doctrine-changers in the Temple
were turning the Church into a den of thieves, and the politi-
cians on the hustings were inciting people to rebellion, the
innkeepers of England in their several generations were keeping the common people sane and tolerant and were preserving
good fellowship.   Whether his intention was sardonic or not,
Housman wrote sense when he rhymed:

And malt does more than Milton can
To justify God's ways to man.

It is true that rival factions have resorted to their separate
taverns, that murders have been committed in inns—even in
Essex inns—and that most of the commandments have been
broken in them.   It is even true, as Chesterton might have
conceded, that men have been known to get drunk in inns.
But in spite of this, or perhaps because of it, the inn has
preserved humane and tolerant traditions, and upheld the
rights of a free people.

Let us be clear about this.   No proper-minded person
would allow every reeking pot-house and drinking-den to be
an inn, for an inn must provide rest and refreshment, and
those provide neither.   An inn must afford safe lodging.

This ancient institution has been gravely abused. Even the translators of the Authorized Version slighted it, and in doing so discarded one of Miles Coverdale's most beautiful sentences. 'And my people shall dwell in a peaceable habitation' is a poor substitute for 'My people shall dwell in the inns of peace.' The intoxication of religious enthusiasm has never been congenial to the sober spirit of the inn. We have an illustration of this in the tale of George Eagles, the Essex martyr, as Foxe in his account of the Marian persecution tells it. The capture and killing of this simple hedge-preacher as related in the original Foxe is a very different story from that of his pious putting to death as related in Sunday school editions of the book. But both are severe in their treatment of the Chelmsford innkeeper, so joyously named Richard Potto, who tried to make Eagles see reason, and thus save his life.

This brutally murdered man, George Eagles, was a poor tailor who went about the countryside preaching the gospel, 'now tarrying in this town, and sometimes abiding in that, certain months together, as occasion served, lodging sometimes in the country, and sometimes, for fear, living in field and woods, who for his immoderate and unseasonable going abroad, was called Trudgeover. Oftentimes he did lie abroad in the night without covert, spending the most part thereof in devout and earnest prayer.' One day he was heard praying that the heart of the queen might be turned, or else that she might be taken away. After this he had to go into hiding, for a reward of £20 was offered for his capture, and there were many people ready to take sides with the bishops if they could get £20 by it. That a man must lose his life mattered little. So when George Eagles went into Colchester for the fair on St. Mary Magdalene's Day he found the town full of enemies, and had to run for his life. First he found shelter in a copse; but the angry crowd still followed him. So, taking advantage of the screen of trees, he crept into a cornfield where he lay completely hidden. After fruitless search in the copse the crowd went back to the fair, and George Eagles, believing himself safe, got up on his knees to thank God for his deliverance. But one man had stayed behind, and had climbed a tree to get a view of the surrounding fields, in one of which he was sure the preacher must be hiding. As soon as George Eagles moved he was seen and taken prisoner. Subsequently he was tried at Chelmsford and condemned to death.

The innkeeper, Richard Potto the elder, comes into the story at this point. Foxe tells us that Eagles was taken to a new inn at Chelmsford called the 'Crown,' and that there he was visited by Potto, the licensee of another inn called the 'Cock,' who tried to persuade him to confess that he had offended against the queen in his prayer, and to beg her to pardon him. Eagles stood firm, and he may have been right in so doing. He was certainly heroic. In Foxe's view, Potto was the devil who tempted him, and who continued to tempt him by begging him to relent until, at the very last, the sheriff ordered the innkeeper to hold his peace and retire. Foxe records with devout satisfaction that when Potto's turn to die came, this would-be maker of peace between the rival religious factions lay for several days 'as senseless as it had been a very dumb beast,' which he took to be a sign of divine disfavour, not pausing to reflect how many good men have died in greater suffering. I must confess that my own heart is with the innkeeper, the one man in all this noisy company who tried to save the life of this poor preacher, even at the risk of being arrested as a man well disposed towards Protestants himself, and of certain injury to his trade. The peacemaker, as so often happens, was belaboured by both parties. He was silenced by the sheriff to whom Eagles was a criminal, and abused by Foxe to whom he was a martyr. It is therefore good to learn that this Richard Potto, whose inn was later pulled down to make room for the Methodist chapel on the east side of High Street, near the bridge, was highly esteemed by his fellow townsmen, and was more than once elected people's warden, an important office in the sixteenth century.

In the abridged versions of Foxe we get none of the horrible details of the last act. Instead, we get a few piously sterilized phrases informing us of the passing. It we would know what the kindly innkeeper was trying to prevent, we must refer to the complete edition. There we read how Eagles was dragged on a hurdle to the place of execution. The hanging is described in detail right through to the last gruesome circumstance, which was that when Eagles was cut down he was found to be still alive, whereupon a Chelmsford bailiff named William Swallow drew the body over to the hurdle, 'and laid his neck thereon, and with a cleaver (such as is occupied in many men's kitchens, and *blunt*) did hackle off his head, and sometimes hit his neck, and sometimes his chin, and did foully mangle him.'

But the true spirit of the English inn must be expressed in more homely terms than these. Heywood got it best when he resolved 'To let the world wag, and take mine ease in mine inn.' That is what is to be understood by the sobering influence of the English inn—a place to take one's ease in while the world wags.

It is for this reason that we prefer our inns to be well established. They must have survived a few of the world's wags. If they have survived them through three centuries or more, as many of them have done, so much the better. Even those who prefer everything else to be of the latest design and fashion glory in the stout timbers and ancient fittings of their favourite inns, while landlords quarrel over the ages of their respective houses like pensioners at a tea-party. There is a reason for this. It is that we want to be at ease in our inns, and we are most at ease with old things. They have attained composure, or rather they bestow composure. By their familiarity of feature they release us from self-consciousness. Perhaps it is their freedom from the trammels of time rather than their actual antiquity that makes their appeal universal. In their businesses and professions men are kept at full stretch. In their leisure they want to relax, and for this they need easy clothes, easy chairs, easy talk, and easy rooms. And easy things, they find, are those that have survived the intolerance and restlessness of their youth, the ambitions of their early maturity, and

F

have come to that mellow state of genial give-and-take that
is at the heart of English hospitality.

The inn as we know it to-day, like the whole set-up of
English life as we know it to-day, came with the Tudors and
ripened under the Stuarts. There were few inns in the
modern sense outside large towns or on famous highways
before the monasteries were suppressed. The monks had
themselves given hospitality to travellers before that time,
or had provided for it by building guest-houses such as
the 'Stables' at Audley End may have been. But the
number of inns that must have sprung up overnight at the
Dissolution is astonishing. What is not surprising is that
so many of them should have been in the old abbey towns,
where wayfarers had been accustomed to find lodging and
food. There were always a great number at Waltham
Abbey. Indeed, many licences there have been withdrawn
within living memory. Some of these former inns can still
be recognized. There is, for example, a shop at the corner of
Sun Street nearest the market with a relic of its hospitable
past in a corner bracket carved to represent a grotesque
crouching woman holding a jug in her hands. Fortunately
the oldest Waltham inn, the fifteenth-century 'Welsh Harp,'
is left.

Market towns were always full of inns. Others are to be
found in numbers for other reasons. At Blackmore, where
Henry VIII had his favourite pleasure-house, Jericho—the
place where he installed his mistress Elizabeth Talbois, and
where his natural son, Henry Fitzroy, was born—there were
five inns, as we know from a record that when Jericho was
abandoned as a royal resort the inhabitants of Blackmore
petitioned for three of its inns to be suppressed and the
other two reformed. It is true that Blackmore was an old
centre of the leather trade, as its present inn, 'The Leather
Bottle,' reminds us, but that would not account for five
inns.

Besides inns, which were required to have beds and stables
for travellers, there were ale-houses, which need not have
either. They were for the sale of ale and bread, and the need

for bread was commonly as important a reason for granting a licence as the need for ale, which was then the universal drink. A certificate from Little Birch will serve as an illustration:

'4 May, 1614. CERTIFICATE by the inhabitants of Great and Little Birch that John Bundock of Great Birch being desirous to be licensed to keep an alehouse is one who from his childhood hath been well known to them to be of good conversation and dwelleth in a house the farmers whereof have victualled from time to time for 20 years; "and howsoever it may be objected that ther is one in the parishe allredy aucthorysed in a more convenyent place beinge in the mayne rode, yet experyence dothe demonstrate that for the good of the poore of the parishe who in regard to the price of corne are constrayned to bye bread by the penny, that both the house of this Bundocke as allso for his promptnes in the faculty is more fittinge and convenyent than the other, who partly for want of abylyti, but chiefly through nastines, dyvers passengers havinge beene overtaken with approaching night and werysomnes being constrayned to enter and intendinge to have lodged, through the want of clenly lodging and diet have been compelled to trouble some of the next neighbours suddenly at unseasonable hours, wherefore if it shall please this sacred court to be so propitious and favourable as to grant to the above named Bundocke at our entreaty this his request." '

To this the signatures of many inhabitants were appended.

Far more than we might suppose was required of the man who wished to be an innkeeper. Besides the commonly known function of his calling he undertook neither to use nor allow any unlawful games to be played in his house, not to harbour any person for more than a day and a night without bringing them before a justice of the peace or some other responsible officer of the law. He swore that he would not open his house on Sundays or on holy days, and that he would keep it shut during the hours of morning and evening prayer. He also undertook not to entertain any servant whose master lived in the same town or within a mile of his house. Indeed the qualifications for keeping an inn were so high that we need not be surprised that few were found capable of maintaining the expected standards.   It has even been hinted by those less favourably disposed towards them than honest men ought to be, that innkeepers have traditionally been men of doubtful character, and that the insistence of the justices upon honest dealing, virtuous conversation, and various other attributes that might be thought essential for parsons, but optional for publicans, became customary because the justices required all the reassurances they could get from the rogues before granting them their licences.   To be quite frank about this, there is a vast amount of evidence to show that all through the Middle Ages the miller, the maltster, the baker, and the brewer, and every one connected with them for that matter, were regarded as rascals.   At best they might be the kind of merry rascals we get in Chaucer, at worst they might be mean and false scoundrels who adulterated ale and gave short weight in bread.

'Whereas by Act of 23 Henry VIII,' reads a memorandum in the sessions rolls at Chelmsford, 'no "beerebrewer nor alebruer should put their beere or ale to sale" in any barrels, "kilderkyns or firkyns" other than those "marked by an artificer de lez Cowpers," and that the rates and prices therefor should be assessed and that "alebruers or beerebruers" who at any time thereafter sold their beer or ale at other rates or prices should forfeit penalties [specified]; and whereas at the Easter Sessions 23 April 10 James [1612] the justices assessed "the prices of stronge beere and strong ale" at 8s. a barrel and not above, and of "smalle beere and smalle ale" at 4s. a barrel and not above; nevertheless Robert Taylor of Horndon-on-the-Hill "beerebruer" between the said 23 April and the present time, sold "his stronge beere brued" by him to divers persons whose names are unknown to the informer, at greater prices than those assessed by the justices, viz. 100 barrels of his "stronge beere" at 10s. a barrel, for which he has forfeited £30, viz. 6s. for every barrel, whereof the informer sues half the sum.

'John Neale of Orsett "beerebruer" for the like, "mutatis mutandis."

'John Shelton of Barking "beerebruer" for the like, "mutatis mutandis."'

Of the offences of the bakers we may take a representative example from Aveley in 1613, when Christopher Wells, 'being a common baker, was presented because on the third of April and divers other days and times before and since, made and sold there "his penny white looffe" under 5 oz. and "his penny wheaten loaffe" under 8 oz., viz., on 3 April made and sold 5 dozen white loaves, every loaf being under 5 oz. and 5 dozen wheaten loaves, every loaf being under 8 oz., being under the weights and assize fixed by law, best wheat being under the price of 43s. a quarter, viz., 42s. 6d. a quarter. Confessed and submits himself to the Court. Fined by the Court 5s. Witnesses: George Moody. Edward Udall.'

The poor man's bread, we may note, was not always of wheat. It might be of rye and barley, and sometimes of beans and oats. In hard times it might even be of acorns from the forests.

The fact is that the history of the inn is not dissimilar from that of the Church. It might be argued that the true English inn came in with the true English Church, as the rhyme already quoted,

> Hops, Reformation, Bays and Beer,
> Came into England all in a year,

suggests. Certain it is that the story of the old unreformed inn had many things in common with the story of the old unreformed Church. Monks and ale-wives share the scandals between them in the old comedies. We may believe the tales or not as we choose. They were the stock properties of the medieval comedian just as the mean Aberdonian and the interfering mother-in-law are the stock properties of the modern comedian. The laugh is on ourselves if we take them too seriously. For all that we need not be traitors to the cause if we admit that most of the old ale-wives seem to have been fraudulent. In the Chester morality plays the pageant called *The Harrowing of Hell* was for cooks, tapsters, ostlers, and innkeepers. In it the ale-wife is made to confess:

Some time I was a taverner,
A gentle gossip and a tapster,
Of wine and ale a trusty brewer,
    Which woe hath me wrought.
Of cans I kept no true measure,
My cups I sold at my pleasure,
Deceiving many a creature,
    Though my ale were naught . . .
Therefore this place ordained is
For such ill-doers so much amiss.

Sometimes an offending ale-wife would have a turn in the cucking-stool, to the great amusement of her customers. Or the people might take the law into their own hands. One favourite method of punishing an offending baker was to tie a stale loaf round his neck and drag him round the town on a hurdle. But as a rule the whole community had to rise against a miller or a baker before drastic measures could be taken. Few were bold enough to bite the hand that fed them.

The method of regulating the prices of ale and bread made supervision difficult. It was done on a sliding scale. The price, or assize as it was called, was regulated in the case of bread by the price of wheat, and in the case of ale by the price of wheat, barley, and oats together. With the bread the weight was adjusted, with the ale it was the price.

The fixing of prices under the assize was a delicate matter. The phrasing of a justices' order of 11th April 1613 is an indication of this. It runs:

'Whereas the prices of grain are now dearer than in former years, whereby it appeareth that the brewers cannot (without great loss) brew their beer and ale at the rates and prices which were lately assessed at the Easter Sessions, 23 April 1612; it is therefore at this Sessions advised and upon deliberate consideration ordered that from henceforth the brewers and such other brewers as shall hereafter sell and utter any beer in the said county, shall not brew nor sell any beer or ale above these 3 several rates and prices, viz., the strongest beer at the rate of 10s. the barrel to be delivered at the house of the buyer, the middle sort at 6s. the barrel so delivered, and the smallest at 4s. the barrel so delivered; and so after that rate and not above for a greater or lesser vessel until other order shall be taken therein, and to the end His Majesty's subjects may take certain knowledge hereof the same rates and prices were publicly proclaimed in this open Sessions.'

The imposition of price control and commodity rationing in the periods of scarcity caused by the two great wars of this twentieth century make the controls of the Middle Ages matters of topical interest. The assize of bread actually remained in force until 1822 in London, and elsewhere until 1836, though it was modified several times. To appreciate the operation of the modern system properly we need to see it in relation to a longer period of history than our own two wars provide. The basic principle behind twentieth-century food price control is exactly the same as that behind the assizes of bread and ale, namely that for commodities of prime necessity the price must be kept moderate. Only during the privileged period of trade expansion in the nineteenth century were we able to discard the principle of regulating prices by controlling supply, and instead to allow supply freely to control the market. Perhaps a better knowledge of history would have saved twentieth-century planners and their victims several mistakes. What the seventeenth-century justices appear to have understood better than some of the twentieth-century ministers of state is that in fixing prices for commodities in general use it is essential to have the co-operation of all the principal branches of the trade involved. Sometimes co-operation in the old days was obtained by bribery, which in earlier days was practised to an extent we should not allow to-day, but promise of co-operation was obtained somehow before an important price was agreed upon. If it were not, these justices discovered, one of two things happened. If the price fixed by the justices was higher than necessary many traders cut their prices to gain an unfair share of the trade available. If it was lower than necessary, supplies immediately disappeared from the markets. Two tricks, these, that modern traders appear to have discovered for themselves without taking refresher courses in history.

We may bless or curse men for being the creatures they are, but it is no use being rebellious about human nature. It is much the same through the ages, and on the whole it is good honest stuff. We hear too much of the black sheep. Here is a pleasantly human petition from the people of High Easter who wanted a licence to be granted to Edward Besse. It recites that:

'Edward Besse their neighbour is of the age of three score years, and his wife being an aged motherly woman who hath kept victualling where they now dwell 50 years, and she doth bake brown bread and brew small beer to sell to a great number of the very poor people, who could not otherwise know how to be maintained, and they do sell such weight and measure as no other victualler in the parish will do the like, furthermore he hath a house which is very fitting and convenient to be enrolled for an inn, for there is at all times horse meat and man's meat and lodging for all passengers and wayfaring men, and it standeth in a road leading from Great Dunmow to Ongar and so to London, and many passengers do travel that way, both horse men and footmen, the honesty of this man and his wife with the civil government and zealous religion of them both and the conveniency of their house being considered, they request that Besse may be licensed to keep an alehouse.'

*Signatures (or marks) of the inhabitants.*

*Added at foot in a different hand:* 'Granted. "I have entered it as an inne according to this peticion and delivered him a coppie."'

It is such quiet, decent couples as Edward Besse and his wife that have given the innkeeper and his lady so warm a place in English hearts. Harrison of Radwinter said that England before the Reformation was the best pair of bellows the pope had to blow his kitchen fire and make his pot boil.

Later it blew King Henry's fire to a fine flame. And since his day the English bellows have been most effective with the fires in English inns. The poets and playwrights of Elizabeth's England were quick to see the popular appeal of the inn, and since then practically every book that has come to be regarded as characteristically English has had an inn at the heart of it. Dickens, who knew better than any one else how to make capital out of sentiment, came into Essex for what is perhaps his best inn story. The old ' King's Head ' at Chigwell, the Maypole Inn of *Barnaby Rudge*, an early seventeenth-century building with the original central chimney stack and much old panelling, is perhaps our best loved Essex inn. It has been written about over and over again. It belongs to Dickens now, and can never be forgotten while *Barnaby Rudge* is read.

Though the present house was built about 1620, it stands on the site of an earlier inn, and my own imagination plays about the earlier house no less fondly than about the later. In 1603 Samuel Harsnett, vicar of Chigwell, published *A Declaration of Egregious Popish Impostures*, from which Shakespeare took the names of the spirits in *King Lear*. Did Shakespeare visit Chigwell? Or did the spirits get into *Lear* by way of Edward de Vere, the seventeenth Earl of Oxford? It was in 1603, the year in which Harsnett's book was published, that the lord wardenship of Waltham Forest, as Epping Forest was then called, was restored to the Earls of Oxford in the person of the seventeenth earl. The office of lord warden had been held by Earls of Oxford from time immemorial until Henry VIII, in the twelfth year of his reign, decided to reserve the rights of the office for himself. The succeeding Tudors kept them, and not until James came to the throne were they restored to the de Veres. The seventeenth earl could not fail to experience a measure of pride on resuming the ancient office, and as the forest court of attachments was held at Chigwell he would visit Harsnett's parish. The pamphlet may well have come to his notice there. It was not the kind of work that either Shakespeare or Oxford would normally be certain to read.

\* F

What better fancy could be indulged in an Essex inn than the fancy of an Essex de Vere as author of Shakespeare? And should we find an inn more favourable for such day-dreams than the 'King's Head' at Chigwell? But such fancies are not every man's. It is for traces of Dickens, not for traces of de Vere, that we go to Chigwell.

No character has changed less in the national eye during the past three hundred years than that of the innkeeper. John Willett of the 'Maypole' might have been one of the genial company addressed by John Taylor the Water Poet in his book of *Tavernes*, published in 1636, which, incidentally, had references to a number of Essex inns. 'To all the good fellows in general and particular,' wrote Taylor, 'that do keep, inhabit, allow, or maintain the wine taverns or inn taverns in the ten shires. Mine hosts, I hope I am not much mistaken in calling you gentlemen, or kind friends, you only are the men that do truly merit the name and title of mine hosts, for alas our city taverns have no other entertainment but "Welcome Gentlemen—a crust and what wine will you drink?" But you brave minded and most jovial Sardana-palitans have power and prerogative to receive, lodge, feast, and feed both man and beast. You have the happiness to boil, roast, broil, and bake, fish, flesh, and fowl. Most of your customers come riding to your houses, where almost all our guests are footmen.'

It is in this book that Taylor describes Romford as 'a sweet, savery, clean and gainful market for hogs, and all sorts of swine, and what else is needful for man's life. It hath,' he says, 'these taverns, the Angel, the Bell, the White Hart and the Cocke.' Which of these, we wonder, inspired Romford's poet, Francis Quarles, to see the whole world as an inn?

> The World's an Inne; and I her guest,
> I eate, I drinke, I take my rest;
> My Hostesse, Nature, does deny me
> Nothing, wherewith she can supply me;
> Where, having stay'd awhile, I pay
> Her lavish Bills, and goe my way.

Whatever the inns of earlier times had been, practically every traveller was eloquent in his praise of them in the seventeenth century. A notable exception was our own Mary, Countess of Warwick, who had consorted too much with chaplains to have the right spirit to enjoy an inn. On one of her journeys from London to Leighs she stayed at Brentwood, a place famed for inns, and wrote in a vein that might have gratified Mrs. Varden, with her *Protestant Manual* and simpering Miggs: 'With what cheerfulness and serenity of mind did I bear with all the inconveniences and ill entertainment of this inn, upon this consideration, that what I met with there was not to last, but at night, when I came home to my own house, I should have abundant recompense made me by the good things I should there enjoy. O, my soul, turn this into spiritual advantage and consider that all the ill entertainment I meet with in this vain world is but the ill accommodations of this great Inn; and when thou hast past through this howling wilderness and hast finished thy great journey, thou shalt come to Heaven to thy home where, when thou hast been but one hour, it will make thee forget all troubles thou meetest with in the way.'

From this we may turn to one who knew better than the countess how to work his innkeepers, to Fynes Moryson, who in his *Itinerary* of 1617 had a better tale to tell. Even in poor villages, he said, good and cheap entertainment was even then to be had, and everything possible was done for the traveller's comfort. As soon as he arrived, the servants would run out to meet him. One would take his horse while another conducted him to his room. Someone else would take his coat and help him off with his boots, and by the time he had been made comfortable the host and hostess would be at his service to discuss a meal. Moryson goes so far as to say that on leaving next morning the guest would receive his reckoning in writing; but it is hardly likely that many innkeepers would be equal to that fine point in the first quarter of the century.

Not until the coming of the stage-coaches in the closing years of the seventeenth century did the great hostelries that are now the glories of our towns begin to flourish. Many of these suffered disfigurement when the railways took the traffic off the roads, and gave place to those monstrosities of a barbarous age, railway hotels. Motoring has so fully restored the wayside inn to its former and proper status in English life that even the old stables, curiously enough, have come back into use, for riding schools are now established behind many of the best, and few sights gladden a true-born English heart more than a party of smartly dressed riders on well groomed horses drawn up outside a country inn.

But while proud of our large inns, most of us find a peculiar interest in the smaller houses, because these have always been the ale-houses of the local people. The larger inns were for travellers, and primarily for wealthy travellers. Only in the smaller houses could the dialect and conversations of the village folk be heard. And so it is still, for the character of the inn has changed as little as the character of the innkeeper, in spite of the different modes of transport. It is more than probable that the principal topics of conversation have been no less constant. The weather, the growth of crops, the price of property, wages, and the latest news of a sick neighbour have been the topics in every generation. There would, of course, be variations on these ancient themes. In the seventeenth century there would be much indignant talk about rising rents, though apart from the disturbed period of the civil wars the age was a prosperous one for farmers. They did well until their leases ran out; but when that happened the lord of the manor increased the rent, so that at the next harvest, as Harrison of Radwinter put it, he swept off all the ready money as clean as a barber shaves a chin.

At each different season the conversation would come into line with the work on the land. At Michaelmas, when rents fell due, all the talk would be of the poor men who were compelled to sell their crops in order to pay. There would be hearsay reports of the rich farmers who were buying up crops at low prices from less thrifty neighbours, and speculations on the way this would affect winter prices—because the rich farmer could always hold his crops until he could command a higher price. As likely as not, in the same room with them there would be a man who, unknown to the rest, had been tipped to sound the farmers on the length of their pockets, and even to buy crops for ready money if the chance came. The man who paid these hangers-on had probably been in the neighbourhood before, and had not the courage to show himself again.

Then all the old superstitions would be discussed regularly. Did the position of the moon at the time of sowing affect the growth of the crop? Or did such and such a sign foretell good weather? Perhaps the rooks were building high, or the new moon would not hold water. These questions have all been discussed in every generation for centuries. Or it might be the price of timber. As there was much building in the seventeenth century, timber was a topical subject. It was said that park oaks were more brittle than hedge oaks, and one old greybeard would be sure to wag his head and say that at the present rate of building there wouldn't be an oak left in the county in forty years' time.

In the corner, we may imagine, a more private conversation might be overheard. It might be between lovers, or it might be along the lines of one I found recorded in the sessions rolls recently, in which a traveller took aside a serving man and asked him why he stayed at home to be a drudge and a slave, when he might have a horse under him and ride among gentlemen.

Such talk would be heard everywhere, in the smallest ale-house in the Roothings and in the 'Red Lion' at Colchester, which is, I suppose, the finest of all our Essex inns. It has been a licensed house since 1500, and if we had the atmosphere of certain phases of *A Midsummer Night's Dream* at Coggeshall, at Colchester we may have the spirit of Falstaff, whose loftiest sentiment was expressed in the line 'Shall I not take mine ease in mine inn?'—a sentiment identical with Heywood's already quoted. Falstaff's would be the best conversation we should ever be likely to hear in such a place. Or is it Mistress Quickly we hear speaking? Falstaff has just asked for his reckoning, and she reminds him of a proposal of marriage: 'Thou didst swear to me upon a parcel-gilt goblet, sitting in my Dolphin-chamber, at the round table, by a sea-coal fire, upon Wednesday in Whitsun-week, when the prince broke thy head for liking his father to a singing-man of Windsor; thou didst swear to me then, as I was washing thy wound, to marry me, and make me my lady thy wife.' That, perhaps, is the oldest tale of all—and the newest!

## CHAPTER XI

## WITHOUT THE LAW

*There 's likewise in mine host sometimes deceit.*

CROMWELL commanded his judges to suppress all nuisances, including 'alehouses and the Prayer-book.' They were equally obnoxious to the Puritans. And to be just we must allow that even among innkeepers there were scoundrels to be found, just as there were scoundrels to be found even among parsons. There was the landlord of the 'White Horse' at Chelmsford for one. On a night in April 1654 he murdered a guest in his house, a Mr. Kidderminster, who was travelling through Chelmsford on his way from Cambridge to London with £600 in his pocket. The crime was not discovered until nine years later, when the bones of an unknown person were dug up in a Chelmsford back yard. The discovery was brought to the notice of Mrs. Kidderminster, who felt suspicious and decided to visit Chelmsford. She was not a rich woman, so was obliged to travel on foot. On the first day she walked from London to Romford and slept at the 'Black Bull,' where she chatted with another woman walking to Chelmsford. Inevitably, the conversation came round to the 'White Horse,' which the woman knew well. It was kept, she said, by a very respectable man named Turner. But the previous licensee, a man named Sewell, had been a rogue, and, whispered the woman, unless she was much mistaken, a murderer.

The conversation of these two women during the next half-hour or so can be imagined, and need not be followed. Eventually the woman from Chelmsford remembered that a former ostler at the 'White Horse' was now living in Romford and could confirm her story of suspected murder. This man was sent for; but he wisely made his excuses and stayed at home. The person who carried Mrs. Kidderminster's polite message had overheard the conversation of the two women and told the ostler why he was wanted.

The next day Mrs. Kidderminster, stimulated by her conversation at Romford, reached Chelmsford in good time and went straight to the 'White Horse.' The landlord smiled at her story. He advised her to visit Mrs. Sewell, the previous landlord's widow, who now kept the 'Shears.' She thanked him for this help and did as he suggested, but found that Mrs. Sewell was no more inclined to talk than the ostler had been. But in the town itself she heard enough to rouse all her suspicions to a dangerous pitch of excitement. No one who knew anything about the 'White Horse' and its late landlord, or about the bones that had been found so mysteriously in the back yard, had any peace until the whole story was pieced together. The gossips of Chelmsford told her that strange tales had gone about for a great many years —for nine years, in fact; but it had never been possible to pin anything on to the rogue Sewell. Suspicions, however, had been so strong that, when the bones were found, warrants were issued, and the Sewells put on bail to appear at the assizes. But before the assizes came round Mr. Sewell died, and every gossip said—with suitable reminders that she was only repeating what she had heard—that there was strong suspicion that his wife had poisoned him for fear he said too much. More than one could testify that Mr. Sewell, who, though a rogue, was a better-hearted person than his wife, had often said after a glass or two that he had something on his mind, that one day he would talk, and that when he did he would surprise them. More than once Mrs. Sewell had silenced him, and when the news went round that he had died, well, how could they help wondering? Mrs. Sewell was examined at the assizes; but it was impossible to prove anything against her, for the very good reason that no evidence was produced at the trial of any one having been missed from Chelmsford at the time of the suspected murder. She was therefore remanded on bail, and the announcement of the discovery, which Mrs. Kidderminster had been shown, was ordered to circulated.

Mrs. Kidderminster was determined that the ostler, whose name was Moses Drayne, should be made to talk, so she returned to Romford. But she was still unable to persuade him to discuss the suspected murder, though he did admit that he remembered a gentleman of the appearance she described staying at the 'White Horse.' He pointed out that nine years was a long time for a man to carry a face in his memory, and he could hardly be expected to say what happened to every one who called for a night's lodging. When asked if there was any one else still living in the neighbourhood who had been employed at the 'White Horse' in those days, he said there was a Mary Kendall, who had been chambermaid at the time in question. Mrs. Kidderminster reported all this to the officers of the law in Chelmsford, and warrants were issued for the arrest of both the ostler and the chambermaid. The chambermaid's story cleared up the mystery, and took Moses Drayne to the gallows. He was found guilty of participating in the crime and hanged at Brentwood.

This is what the chambermaid told the jury: On the night in question she saw the guest, a man of the height, age, and dress described by Mrs. Kidderminster, hand to the landlord a cloak-bag with a request that it should be placed in a safe place because it contained nearly £600. She remembered the night well. In the first place, she was put into a bedroom at the far end of the house that night, and locked in till breakfast time next morning. When she inquired about the visitor, her mistress told her that he had gone. When she went to the bedroom he had occupied, she found it locked. It remained locked for eight weeks, though it was the best bedroom in the house and constantly in demand. These things, though suspicious, proved nothing. But one day her master was in a hurry to leave the house and sent her to his bedroom for a cloak. She took advantage of the opportunity to peep in a few corners, and saw, she alleged, the clothes and cloak-bag of the missing man. Later she discovered also his hat, sword, and boots. These she actually took downstairs, and confronted her mistress and the ostler with them. For this she was beaten; but enough was said during the angry scene to convince her that the guest had been murdered, and that Moses Drayne as well as Mr. and Mrs. Sewell knew it.

It was disclosed also that Mr. Sewell, who had been in arrears with certain payments before that day, paid off his creditors and seemed to be in easier circumstances suddenly. Moses Drayne, furthermore, was known to have lent a friend £60 about the same time, and £60 was a large sum for a man in his position to save. The jury were satisfied that the guest of that night had been murdered, and Mrs. Kidderminster was convinced that this man was her husband.

That, of course, is an exceptional case; but while looking at the darker side of ale-house records it has to be confessed that many ruffians were found in them. In the eighteenth century the notorious Dick Turpin, a hero to schoolboys, perhaps, but nothing to be proud of, was bred in an Essex ale-house. Several of his family were presented to the justices at various times in the seventeenth century for selling ale without licence. There was a William Turpin, butcher, of Great Sampford, and a John Turpin, joiner, of the same village, both charged with this common offence. Indictments for keeping ale-houses without licence were, in fact, only second in frequency to those for neglect of highways during the seventeenth century. The offence was common everywhere, but its exceptional frequency in Essex was due to the wool trade depression. The poor kept ale-houses because they could make so little at their looms.

Ale-houses have been controlled in England longer than in any other country. As early as 1495 an Act was passed empowering justices of the peace to suppress disorderly ale-houses, where, it was said, those who disliked work spent their time 'dicing and drinking,' and in 1551 a licensing system was adopted. At first its application varied greatly between one county and another; but all through the reign of James I efforts were being made to bring the whole country into line, and all the Acts passed were intended to promote the ancient and proper use of inns and ale-houses as places of lodging and

refreshment instead of places for 'entertainment and harbouring of lewd and idle people to spend and consume their money
and their time in lewd and drunken manner.' It was
recognized from the start of licensing that however many
laws were passed for the control of ale-houses, the licensee
himself was the only man who could guarantee orderly and
decent conduct on his premises. There were many shocking
cases. One of the worst, perhaps, was that of Silvester
Rayment of Thaxted.

In July 1610 the mayor and vicar of Thaxted—Thomas
Collin and Thomas Crosbie by name—headed a list of townspeople petitioning for Rayment's ale-house to be suppressed
so that they and their neighbours could live in peace. They
complained that he allowed excessive drinking on Sundays as
well as other times, and dicing and carding day and night.
Many other offences were enumerated, so that it was made
quite clear that Silvester Rayment was a dissolute and un-
bridled character. When summoned to answer the charges
brought against him, he said in 'gross words unseemly to be
rehearsed that he cared not for the warrant, the justice, nor
the king.' He had told the mayor that he would like to see
him in the stocks and had 'often miscalled and abused' the
minister 'with disgraceful terms saying that when he is out
of the pulpit he doth nothing but study and devise lies.'
That this should be mentioned specially shows how sacred
the person of the minister of Thaxted was at that time held
to be.

Later in the century the clergy combined on this issue
of ale-houses and suggested that they should themselves have
a say in the granting of licences. In 1643 no fewer than
sixteen Essex clergy in Chelmsford and the surrounding
villages and small towns presented a petition which:

'Humbly sheweth that your petitioners, having had serious
and sad thoughts upon the grounds of the growth of profane-
ness, do find our alehouses to be one of the chief roots upon
which a world of diabolical wickedness grows, which spreads
into the whole kingdom and doth poison many towns, families,
and persons, and unless some sharp course be taken for

prevention threatens ruin, if not total yet to many places and families in this land. Your petitioners are therefore bold to present our humble desires to this honourable bench that all alehouses may be suppressed, and then those that shall be judged fit for situation, and have persons fitly qualified for the keeping them, may be licensed upon the approbation of the ministers and other chief inhabitants, and the rest finally suppressed, and we shall ever pray, etc.' This is surely a rare if not unique petition. Imagine the parson standing in the bar to pronounce judgment, using perhaps, since a parson must have his text, Massinger's words in *A New Way to Pay Old Debts* (Act IV, sc. ii, ll. 76–9):

> For which gross fault I here do damn thy license,
> Forbidding thee ever to tap or draw;
> For, instantly, I will, in mine own person,
> Command the constable to pull down thy sign.

As the complaints against Silvester Rayment were not suitable for detailed quotation, the presentment at Chelmsford, on the 11th January 1621, of Robert Prentise of Hadleigh may be given to show the kind of conduct that occurred. He was charged with victualling without licence for a whole year, using in his house 'dyseinge' with other unlawful games, and harbouring poor men all day and night. One poor man confessed that he had spent and wasted £4 in Prentise's house, and owed 20s. 'on the skore' for black pots of beer, 'all within a twelve month space.' The presentment then continued:

'The parishioners brought Prentise and this poor man before "Master Ware." The poor man should have been sent for his misdemeanour to the House of Correction, but on hope of amendment he was spared. Since that time Prentise hath called him out of his bed at midnight to drink with other unruly company the other part of the night, and the next morning, being very drunk, this poor man went home to his house and beat his wife and misused her pitifully. A neighbour came in to rescue her, and he set on this neighbour and beat him like to have killed him.

'Prentise hath been suppressed and since that time hath sold again and poor men have been drunk in his house since that time.

'Another poor man, a tailor, hath confessed that he could not keep his work hardly three hours in a day, for Prentise would send his children to come into the street and whistle him. If he came not with whistling, then Prentise did come to his shop for him.

'An honest man, being constable in the parish, awaking out of his sleep, and upon occasion, did call for some of his servants, and hearing no answer among them did rise and going to Prentise's house did find there at midnight his children and his servants drinking and playing with other men's servants of the same parish, though he had given Prentise warning.

' Joseph Camber of Hadleigh, being in Prentise's house and very much drunk, little better than mad drunk, caused his wife to fetch a pound and a half of gunpowder, and, when he got into the house, he got this powder to fire his wife out of Prentis's house, and was held by strong hands for not doing this act, to the great danger of burning the whole street.

'Mary, the wife of the said Joseph Camber, for breaking open the Pound of Hadleigh, and for calling of her neighbours rogues and other names.

'Geo. Clarke, churchwarden of Hadleigh, for "settinge fiddelers to playe" on the sabbath day in the time of divine service, and for "dauncinge," all in the said Robert Prentise's house.

'The said Clarke hath had his own servants drunk in Prentise's house, and hath "a fallen to gether by the eares lyke to kyll one an other" and yet he doth manage Prentise in his ale house-keeping and other wretchedness.'

Silvester Rayment and Robert Prentise were wicked and dissolute men whom no decent person would wish to defend. But we had in Essex a couple of rogues well known to innkeepers who were treasures indeed. They were Davy Bennett and Tony Whiting, and they lived by counterfeiting licences. Over and over again men to whom no justice of the peace could recall that he had granted a licence came up for examination and produced one duly signed and sealed. It was a puzzle to all officers of the law until the constables of Terling, in the December of 1581, examined a man named Edward Symson and in due course carried him before the justices. This Edward Symson said that he knew two clever men who went about counterfeiting licences. One, Davy Bennett, 'did make divers and sundry counterfeit passports' for a man named Bartholomew Newell, otherwise John Johnson, who travelled about the country with a young lady named Mary Anderson, who was known to her acquaintances as 'Fine Mary.' Edward Symson knew Bartholomew Newell well, and had seen the passports provided for him by Davy Bennett. One represented him to be a soldier of Berwick come from his captain, another to be a man visiting friends. Symson testified that Bennett could 'counterfeit any justice of peace seal, or any other seal if he seeth it in wax.' He would, said Symson, 'lay it afore him and carve it out in wood very perfectly.' He would then forge signatures, 'for that he writeth sundry hands, and hath most commonly about him a little bag full of these counterfeit seals. And these be the marks which most commonly you shall know him by: first, he is about the age of twenty-four years, and his face is something full of pockholes, and [he] goeth sometimes in an old cloak, and likewise hath in his company at times one Mary Philips, who hath now a young child two months old, and doth many times frequent the parish of Ugley at an old man's house, whose name he doth not now remember, but this he saith, that the old man's house hath a glass window by the door,' and so on. It was somewhere near Ugley Hall. Of Tony Whiting, the other counterfeiter, he gave an entrancing description. He said: 'Tony Whiting, the other counterfeiter, is an old man, and goeth very simply, and hath over his head a white woollen nightcap with two ears, most commonly tied under his chin. And where he lieth he usually maketh a mark with a white chalk, like unto a whiting, to the intent if any chance to lodge there [they should know] that it was not long since that he was there, to the end if any would have counterfeit licences, they might seek after him.'

And what of these two Marys? Should not a word be said occasionally in defence of the doxy, the beggar's and the tinker's trull, who follows her chosen master for no better reward than to share his straw by night and to tramp the road by day with him? Even Breton, in the poem already quoted, mocks her:

> Look on old Beatrice with her beetle brows,
> Begot betwixt a tinker and his Tib,
> And but of late a silly cobbler's spouse;
> If she have played the thrifty prowling scrib
> To purchase grass to grase the bullock's rib,
> She shall be fed with fine and dainty fare,
> And wooed and wedded ere she be aware.

But civilized society has no use for such gay and wanton characters as these, and in course of time the licensing system in Essex was reduced to order. In 1656 the justices at Chelmsford issued a recommendation addressed to 'the justices of peace in their several divisions to be only and speedily put in operation.' The terms were:

'1. That no alehouse be hereafter licensed but at a public meeting of the justices in their several divisions, and that all licences be signed by the justices there present or two or more of them according to the law.

'2. That no persons be licensed but such as are well affected to the Government, of honest life and conversation, and such as bring certificate of the same under the hand of the minister of the parish of three or more well affected persons of the neighbourhood.

'3. That no person be licensed but upon entering into recognizance with two sureties, the alehouse-keeper to be bound in £40 and the sureties in £20 apiece, which sureties shall be persons of honesty, having each of them £10 per annum of real estate, or £200 personal estate and living within the same parish or parishes adjacent. And that they be not innkeepers, alehouse-keepers, bailiffs or servants.

'4. That no person be licensed but such as have sufficient

accommodation for travellers, viz.: two spare beds at the least and stable-room for four horses. And that every alehouse-keeper have a sign over his door.

'5. That there shall be none licensed but in thoroughfare towns and in such towns as stand upon the seawalls or near navigable rivers or on common roads three miles distant from any town. And that they be such as live near neighbours and not in blind alleys or corners out of the roads.

'6. That the justices of the peace in their several divisions do reduce the number of alehouses to as few as may be. And that they do ascertain the number in every town and parish and certify the same to the next general sessions of the peace together with the several recognizances of the said alehouses, to the end the same may be read by the clerk of the peace at a full court at the beginning of the sessions. And that the said court may have a view of all the alehouse-keepers in every division. And that no addition to the number so ascertained be made but in open sessions, and that to be first certified by the justices of the division.

'7. That upon suppression of any alehouse-keeper, certificate thereof be made to the next sessions and whether it be first, second, or third conviction, the same to be also publicly read as aforesaid in open sessions.

'8. That the justices of peace do keep their monthly meetings, and at the said meetings and otherwise do by all possible diligence and care in the vigorous execution of the laws for the suppressing of all unlicensed alehouses, and in causing constables and other officers to be dexterous in discharge of their duties for the discovering, presenting, conviction, and punishment of all such offenders.'

In framing this well-meaning testimony the justices were doubtless imbued with the same thought as that which inspired Henry Farley to write *St. Paul's Church, her Bill for the Parliament*, 1621; but they had of necessity a much duller way of expressing themselves. Farley, in his complaint about the way the money was going to the brewers, sets out the attractions to be found in alehouse yards and similar places in merry fashion:

To see a quaint outlandish fowl,
A quaint baboon, an ape, an owl,
A dancing bear, a giant's bone,
A foolish engine move alone,
A morris dance, a puppet-play,
Mad Tom to sing a roundelay,
A woman dancing on a rope,
Bull-baiting also at the *Hope*,
A rimer's jests, a juggler's cheats,
A tumbler's showing cunning feats,
Or players acting on the stage—
There goes the bounty of our age:
But unto any pious notion
There's little coin and less devotion.

In the seventeenth century we did, however, turn from these frivolous pastimes in Essex. To be frank, Essex was rather conscious at the beginning of the seventeenth century of being a county with a past. The memory of Henry VIII's revels were still fresh in the popular mind. Besides Jericho, where his favourite mistress, Elizabeth Talbois, lived, houses at Shenfield, Roxwell, and Chigwell had been associated with the king's more private pleasures. In fact, the sixteenth-century wild oats had become mildewed, and to find new sources of entertainment the people were obliged to reform. So from ribaldry they turned to religion and were as extravagant in this as they had formerly been in the other. Every one shared in the fun; but the liveliest passages occurred between the Puritans and what Milton, with the restraint of his party, called 'All the hell pestering rabble of Somners and Apparitors.' On 17th January 1616 a typical rhyme of the period, composed, no doubt, in a pot-house, was 'maliciously and scandalously published and recited by two tailors, a joiner, and a labourer, all of Newport, against the church-wardens and lecturer or preacher of the parish.' It was entitled *A Citation Sent to To-bad the Paritor*, and ran:

I charge you that speedily to the Corte you bringe,
Will the prowde butcher and Tom with no thinge,
For that they present poore men to their great losse,
And leave out the Sheperde for not signing with the crosse.

This is their oath and to this they are sworne,
To see the Holydaies kepte and the surples worne,
Also they are to present so many as they shall see,
Which take the sacrament on their tailes and not on the knee,
And to ther oath this is a great breache,
To suffer any Sheperd without a lycense to teache.
They can spye a moate in another man's eye,
And suffer great beams in others to lye.
Also cyte the Sheperd at the court to appeare,
For gettinge two children within one yeare,
Wish him from his pleasures a littell to abstaine
And knowe how the towne shall be discharged of thes twayne.
The Sheperde should be an example of holyness of liffe,
And not stande playinge with his dogg and kissinge of his wiffe.
Item for that he dwelt by an hoste above two yere,
And was indebted to him for ale and strong beere.
They gave him an angell to make a funerall exhortation
And then in truth shee did not know his life or conversacion,
But a sudden death to a pore cobler befell,
And he 's made his Mittimus and sent him to hell.
Oh do not judge nor up so high clyme,
Remember Noah was overtaken with wyne.
The theefe to repent had but a short space
And yet Christ received him into his heavenly place.
And so for you to make an end of this rime,
God's mercye is not restreyned by shortness of tyme.

Which libel was endorsed in English:

Deliver this to the Townes Jewell,
Whose elboe cushen is of crewell,
To him I meane who at the poore barks,
And eats nothing but cock sparrows and larks,
To him I say who no compassion feeles,
But cries let the poor starve and kick up their heeles.

These rhymes, though crude, are worth more than we may
think.   They show the genius of the common man in its
natural state.   At Coggeshall we had in the carving along the
great beam at Paycocke's another expression of the spirit
that gave life to *A Midsummer Night's Dream*.   At Colchester
we supped with Falstaff.   Here we are closer to Bunyan.

To-bad the Paritor is not so far removed from Mr. Badman as at first he may appear to be, and Bunyan was no stranger to the Essex countryside. He was a frequent visitor to Bocking, and preached in a grand old barn there, as well as in front of the 'White Hart' at Braintree. The people of the north Essex weaving towns were for easily understood reasons 'censorious and factious to the greatest degree' at this time. They were badly paid and often without work. At Bocking, their parson was a wealthy and exalted cleric enjoying an income with a purchasing power greater than that of an archbishop to-day. We can readily understand the discontent that produced conditions well suited to religious revolt, and even its more irresponsible expressions can help us in studying the prevailing moods in the folk spirit of the day.

To-day it seems strange that religion should be mingled with ribaldry, inns be discussed with churches, and priests be cited with poets and potmen. There was nothing strange in the seventeenth century about such jovial mingling. The connection between the ale-house and the Established Church was very close indeed. The favourite method of raising money for a charitable object in those days was to hold an ale, or drinking party. Peter Mews, Royalist Bishop of Winchester, in *Ex-ale-tation of Ale*, 1671, says:

> The churches much owe, as we all do knowe,
>     For when they be drooping and ready to fail,
> By a Whitsun or Church-Ale up again they shall go,
>     And owe their repairing to a pot of good ale.

The holding of church-ales was not peculiar to Essex; but in one traditional association of ale-house and church, that of the bellringers, Essex was outstanding. In the first place it had in Miles Graye of Colchester, who made bells from 1600 to 1648, and was succeeded by a second and third Miles Graye, one whom Canon Raven, the Suffolk historian and campanologist, called 'the prince of founders.' Our Essex churchwardens' account books are full of references to money paid to the bell-ringers for beer. Sometimes genial parishioners provided for bell-ringing in their wills.

The Rev. G. Montagu Benton, the well-known Essex antiquary, records such a bequest made by a Saffron Walden mercer, Thomas Turner, whose will is dated 10th June 1623. He willed that twenty shillings should be bestowed annually upon a preacher for a memorial sermon on the anniversary of his burial, thirty-three shillings and fourpence upon the bell-ringers, and six and eightpence to the parish clerk for preparing the bells for ringing. The ringers seem to have made a day of it, for there are entries showing how the money was spent, and on one such merry occasion we find payments for every meal from breakfast to supper, including both. It is worth noting that this will is still honoured in Saffron Walden, and the occasion known there as the Great Ringing Day.

Change ringing was thirsty work, so ringers' jugs, peculiar to the eastern counties and not to be confused with the marriage-jars found elsewhere, were provided to contain ale for much-needed refreshment. Four of these survive in Essex. The largest, which was made in the county in 1658 and holds four and a half gallons, is in St. Andrew's Church, Halstead; others are in Colchester museum. These two-handled jugs were carried round the village to collect ale in the way a hat is sometimes passed round to collect coppers. It probably went round most effectively when there was a contest in the belfry between rival teams. Though several such jugs are now preserved in East Anglian churches, there is plenty of evidence to show that the parson did not always approve of the freely flowing ale at bell-ringings. The jug, or gotch, as it is sometimes called, a gotch being a big-bellied jug, was not kept in the church until it became a curio. When in use it was kept at the bell-ringers' favourite ale-house, where one or two still remain, though not in Essex. Most of them have quaint inscriptions. The first four lines of that on the Halstead jug go:

> Be merry and wise and breake me not
> For I am but an earthen pot.
> As we sit by the fire to keep ourselves warme
> This pot of good liquor will do us no harme.

Occasionally the bell-ringers would get more than commonly merry and give trouble. On New Year's Day, 1641, the ringers of Latton, near Harlow, played a prank that brought several of them before the justices assembled at Chelmsford for the Epiphany sessions. John Starkys of Latton, servant to Mr. Den, the parson, gave information that 'two of the sayde ringers, namelye, Jeremye Reeve, servant to William Stracye of Latton aforesayde, yeoman, and William Skynner, sonne to Widow Skynner of the sayde towne, did from the belfreye repaire to the Communion table in the Chancell of the sayde church, and in the sight of this Informant, as hee was standing in the bellfreye, pull down the rales from about the sayde Table with theire hands. And sayeth that hee this Informant goeing out into the Churchyard did see the sayde Reeve and Skynner together with Henrye Wennell, apprentice to John Starkys of the sayde Latton Potter, and one Henrye Vinton, servant to one, Poole, a dish turner of the same, bringing the sayde rales out of the Chancell into the Churchyard and from thence throwe them over the Churchyard wall into the Highewaye. And hee further sayeth that hee did see the sayde persons carrye the sayde broken rales neare to the whipping post of that towne, and there set them on fire.'

John Case, servant to James Altham of Mark Hill, said that John Wright, a carpenter of Latton Potter, was also 'at the drinkeing of the sayde beere, and payed for part thereof, and that theye did send for it to releeve theire necessitie.' In the course of a lengthy examination of four bell-ringers 'touching a supposed riotous misdemeanour done by them in Latton Church' on this ocasion it came out in the evidence of William Skynner that the ringers 'did laye their moneyes together to the summe of two shillings, and sent Wennell for beere. And the sayde Wennell brought a Kilderkin, or such like vessell of beere, for the sayde moneye from the Black Lyon, an alehouse in Harlowe, on his shoulders, and sett it downe neare the Highe waye, where the rales were fired. And hee, the sayde Skynner, further sayeth that the sayde vessell was carryed thence (but hee knoweth not by whome) into the sayde Church porch, where the greater part of the sayde beere was dranke by them, the other Examinats, and divers others. And sayeth, that Henrye Vinton above sayde did carrye it into the Church, and into the belfrye, where the remainder was dranke up by themselves and the ringers. And hee lastlye sayeth, that the reason of his so pulling downe the rales was, because theye gave offence to his conscience, and that the placeing of them was against Gods lawes and the Kings: as appeareth by the twentyeth chapter of Exodus, and about the twentyeth verse: and lastlye because the rales had been pulled downe in other places without punishment therefore. And this Examinat lastlye sayeth that he, and the sayde other persons had no weapons at all, or anye offensive matter about them: and is verye sorye for his sayde offence, and confesseth it was most inadvisedlye done. And this Examinat doth not knowe of anye other persons counselling, countenancing or assisting thereunto.'

These stout Protestants had removed the table, railed off by an order of Archbishop Laud, and had set it again in the chancel, where formerly it had stood.

## CHAPTER XII

## THE KING'S HIGHWAY

Forth issuing on a summer's morn to breathe
Among the pleasant villages and farms.
JOHN MILTON.—*Paradise Lost*, ix. 447–8.

THE inn and the road should be thought of together. Ale-houses might be for lewd and idle fellows; inns were for travellers. The number of inns in a town along a highway was a clear indication of the amount of traffic it carried, and consequently if the number of inns increased in a given period it could be taken that the traffic had increased in proportion. We have an illustration of this in the development of the Newmarket road through Essex at the beginning of the seventeenth century. Newmarket was a Stuart creation. It was first visited by James in 1605, and afterwards he and his Scottish nobles, assisted as time went on by the more sporting of the English favourites, applied great energy to establishing in this breezy East Anglian town the capital of the turf.

The principal settlement along the Newmarket road as it runs through Essex is Epping, which owes at least half its growth to the needs of travellers. In 1605 Epping had not one innkeeper among its ten victuallers. Six years later it had four. Soon after 1607, when James took Theobalds from Robert Cecil, first Earl of Salisbury, in order to shorten the journey to Newmarket, a road was cut through the forest to Epping, starting at the point on the old Waltham to Theydon road where the 'Wake Arms' stands now. The whole of the northward road across the east of the county was either made or greatly improved at this time, though the principal highway from London to Newmarket and Cambridge continued to be on the other side of the River Lea.

The Newmarket road through Epping and Harlow is now

one of the busiest in the county, but its popularity was slow in developing. After a moment's reflection the reason becomes obvious. It passes through Epping Forest, which long continued to be the haunt of highwaymen and other disturbers of the peace. The effect of this fear of passing through the forest is to be seen in the lay-out of Harlow, the oldest town along this Essex stretch of the Newmarket road. It is built across and not along the present highway, which makes it clear that its trade came, not from those who had travelled from Epping, but from the people of Dunmow and the Roothings, who passed through on their way towards Hoddesdon and Ware. It is also evident that those who came in from London by Hoddesdon and wished to turn north at Harlow used a different way from the one we take now. A glance at John Oliver's map shows that there was no bridge across the Stort at Harlow Mill in the seventeenth century, though there was probably a track of some sort leading down to it at that point. The road to Sawbridgeworth and Bishop's Stortford went through Mulberry Green. On the other hand, Epping, which developed later than Harlow, is built in the expected direction, though it is to be noted that here again the oldest buildings run east to west. The original Epping was the present Epping Upland, which was fed by the road from Ongar and Coopersale into Hertfordshire by way of either Roydon or Waltham Abbey. It passed near Gaynes Park, in Theydon Garnon parish, the old home of the FitzWilliams, and Coopersale House, which belongs to the late seventeenth century and has both good panelling and plaster work (a chapel on the ground floor has a ceiling showing William III casting out popery). After crossing the main road, this older way runs down to Eppingbury, then up the hill to the old church and Chambers manor house, once held by fealty and rent of one red rose. From Chambers one road goes north-west to Roydon, another south-west to Waltham Abbey, from which in older days the monks would come to serve the chapel at Epping.

In 1611, or soon after that date, a road was made from Loughton to 'Wake Arms,' and when completed it altered

Loughton as thoroughly as the continuing stretch altered
Epping. Loughton was swung up from the Chigwell side just
as Epping was swung up from the Roydon side, and eventually a new road from London into East Anglia developed,
which was to alter the whole lay-out of west Essex.

This weather-cock, or rather trade-cock, movement of
Epping, which swung the blade of the town round from the
old road to the new, was not affected without local stress.
Epping long continued to be an instance of a parish pump
split into two contentious halves. What the new Epping
wanted the old Epping did its utmost to veto. For civil administration the parish was divided into Epping Upland
and Epping Street or Town. In 1642 a certificate was sent
to the justices at Chelmsford which illustrates this. 'We the
inhabitants and formerly constables of the township of
Epping,' it recites, 'whose hands we have hereunto subscribed
do certify that all compositions for His Majesty's and other
taxes levied upon the parish of Epping, have constantly been
paid in two equal parts by the upland and townside of the
said parish.' There is something behind this. As the 'town'
or 'street' grew and the 'upland' dwindled the agreement for
equal contributions from each came to be regarded as unfair.
The certificate already quoted was to support by argument
from custom the demands being made for the contribution
to that year's taxes of the 'upland' part of the parish. Martin
Masters, the constable of Epping Town, sent a petition at the
same time, in which he 'humbly sheweth' that he has collected
'according to a warrant to him directed,' the half from the
'town,' but can do nothing about the 'upland.'

A far worse case of local division, and one without the
same excuse, was to be found in Chelmsford and Moulsham,
the two parts of the county town separated by a narrow
and apparently inoffensive river, the Can. Moulsham even
appointed its own churchwarden to Chelmsford parish church.
Yet for nearly eight and a half centuries both depended upon
the one life stream, namely, the traffic that flowed through
the town along the London to Colchester road, which all that
time passed over the bishop's bridge, the point where these

G

two disagreeing brethren met and parted. Before the Reformation Moulsham had been the manor of the abbots of Westminster, Chelmsford the manor of the bishops of London, one of whom, Maurice, in 1100, built the bridge that brought prosperity to the town. Even to-day there is a marked difference in character and social atmosphere between Moulsham and Chelmsford, though they form one town, and that a remarkably progressive one.

This London to Colchester road, which continued to Harwich at the north-east tip of the county, was not only the most important road in Essex, it was one of the most important in England in the seventeenth century. Harwich, now a decayed and sorry port, was then thriving. Its shipbuilding yards were full of work, and it was busy with people coming and going between England and the Low Countries. Successive waves of refugees from political and religious persecution on the Continent came to England that way to settle in the eastern counties. Consequently there was life on the Harwich road. Of the port itself, we might still in the twentieth century accept Defoe's description of it as it was early in the eighteenth: 'A town of hurry and business, not much of gaiety and pleasure; yet the inhabitants seem warm in their nests.' But we can only smile at the story of the departure of Queen Elizabeth at the end of the sixteenth century, when, as Samuel Dale, friend of John Ray and historian of Harwich, records, 'being attended by the magistrates at her departure as far as the windmill out of town, she graciously demanded of them, what they had to request of her, from whom she received this answer: "Nothing, but to wish her Majesty a good journey." Upon which she, turning her horse about and looking upon the town said, "A pretty town and wants nothing," and so bade them farewell.'

The best account we have of this Harwich road is by Daniel Defoe, who, in an appendix to the second volume of his *Tour through Great Britain*, says of it: 'First, that great County of Essex, of which our first Tour gives an ample Account. The great Road from London, thro' this whole County towards Ipswich and Harwich, is the most worn with

Witham

Ingatestone

Maria de Medici arriving at Gidea Hall

Waggons, Carts, and Carriages; and with infinite Droves of Black Cattle, Hogs, and Sheep, of any Road (that leads thro' no larger an Extent of Country) in England: The length of it from Stratford-bridge by Bow, to Streetford-bridge over the Stour, on the side of Suffolk, is 50 Miles, and to Harwich above 65 Miles.

'These Roads were formerly deep, in time of Floods dangerous, and at other times, in Winter, scarce passable; they are now so firm, so safe, so easy to Travellers, and Carriages as well as Cattle, that no Road in England can yet be said to Equal them; this was first done by the help of a Turnpike, set up by Act of Parliament, about the Year 1697, at a Village near Ingerstone. Since that, another Turnpike, set up at the Corner of the Dog Row, near Mile-end; with an additional one at Rumford, which is called a Branch, and paying at one, passes the Person thro' both: This I say, being set up since the other, compleats the whole, and we are told, that as the first expires in a Year or two, this last will be sufficient for the whole, which will be a great Ease to the Country: The first Toll near Ingerstone, being the highest rated public Toll in England; for they take 8*d*. for every Cart, 6*d*. for every Coach, and 12*d*. for every Waggon; and in proportion for Droves of Cattle: For single Horsemen, indeed, it is the same as others pay, *viz.* 1*d*. per Horse, and we are told, while this is doing, that the Gentlemen of the County, design to Petition the Parliament, to have the Commissioners of the last Act, whose Turnpike, as above, is at Mile-end and Rumford, empowered to place other Turnpikes, on the other most Considerable Roads, and so to Undertake, and Repair all the Roads in the whole County, I mean all the Considerable Roads.'

This must have been one of the first turnpikes in England, and its setting up is proof of the importance of the road it served. The seventeenth century saw a marked increase in the size of carts. Already in 1622 we find the people of Chelmsford complaining of the state of the road between that town and Brentwood, which, they said, was caused principally by 'drugges and foure wheeled carts' bearing thirty- to forty-hundredweight loads. These did so violently 'frett and pierce into the ground' as to plough up the gravel. This road had been 'as commodious as any other roadway a like distance of miles from the city of London' until these 'drugges with foure wheeles' came into use in these parts.

The repair of highways was the greatest worry the justices had in the normal course of their administration. Indictments for highways out of repair, ditches overflowing, watercourses obstructed and causing floods on the roads, and bridges out of repair or broken exceed in number every other class of offence in the first half of the century. At the beginning of the seventeenth century even the important Roman roads through Essex—the one through Dunmow and Braintree, and the one through Broomfield and Little Waltham, as well as the one through Chelmsford to Colchester—were in poor condition. They had not been required to carry much heavy traffic. Bays and says from the north Essex towns were carried to London by water from Colchester, not by road. Elsewhere there was little transport. Such roads as existed in addition to these were of two kinds: those which long usage had defined, and mere rights of way with no clearly marked track, such as may still be seen as green rides. The more frequented roads were bordered by ditches and sometimes by hedges to mark them. Both were jealously guarded, as an examination of the sessions rolls will show. The vigilance now required to preserve footpaths was then needed to keep open the tracks that have since become roads.

Essex roads, because of the low-lying, marshy nature of much of the county in the south, the heavy clay in the north and centre, and the absence of solid stone for repair work everywhere, were more difficult to maintain than those in most counties, though there were obviously some in worse plight. As a maritime county, with shingly beaches and many useful deposits of gravel, Essex was better placed than a number that could be named. Perhaps the rivers that intersected the roads raised the worst problems. Where bridges had been built they were usually poor, and not infrequently submerged in time of flood. An example is to be found in a letter from the justices of peace in what is now a densely populated part of the county to the justices at the quarter sessions held at Chelmsford on 23rd and 24th April 1612, reciting 'that whereas a petition was exhibited at the last Michaelmas Sessions touching the repairing of "certen decayed marshe bridges leading over Walthamstow and Layton Marshes," in the half hundred of Becontree, to Locke Bridge on the River Lee, over which bridges is and hath been time out of mind a common highway for market folks, travelling afoot 4 days in the week to London market from a great many towns and parishes adjoining, as also for all other foot passengers travelling to and from London that way out of those parts of Essex, Cambridgeshire, Suffolk and Norfolk, which passage, for lack of the said bridges is and will be very hurtful and dangerous for his Majesty's subjects in the winter time, and also in summer in the time of floods and great waters; and whereas also upon the said petition, order was given at the said Sessions, that they and some other of the Justices near there inhabiting, should view the said decayed bridges and examine witnesses, who ought to repair the same, which hath been done accordingly; and have certified at the last Sessions held after Christmas, that the same bridges are in great ruin and decay, and that it cannot be known what persons ought to repair the same; and whereas order was given at the Christmas Sessions that at the next Sessions to be held after Easter, further order should be then given for the speedy repair and amendment of the said bridges; they therefore still pondering the great use, ease, benefit, and safety that His Majesty's subjects do reap and receive by the daily passage over the said bridges, have thought good to write this much, praying that the Court would be pleased to give order for the speedy repairing of the same, this summer following, according to the statute of 22 Henry VIII., wherein shall be done a deed of great charity for the poor market folks, and also will be for the public good of the country thereabouts.'

It was signed by Robert Leigh, Michael Hickes, and Nicholas Coote.

Each parish was responsible for the maintenance of the roads within its boundaries, and surveyors were elected to see that the work was properly carried out. It cannot have been a popular office. Rich and poor were alike in being liable for service, and in many places they were alike in their determination to withhold it. Here for example, in the first year of James's reign, we find the surveyors of Marks Tey, chosen in Easter Week 1603, complaining soon after their election that the two principal landowners in their parish neglected to send their teams to repair the main Colchester to London road though cottagers and labourers had done their share. One would do nothing at all, the other, William Perry of Marks Tey Hall, would only do six days' work. Both were presented again the following year. Danbury in 1610 had a long list of defaulters, including Humphrey Mildmay himself. Perhaps the surveyors contented themselves that year by reporting every one and left it at that. Or perhaps the parson had not announced in church when the work was to be done. The Marks Tey surveyors were careful to state that warning had been given in church there on what day the teams and draughts of men and horses were to be set at work.

Sometimes the surveyors themselves were in trouble because they could not procure the gravel they needed. The reports from the different parishes vary greatly. Some places were obviously full of disaffected people, others exemplary in their public-spirited zeal. Every one in Theydon Bois does, or offers to do, his work in a number of certificates before me for 1609, with Mr. Elrington heading the list. Doubtless this would be Edward Elrington of Birch Hall, Queen Elizabeth's chief butler. But Harlow bears away the palm. Could anything be more satisfactory than this? It was received at the same sessions:

'We certify that all the inhabitants have done their work, and that the highways are sufficiently repaired. As for money given to the reparation of our highways, there is none, but some money we have received from the labourers which did not work, and some we are to receive, part whereof goes to the discharge of the gravel, the rest that remains (if any remain, for as yet we know not), we will bestow to the mending of the by-ways within our parish.

'Subscribed by Thomas Wood and John Tyle.'

And again:

'We the surveyors for the year 1608 certify that the parishioners of Harlow, both carts and labourers, did their work three days, and so continued twelve hours in every day, and also for the money which we received of any labourer, it was employed for picking of stones and repairing a bridge in Potter Street belonging to the highway in Harlow.'

There is much to be read into the way the different parishes attended to their roads. Self-interest counted for most. The farmers of Marks Tey may have felt that there was some injustice in their having to maintain a road for the use of so many travellers who had no connection with the parish. The wagons that ploughed up the road they were required to repair left nothing in Marks Tey. As Colchester was so near and benefited so greatly from this road, they may have felt that Colchester ought to take care of it. Perhaps the Danbury people looked after the road into Chelmsford, their market town, but cared nothing about the road towards the coast, which did them no service. They may even have thought that it might be in their interest to keep this road in a bad state. If an enemy happened to land at Maldon or thereabouts they might be glad enough to have that way closed.

The roads most carefully watched were those to church or market. It was for this reason that so many complaints came in about the roads leading into Chelmsford and every other market town. Sometimes descriptions of the places complained of give us knowledge of other things we are glad to learn about. We learn of a horse fair being held on a green at Blackmore in a complaint about a noisome ditch in a lane near by. One of the persons whose land it lay on was appropriately named Nicholas Horsenayle. 'In the noysomnesse thereof' this offensive ditch was in length about twelve rods or perches. This horse fair was probably connected originally with the tanning and leather trade of Blackmore.

The statute by which the separate parishes were thus made responsible for the maintenance of their roads was of 1555. The arrangement was for those who occupied 'ploughland in tillage or pasture' to furnish a cart, horse, and two men, while other householders were to labour themselves or provide substitutes four days a year, or, after 1563, six days. It never worked satisfactorily, and at a quarter sessions held in 1654 the justices empowered the surveyors to hire labourers and carts, supervise the work themselves, and raise the cost by laying an assessment on the householders who had previously been required to do the work with their own hands.

After so much has been said in various places about the injustice of the gentry alone administering the laws that affected all, a word should be said about the enlightenment and impartiality they exercised when religious or political issues were not at stake. A careful examination of the records of the courts held at Chelmsford would convince any fair-minded person that either Essex was unusually fortunate in its justices, or that the services of the landed gentry as magistrates had not been adequately appreciated. It has yet to be proved that a different system would be more humane. Much could be said about this in many aspects of the administration of the law; but, to keep to the subject of highways, an example of clemency shown to a poor weaver of Bocking may be given as an example. Osias Goodwin had been presented for neglecting his work on the highways, but when the 'chief inhabitants and headboroughs of Bocking,' where he lived, asked the justices to take into consideration 'that he ys at some charges in keeping his father, being an old man of an hundred yeres old or there about,' and was a poor weaver with 'little towards his maintenance but only his work,' they let him off with a fine of fivepence.

If this had been a rare offence there might be nothing remarkable about the leniency shown in a special case; but when every one had to do his share, and nearly every one could think of a reason for not doing it, these busy magistrates might well have said it was impossible to pick and choose. Sometimes the surveyors themselves, who were not of the privileged class, adopted this attitude. Anthony Sammes and John Thwaites—the variety of Essex surnames, as we have already noted, is astonishing—in presenting defaulters at Hatfield Peverel on the London to Colchester road, 3rd July 1623, said: 'There are certain other poor men of a lower form but a higher spirit, as old Mason, old Dunsted, and Meadows. Their plea is that not having wrought these seven years they will keep their custom. However these of the poorer sort may find your favour, there are divers able cottagers also [who] if they escape will stand for precedents in the years following. But we hope assuredly to prevail in the case of outdwellers, that having a long highway to amend upon the road we may have the assistance the law allows us.'

The term 'chief inhabitants and headboroughs of Bocking,' used a moment ago, calls for a brief comment in passing. The adjoining towns of Braintree and Bocking, which were joined together like Siamese twins, were an interesting example of the system of government by headboroughs. In their work on *Local Government* (i. 221–7), Sidney and Beatrice Webb say: 'A more complete example of the government of all the town business by the headboroughs, acting as a municipal council, and not simply through the leet, is that of the four-and-twenty headboroughs of Braintree in Essex, a town famous for its bay making. . . . At their monthly meetings, these headboroughs transacted all the important town affairs. The fact that they usurped all the public offices, both of the church and of the town, must have meant enormous work for them. The constables and other less important officials were appointed in the court leet; but they were apparently nominated by the Four and Twenty, who, for the most part, made up the jury. Although the headboroughs did much good work, they were regarded with great jealousy, and disappeared as a body in 1716.'

Whatever the system was worth, and whether the headboroughs were or were not regarded with any more jealousy than officials armed with power at any time are regarded, the willingness of headboroughs, justices of the peace, and

* G

constables also, to undertake public responsibilities, and to try to evolve new and better methods of conducting affairs, is evident and worthy of praise. They were not alway far-sighted, but then neither are we. The empowering of the surveyors to engage men to do the work and to levy a rate to cover costs was a progressive measure, but the arrangement was still unsatisfactory because the surveyor himself rarely had any special knowledge. He could only level the roads and fill up the holes with gravel. They were still appallingly bad when the stage-coaches of the eighteenth century rocked and rumbled across the county to Ipswich and Norwich. But it was one step forward, and prepared the way for the advent of the professional surveyor.

The seventeenth century was far from being an age of easy travel in England, but it was an interesting one in the development of facilities for it. There had been a break in progress since the dissolution of the monasteries put an end to the pilgrim age. The growth of trade and the development of marketing brought the people back to the roads, and in the middle of the century the movement of troops during the civil wars brought home to Parliament the badness of English highways as they were at that time, as well as making them worse. At the end of the century the stage-coaches came, and the highways thrilled into life.

For a vivid account of a journey across Essex at the be-ginning of the century, or, to be accurate, in the spring of 1599, we should read William Kempe's *Nine Daies Wonder*. Kemp was a comic actor of renown, who spent his life 'in mad jigges and merrie jestes,' and who is known to have played the part of the fool in several of Shakespeare's plays.

'Well, you merry knaves,' he cries in starting, 'you may come to the honour of it one day: is it not better to make a fool of the world as I have done, than to be fooled of the world as you scholars are? But be merry, my lads.'

In that spirit he set off in the company of Thomas Slye, his tabourer, William Bee, his servant, and George Sprat, who served as overseer, on his morris dance from London to Norwich, or, as he put it, 'frolickly to foot it from the right honourable the Lord Mayor's of London towards the right worshipful (and truly bountiful) Master Mayor's of Norwich.' He got a lively send-off in London. A great throng accompanied him to Bow Bridge, over which he danced into Essex. At Stratford he heard the bear roar and the dogs howl at a bear-baiting. Treading his hey-de-gaies he went on to Ilford, where he was offered refreshment from the town's great spoon, an enormous ladle that held a quart. By moonlight he proceeded to Romford, where he allowed the townsfolk, and those who had followed from London, to make a fuss of him. Then he rested. From Romford he danced into Brentwood, and from Brentwood to Chelmsford, where he records a pleasant incident. Sir Thomas Mildmay of Moulsham Hall, standing at his park paling, graciously accepted a pair of garters from the dancer as he stepped into the town. There again he was greeted royally and enjoyed some merry capers at the inn where he stayed the night. His next stretch of road was to Braintree, and here, he tells us, there were thick woods on both sides of the highway, which was so full of deep holes that he was thankful to reach Braintree and rest there before going on to Sudbury. The trees may have frightened him as much as the potholes. The road through Epping Forest—such as it was—was not the only one infested with robbers. On 16th May 1603, Daniel Baisie, a collar-maker from Huntingdonshire, at a court presided over by John, suffragan bishop of Colchester, confessed that 'on Saturday was a fortnight in the evening, he with two others stood in the King's highway by Faulkbourn Park, that leadeth from Witham to Braintree, and there intended to rob such of His Majesty's subjects as should pass that way.'

There were numerous highway robberies then, but far more later in the century, especially at the end, when more wealthy travellers were to be met with, either on horseback or in the new stage-coaches. Earlier it had been the custom for the rich to travel always with a numerous retinue in attendance.

One of the most important dates in the history of these roads was 1635, when the royal post was established and the postboy's horn became a familiar and eagerly expected sound. There were also the carriers' carts that John Taylor about in his *Carriers Cosmographie* of 1637.

How much valuable property must have been carried along this Harwich road in times of political stress! In *The Court Life of Charles I* we read that in July 1627 Lord Petre's son was apprehended while trying to carry across the sea to Flanders bundles of letters and 'two barrels of treasure, gold and silver, in a pink.' On page 224 of Sir John Bramston's *Autobiography* there is an account of a mail hold-up in 1685 or 1686, 'which gave occasion to the grand jury to present as a grievance the conveying of great sums of money in the post mails.' Sir John met Mr. Frowde, then head of the post office, and mentioned the complaint to him. Mr. Frowde said that the Jews were in the habit of sending money in coin rather than by bills of exchange. As the stolen money could then be recovered in damages from the hundred through which the mail was passing, this was a serious matter. Sir John sought an interview with the lord treasurer about it, and suggested that the mails carrying money should not be allowed by day. If they travelled by night and were robbed, damages could not be recovered. The lord treasurer was taken aback: ·

'"What," says he, "you would have them goe by night?"

'"Aye, my lord," said I, "for then we are safe."

'He laughed heartily, and said he would speak with Frowde, and take order in it. That very night, about ten o'clock, the mail was robbed, and £5,000 sterling, in foreign gold, coined and uncoined, taken by two men from two post-boys who carried the mails.'

Highway robberies were not confined to places where the cover of trees was provided. In 1643 the inhabitants of Chadwell, in the parish of Barking, petitioned the justices at the quarter sessions for permission to levy a rate to enable them to build a watch house near the Whalebone, the whalebone actually being the jawbones of a whale, which were set up as an arch over the road. Local tradition has it that they came from a whale that was stranded in the Thames near Dagenham during the great storm on the night Oliver Cromwell died, 2nd–3rd September 1658. Fisher's *Forest of Essex*, in a reference to the perambulation of Waltham Forest in 1642, had already proved this inaccurate, by showing that they were already there in that year. A petition brought before the justices at the Epiphany sessions in 1643 confirms this. It 'showeth that the petitioners have been lately enforced to keep a strong watch near the Whalebone in the great road near Romford by reason of sundry great robberies there lately committed. That the constable and watchmen there attending in the night being far from shelter are exposed to the violence of storm, tempest, and cold to the great hazard of their health.' It therefore seeks an order for a watch house to be erected for the shelter of the said watch.

But there were no highwaymen of the seventeenth century about whom we know enough to give them life again as Harrison Ainsworth gave life to the scowling, pock-marked Dick Turpin of the eighteenth century in *Rookwood*. There is a good account of a highway robbery near Ilford Bridge in 1686 to be found in the sessions rolls, but it has no really vivid characters in it. The information came from a trooper in Colonel Hugh Sunderland's regiment, which was quartered in Romford at the time. He said that on Monday, 12th April, about ten o'clock at night, he was sent by one of the officers to London and joined a post that was travelling in the same direction. Just before they reached Ilford Bridge they overtook two men, one upon a bay horse with one white foot behind, the other upon a grey. The man who rode the bay was a short, fat man, with a brown periwig and a light-coloured, loose-fitting coat. The other was in a close-fitting coat of a 'pretty sad colour.' Suddenly the man on the bay turned on him, drew out a pistol and threatened to shoot, then grabbed him by the hair of his head and dragged him off his horse while the other man gained possession of the post-bag, spurred on by the oaths of the first. The scene is vigorous enough, but entirely conventional. There is the more daring exploit of Frank Osborn, a native of

Colchester, who with a single confederate held up the
Duke of Albemarle's coach between Harwich and Manningtree, though besides coachman and postilion there were four
postmen and two gentlemen-in-waiting in attendance. The
duke was robbed of a hundred and thirty guineas. Osborn
was caught later and hanged at Tyburn in 1690. But perhaps
the liveliest among the less reputable characters of the Essex
roads is the nobly named John Milton, a blacksmith of
Stansted Mountfitchet on the highway to Newmarket.

Information about Milton was brought to the justices
from Richard Hubbert on 23rd April 1655. He alleged
'that divers and sundry times he did hear [him] use
divers wicked, seditious, and scandalous words and language to the disgrace of the Lord Protector and present
government, and to the promoting of new insurrections and
rebellion, viz. that about Christmas last past, or a little
before—between Michaelmas and Christmas—seeing divers
in company passing upon the road, some in a coach and some
on horse back, the said Milton used these words:

'"Thieves and Parliament Rogues! And I am to get money
by the sweat of my brow to maintain such Parliament rogues
as these are."'

Milton, whose family still flourishes in Stanstead Mountfitchet, seems to have upset the informant by calling him one
of Cromwell's bastards. This lusty blacksmith must have
been one of the characters of his day. We can imagine the
young bucks who called at his forge to get their horses shod
teasing the old man till the sparks were struck from his
tongue as fast as from his anvil. If we cannot claim the
Parliament's John Milton, we had at least the king's.

But that is not all. There was a pre-Reformation wayside
chapel at Stanstead Mountfitchet, built, it is thought, by
John de Vere, twelfth Earl of Oxford, which, though a richly
carved and notable building, interfered with traffic and was
taken down in 1870. A drinking-fountain with horse and dog
troughs and a signpost was set up in its place. The chapel
had long been used as a blacksmith's shop, and here, we may
assume, the king's John Milton was Vulcan's fiery priest.

## CHAPTER XIII

## CREEKS AND MARSHES

Slee, sla, slud;
Stuck in the mud.

THE proper place for such men as our Essex John Milton was the coast, where odd and defiant characters have always abounded. Essex has the most torn and untidy coast in England. It is in shreds and patches from the Thames to the Stour. The Colne, the Blackwater, the Crouch, the Roach, with their creeks and marshes, their lonely islands and treacherous mud-banks, give it a character that attracts some and repels others. Those who know it best have little to say. But it abounds in interest. Southend and Westcliff flaunt their modern villas and smart hotels; but east of them are the marshes and west of them Leigh, already a well-known haunt of mariners when the seventeenth century opened. A guild of Thames pilots established at Leigh in the fifteenth century was combined by royal charter with one at Deptford in 1514 to form 'The Fraternity of the most glorious and indivisible Trinity and St. Clement,' the union from which came Trinity House. Tombstones in the churchyard are said to have been used by press-gangs to sharpen their cutlasses. Inside the church are memorials to many fine old seamen, in particular to members of the Haddock family, two of whom became admirals and seven captains in a single century. The story is told of Sir Richard Haddock, captain of the *Royal James*, the Earl of Sandwich's flagship at the battle of Sole Bay, that after his ship had been set on fire and all efforts to save her had failed, he threw himself into the sea and was fortunate enough to be saved. After the rescue he was presented to the king, Charles II, who to hearten him took off his own satin cap and set it on Sir Richard's head. With

195

the Earl of Warwick lord high admiral, Essex took pride in
its sailors in the seventeenth century. 'A pretty little town.'
wrote Camden of Leigh, 'stocked with lusty seamen.'

It is a joy in a place so rich in seafaring lore to find that
early in the seventeenth century there was a parson who
refrained from fruitless disputation long enough to record
the lives of some of these seamen. There were, of course, the
inevitable cross-grained Puritans of the age—there was, for
example, John Symmes, a Scot, who ministered with more
than necessary zeal from 1609 to 1638. But there was also
Samuel Purchas, the collector of voyages, who was born at
Thaxted in 1577, the year of Drake's bold venture to circum-
navigate the globe, and was vicar of Eastwood from 1604 to
1614. In his *Pilgrims* he has an account of the Congo, which
he tells us is based on information given to him by Andrew
Battell, 'my neere neighbour, dwelling at Leigh in Essex,'
who was 'taken by the Portugals on the coast of Brasil, and
shipped over to the Congo where (and in the countries
adjacant), he lived very many yeares.' This remarkable
man, Andrew Battell, also supplied William Winstanley with
material for his *Historical Rarities and Curious Observations.*
The information derived by Purchas from Battell about apes
was used by Huxley in *Man's Place in Nature.*

In the fourteenth chapter of the ninth book of his *Pilgrims,*
first edition, Purchas records a curious experience. He says
that on Bartholomew Day, 1613, he was 'in the Island of
Foulenesse on our Essex shore, where were such clouds of
flying pismires, that wee could nowhere flie from them, but
they filled our clothes; yea the floores of some houses where
they fell, were in manner covered with a blacke carpet of
creeping ants; which they say drowne themselves about that
time of the yere in the sea.'

After leaving Essex, Purchas became chaplain to the
Archbishop of Canterbury. At his death he bequeathed £5
to the poor of Thaxted, a messuage and tenement, with
lands and a mill in the same parish to his son and his
heirs for ever, and other land in Thaxted to his daughter,
Martha. He is an example of an industrious man of no

particular talent doing work of considerable importance. Those who knew him well were not impressed by either his person or his ability. He was, if we may believe them, a fawning cleric of the Mr. Collins type, yet his influence is to be traced in the fourth book of Wordsworth's *Excursion*, and from Purchas's *Pilgrimage* came Coleridge's dream of Xanadu. By a stroke of fortune he came into possession of the unpublished papers of Richard Hakluyt, another parson, but a better scholar than himself, and these he was able to incorporate with his own work. It is said that James I read *Purchas his Pilgrim* seven times; but he did not live to read the great *Hakluytus Posthumus, or Purchas his Pilgrimes*, in four heavy folios, published in 1625, with a dedication to the new king. If James had still been on the throne when it appeared our Essex chronicler might have been made a bishop. His son, it is worth noting, who was also an Essex parson and bore the same name as his father, wrote a quaint book entitled *History of Bees, or a Theatre of Political Flying Insects*.

There is a tradition in Leigh that the original *Mayflower* was built there. It is curious that so little should be known about the origin and fate of the ship that carried the Pilgrim Fathers, so many of whom were Essex men. From time to time correspondence appears in newspapers about it, but nothing conclusive has ever been established about either its first or last days. There were several ships of the same name, and these are sometimes confused. What interests us here is that some of them are known to have been built at Leigh, and it is not unlikely that the *Mayflower* we remember was one. But all we know for certain is that its master was a Harwich man.

There were many interesting ships launched from Essex shipyards during the seventeenth century. They can be traced in the *Calendar of State Papers* and various diaries of the period. Harwich, as we should expect, had most; and Harwich, be it noted, once had Pepys as a parliamentary candidate. Sir Anthony Deane, one of the commissioners of the Royal Navy, superintended the building there of several for Charles II. These included the *Harwich*, launched in

April 1674, and described by Dr. Dale, the Harwich historian, as 'a very beautiful ship and swift sailer . . . with balconies and galleries, partly imitating the setting off of the French Men of War.' In 1675 Pepys wrote of her: 'The *Harwich* carries the bell from the whole fleet, great and small.' Two sloops built there in 1666 by the king's orders, the *Spy* and the *Fan-fan*, were useful during the Dutch wars for keeping the sands in front of the harbour clear of the Dutch picaroons that infested them for a time. Prince Rupert wrote to the king on 27th July 1666 that the previous morning, 'it being very calm, and the enemy to windward of them, the *Fan-fan*, a small new sloop of two guns, built the other day at Harwich, made up with his oars towards the Dutch fleet, and drawing both his guns to one side, very formally attacked de Ruyter (in the Admiral's ship of Holland), and continued this honourable fight so long, till she had received two or three shots from him between wind and water; to the great laughter and delight of our fleet, and the indignation and reproach of the enemy.'

Wivenhoe on the Colne, still a yacht-building centre, also has references to its boats in the *State Papers*. There is a record of the *Sunflower* of Wivenhoe carrying a cargo of muskets, rapiers, and belts to Scarborough for the use of the governor, Sir Hugh Cholmley. Boats from Wivenhoe plied for a long time between Suffolk and Kent, and often came into conflict with the light pirate ships from Ostend, which on one occasion at least appear to have sailed up the Colne on a boat-stealing exploit. There is a note that on 3rd March 1656 Captain Richard Country sailed from Harwich in the *Hind*, built at Wivenhoe, under orders to join the *Kent* in search for Dutch ships.

But we must not pretend that all the offences of the day were on one side. The English could be quite as provocative as the Dutch. One Jan Verhulst, a mason of Dunkirk, who in 1659 freighted a hoy of Flushing, the *Fortune*, to fetch lime from England to enable him to repair fortifications, complained that about the Goodwin Sands he encountered a ketch flying English colours, and received orders from the captain, Robert Walker of Wivenhoe, to strike his own colours and come aboard. When he did so the hoy was plundered by the crew of the ketch.

In going through these varied references to Wivenhoe in the *State Papers*, though none of them are of prime importance, we see again how quickly disturbances in London vibrated along the east coast, and how sensitive the coastal towns were in comparison with those inland. A ketch named the *Wivenhoe*, commanded by Captain William Berry, while in search of the Dutch fleet, encountered Dutch men-of-war without warning off the Shetlands and was chased for seven hours. Tales of such exploits would be related in the ale-houses at home, and all through the period of trouble with Holland these apparently remote places in the Essex creeks and estuaries would be kept on the alert.

It must not, however, be supposed that we had to depend on quarrels with foreign powers for excitement. Before the Dutch wars tempers were kept mettlesome by suitable disputes among ourselves. There was always religion to quarrel about. A certain Fred Waggoners of Leigh came before the archdeacon's court for making a profane speech against the Blessed Sacrament, and was fined £300—later reduced to £100—for his Protestant zeal. Religion failing, there was politics to fall back on. So we find Captain Thomas Elliott of Aldeburgh in Suffolk, who was given the command of a frigate built at Wivenhoe and launched on 22nd May 1654, complaining of the abusive conduct towards him of Humphrey White, surveyor, who on coming on board to pass the ship at Wivenhoe before she was launched, called Elliott a knave, a rogue, a malignant dog, and used other abusive terms, finally even threatening to fight him. A more interesting Wivenhoe reprobate was the subject of a petition sent by many of the inhabitants of the town to the justices at Chelmsford, and presented at the Michaelmas sessions, 1641. Unfortunately, part of this interesting petition is illegible now. It begins:

'Right worshipful, whereas we have heard of many untimely and fearful accidents the which have of late fallen out;

not only in our own town but also in our neighbour towns about us, by casualty of fire, we the inhabitants of the town of Wivenhoe do inform your worships of one Edward Mayer the elder of our town, an obstinate and refractory fellow who will not live in rank and order amongst his neighbours in a house, but will live in a boat drawn up on dry land, in which he hath built up a chimney . . . which is near adjoining to a thatched house, and other thatched houses near to it, the which doth cause us to fear the danger . . . of fire to come by his means.'

Edward Mayer has had many successors, as any one may see who cares to visit Canvey Island, which, incidentally, was actually taken from the Thames by a Dutchman named Joas Croppenburgh. In 1622 he was rewarded with a grant of one-third of the island he had made. Two of the original Dutch cottages are still to be seen there. They are octagonal, with a central brick chimney stack, and were first occupied by the engineers who built the mud sea-walls or dykes, faced with stones large enough to withstand the fury of the tides, upon which the island depends. Before 1622 Canvey had been six islands instead of one. These are shown in Norden's map of 1594, but the spring tides submerged them each year.

The fear of fire expressed by the people of Wivenhoe was very real along the east coast in the seventeenth century. A few sparks, alighting in thatch when a high wind was blowing from the sea, have practically destroyed several east coast towns and villages at various times. Southwold in Suffolk is perhaps the best known case. But the fear of fire was much less than the fear of ague. The unhealthiness of the Essex marshes before they were drained is well known. Camden speaks of them 'exhaling unwholesome and noxious vapours.' What is not so well known is that when the marshes were drained and dyked the people who lived near them were afraid that drought would be a worse evil than damp. They knew how much the people farther inland, in the Rooth-ings for example, suffered from lack of water, and they were afraid that this would now be their lot. The feeling is expressed in a ballad popular in the middle of the century. Three of the stanzas go:

The upland people are full of thoughts,
  And do despair of after rain;
Now the sun is robbed of his morning draughts,
  They're afraid they shall never have shower again.

Our smaller rivers are now dry land,
  The eels are turned to serpents there;
And if Old Father Thames play not the man,
  Then farewell to all good English beer.

Why should we stay then and perish with thirst?
  To the New World i' the moon then away let us go;
For if the Dutch colony get there first,
  'Tis a thousand to one that they'll drain that too.

But important as Leigh, Harwich, Wivenhoe, and the rest of them were, they never equalled in interest Maldon, which according to Morant is 'one of the two ancientest towns in Essex.' In spite of its modest appearance, Maldon has, either in itself or in its neighbourhood, practically all the things we can ask of seaboard Essex. Here a frigate was built for the navy which acquired special fame because Pepys became its captain. She was called the *Jersey*, and sailed from Maldon in the August of 1654 under the command of a Captain Terry. Pepys became her captain in 1669 for a special reason which the *Diary* discloses. 'That which put me in good humour both at noon and night,' runs the entry, 'is the fancy that I am this day made a captain of one of the King's ships. Mr. Wren having this day sent me the Duke of York's commission to be captain of the *Jersey*, in order to my being of a Court Martial for examining the loss of the *Defiance* and other things, which do give me occasion of much mirth, and may be of some use to me, at least I shall get a little money for the time I have it; it being designed I must really be a captain to be able to sit in this Court.'

Maldon is not mentioned by name in the *Diary*, but it is related also to another reference, and that under a heading in

the same month. On 29th March 1669 Pepys went with
Sir Richard Browne and Mr. Evelyn to hear Dr. Thomas
Plume, later Archdeacon of Rochester, preach at Greenwich
parish church, of which he was then vicar. Plume was
Maldon's greatest benefactor and most dutiful son. He must
have been a quite irreproachable character. Evelyn, after
hearing him preach on 16th September 1666, relates how
he took 'occasion from the late unparalell'd conflagration to
remind us how we ought to walke more holyly in all manner of
conversation.' No doubt this was all very improving, but we
value him chiefly for his commonplace books. In these we
find odd scraps of gossip, notes on celebrities, rhymes, and
recipes, most of which are dry and lifeless now. Some, however, are fruity. There is a very sound reflection that 'we
put our hands to our mouths too often, and our feet to the
ground too seldom.' A bit of gossip about Sir John Minnes
seeing Shakespeare's 'old father in his shop, a merry-cheekt
old man,' looks like a prize indeed until we find that Sir John
Minnes was only two years old when John Shakespeare of
Stratford died. Dear old Dr. Plume! I never see his name
or think of him without recalling one of E. V. Lucas's
enchanting essays. It describes a visit to Maldon and the
author's discovery that the venerable archdeacon had been
born there in 1630. Lucas knew that Plume had founded the
Plumian Chair of Astronomy at Cambridge, but that was not
what engaged his humour. It was the recollection of the
archdeacon's epitaph, in which he described himself as 'the
greatest of sinners,' adding sorrowfully: 'O that I could say
of penitents.' Lucas smiles at this confession and recalls the
penitent who on his knees protested that he was of sinners
the chief, only to be corrected by his guardian angel impishly
remarking: 'All vanity, my little man, you 're nothing of the
kind.'

Happily for us, Maldon folk in the seventeenth century
were not all so virtuous as Dr. Plume. A curious case of a
fraudulent churchwarden came before an archdeacon's court
in April 1658: 'Upon the petition of the churchwardens
of St. Lawrence, against one, John Pattison, late of the same,

now of Bishops Stortford, for a silver cupp and cover, flaggon, carpet, two linnen clothes, and surplice, belonging to the Church of St. Lawrence aforesaid, carried away by him after possession as a churchwarden there.' It was 'ordered that some justice of the county of Hertford be desired to bind over Mr. Pattison to the next Quarter Sessions.'

In Maldon we are again reminded of the wider concerns of sea-going folk in the petition of a poor woman named Mary Steele. It is addressed to 'the truly pious and worthily ennobled the Right Honourable Robert, Earl of Warwick, Lord High Admiral of England, with all other his well deserved titles and dignities,' and dated 1646. It 'most humbly sheweth' that Mary Steele's husband is 'a poore miserable captive in Algiers in the dominion of the Turks.' The petitioner seeks permission by 'letters of licence to collect and gather within the said county the liberal contributions of good people, for the raising of a sum of money to pay his ransom.' It is a sad and moving petition, too long to reproduce here, but to be found at the Essex Record Office.[1]

The Warwicks were highly esteemed in Maldon in those days, not only because the earl was lord high admiral and the leading figure in the county, but also because the most romantic tale then told in the town was of the earl's aunt, Frances Rich, the second wife of Thomas Cammocke. A figure of Thomas Cammocke, with his wives on either side of him, is to be found under a heavy marble canopy on a wall monument in All Saints' Church, Maldon. The tale of his second wooing is the Essex version of the tale of Lochinvar and the fair Ellen. Morant told it first, and others have copied it from him, but they seem to be muddled over the Rich pedigree. Morant is obviously in error. Thomas Cammocke, it would seem, was in the service of the third Lord Rich, who became the first Earl of Warwick, when he fell in love with his master's sister, Frances Rich. The imperious brother disapproved of the suit, and in consequence the lovers decided to elope. But their plan was discovered. Before they had put a safe distance between themselves and Leighs

*Guide to the Essex Record Office*, i. 56.

they realized that they were being followed, and in the course of a thrilling chase reached Fambridge Ferry only to find the boat at the opposite bank. By this time the angry Lord Rich was in sight, so Cammocke, with Frances in the saddle behind him, rode into the stream and straight across the channel. In other words,

> He staid not for brake, and he stopped not for stone,
> He swam the Eske river where ford there was none,

only the river was not the Esk but the Crouch. When he saw how much the couple had ventured for love, our blustering, impulsive Lord Rich relented and allowed them to marry.

'Seeing she has ventured her life for him, God bless them!' he said, and Frances became the mother of thirteen of Thomas's twenty-two children.

The many-sided character of Maldon's story makes it a fascinating place. A full-length history is long overdue and the man who writes it is to be envied. He will have records of uncommon value to work from. Among the most interesting are those of the Admiralty Court, 1573 to 1638, which was held on Maldon Hythe. The waters of Maldon were jealously guarded and there was no time lost in bringing 'forreners,' or trespassers, to book. In 1575 John Shoote, a fisherman of another parish, was presented for entering the waters of the liberty to fish in them—'anglice dothe trawle and dredge'—to the grave damage and prejudice of the fishermen and fishmongers dwelling within the liberties aforesaid, and to the manifest injury of the liberty.

Some of the trespassers were distinguished gentlemen, whom the court was pleased to try for other reasons besides the offences stated. At a court held in the usual place, on Maldon Hythe, on 17th May 1638, before Thomas Clerke and Jeremiah Browning, bailiffs and admirals, supported by Isaac Dorislaus, doctor of laws, and in the presence of Nowel Hamand, notary public and registrar of the court, Sir Thomas Wiseman, a member of the great Royalist and Catholic family that gave us Cardinal Wiseman, was tried.

'Sir Thomas Wiseman presumes from day to day to occupy

and convert to his own use in dredging of oysters a certain place within the liberty and jurisdiction of the waters of the borough.'

There are some interesting clauses in the Articles of the Court of the Admiralty at Maldon. Inquiry was to be made if any one had 'found in the sea within this liberty any lead, iron, or any other goods lying in the water whereof none is known to be the possessor.' Such flotsam and jetsam went 'the one part to Mr. Bailiff to the use of the borough and the other to the finder.' If any had taken fishes royal, that is to say, sturgeon, porpoise, whales, and so forth, the court had to make sure that these had been delivered to the king as the law required. Inquiry had also to be made 'of and upon the default of beaconage within this liberty, and for the destruction of marks to the sea.'

Other clauses were:

'20. Item, if any have taken with net or trawl any fish whereof every mesh is not two inches and a half within this borough or hath destroyed the fry of fish therewith or with shove nets or engines to the great hurt and prejudice of her majesty's subjects, etc.

'21. Item, if any within the waters of this liberty hath taken any wreck of the sea of his own wrong and hath not answered the same Mr. Bailiff to the use of the borough.

'22. Item, if any, etc., hath broken the assize of fish and hath uttered the same in any market or other place or places within or without this borough, etc.

'23. Item if any, etc., hath used and occupied any false water measure not containing five pecks or any other false measure or balances, etc.

'24. Item, if any hath taken for anchorage over fourpence for a vessel of fifty tons and under ijd. within this port or haven, etc.

'25. Item, if any water bailiff raiseth any new customs or exactions in any port haven or landing place to the grievance or prejudice of Her Majesty's subjects within this borough, etc.

'26. Item, if any hath cast any wastage vizt: Ballast,

rubbish, gravel, or burrow and not upon the land the forfeiture and five pounds.

'33. Item, if any within the liberty of the waters, etc., hath erected any weirs or kydelles to the nuisance of ships, crafts, and other vessels floating upon the said waters, etc.

'34. Item, if any person or persons hath erected any wharfs or cranes upon the banks and the waters of this borough that is to say upon the hythe, etc., against the express inhibition and prohibition of the charter and without licence of Mr. Bailiff, etc.'

How important Mr. Bailiff must have felt! And how well such as he were satirized by Breton in the lines:

> Let but a fellow in a fox-furred gown,
> A greasy night-cap and a drivelled beard,
> Grow but a bailiff of a fisher-town,
> And have a matter 'fore him to be heard,
> Will not his frown make half a street afeared?
> Yea, and the greatest codshead gape for fear
> He shall be swallowed by this ugly bear.

Among common offences, Sir Thomas Wiseman's was the one viewed most seriously. The Colne and the Blackwater are the two most famous oyster-breeding grounds in the county, and none of the old Essex industries is more interesting. We are told by the elder Pliny that Sergius Orata 'first conceived the idea of planting oysters in beds,' and that he built a palace on the shore of the Lucrine Lake near his oyster beds so that he could regale his friends with this new delicacy. Sir Aston Cokayne was inspired by this to write in 1669:

> The old luxurious Romans vaunts did make
> Of gustful oysters took in Lucrine Lake,
> Your Essex better hath, and such perchance
> As tempted Caesar first to pass from France.

The method of oyster culture in the Essex estuaries to-day is to dredge them up in autumn and sell the best. The rest are scattered over the beds again with vast quantities of hard refuse called cultch on which the oysters spawn. Strict rules are enforced in the industry, and to these the undisputed pre-eminence of the Colchester native is due. This control dates from 1634, when oysters had become so scarce that the price had risen from fourpence to two shillings and eightpence a bushel. The lords of the admiralty thereupon instructed the Earl of Warwick not to allow them to be exported by strangers or in strangers' boats. Four years later a report was issued on the state of oyster culture in Essex, and the scarcity was attributed to:

'(a) Taking brood and spat and the shells on which the spat grew from the common grounds to private layings.

'(b) The Corporations of Colchester and Maldon claiming the water of Colne and Pont, which are the best and chiefest places for breeding oysters.

'(c) The extraordinary number of oysters barrelled and sent to London and the North—last year [1637], at least a third more than ever before. Twenty years ago, not one tenth in a year was barrelled as was in 1638.

'(d) Fishmongers and others contracting for all the oysters and keeping them in layings or pits in a few hands, so that none can have any oysters but from them.

'(e) Excessive exporting under pretence of licences for oysters for the Queen of Bohemia [James I's daughter] and the Prince of Orange.'

For the restoration and improvement of the industry it was recommended that oysters should not be taken from the common grounds until they were *wear* or *half wear*, namely, in their third or second year of growth, and in no one week more than one thousand barrels; that no oysters should be barrelled except in Colchester, Brightlingsea, and other places where the best green oysters grew; that no fishmonger was to buy them for resale until they came to the London quays or where common markets were held; that none should be exported except to the Queen of Bohemia and the Prince of Orange, and those under licence. No dredging, it was recommended, should be allowed in unseasonable times. These recommendations were adopted as orders, with the Lord High Admiral, his vice-admirals, and the Lord Warden to see that they were carried out.[1]

[1] Dr. E. P. Dickin, *A History of Brightlingsea*, p. 137.

The result of this control of the industry was immediate and continued prosperity. Dr. Dickin, who went into the subject for his *History of Brightlingsea*, says that oyster dredging, though the chief means of livelihood in the estuaries of the Colne and the Blackwater, did not appear to have been very profitable in the early seventeenth century. In the previous century the grounds in Brightlingsea Creek appeared to have been common grounds, for in the one hundred and thirty-seven wills he searched for references he found no mention of oysters or layings. A 1612 will had a reference to pits and the oysters in them, but not to layings. Later, we find oyster manorial rights, and maps showing the creeks divided up among the lords of the manors bordering them. There is a map of Burnham dated 1675 in the Essex Record Office which shows these oyster lanes.

At the end of the century the industry was thriving, and a perusal of the Colne Fishery accounts, 1700–10,[1] produces a most agreeable picture of the official and civic party going off for a cruise on the Colne, amply provided with brandy and picnic baskets. This is the kind of thing we find:

'Eastertime, when Coln Waters was sett:

|  | £ | s. | d. |
|---|---|---|---|
| A Leg of Veal and a leg of mutton cost | 0 | 8 | 6 |
| Pd. at Burgesses for brandy, beer, bacon & dressing of meat | 1 | 1 | 0 |
| Lemons and Sugar | 0 | 2 | 10 |
| Spent on the Deputy Mayor & Serjant after we came home | 0 | 6 | 6 |
| Pd. the Sergeants horse hire | 0 | 2 | 0 |

Such is the prosperity of the industry now, that before the Admiralty commandeered the best part of the Colne in the 1939–45 war, three to four million oysters were hauled out annually, and throughout the six years, seven veterans of the Colne Oyster Fishery Board, the oldest of whom was eighty-six, tended the beds despite the dangers from drifting mines and other sinister obstructions.

But this has never been a coast for faint-hearts. If there

---

[1] Essex Record Office, D/DRc. F6.

was nothing else to try men, the weather itself was trouble enough in winter. Defoe, it may be recalled, made fun of the wild fowlers who went from London on sporting excursions. He said that they returned laden with game, but often 'with an Essex ague on their backs, which they found a heavier load than the fowls they have shot.' And according to tradition the dangerous craft of smuggling was long practised here:

> Five and twenty ponies,
> Trotting through the dark—
> Brandy for the Parson,
> 'Baccy for the Clerk;
> And watch the wall, my darling, when the Gentlemen go by.

All the way round the Essex coast we find tales of smugglers. In *Mehalah*, Baring-Gould, who was rector of East Mersea for ten years, writes of them using the Essex creeks at the time of his story, as they were said to have done for centuries. Salcott and Virley are believed to have been notorious haunts of wreckers, and Baring-Gould was probably recording fact when he said that the *nots* in the decalogue on the wall of the church at Salcott, where the church itself is said to have been used for storing smuggled goods, had all been erased. There can be no doubt that they had been erased from the consciences of the villagers. Yet the plain fact is that there are few authentic records of smuggling in Essex in comparison with those of Kent and Sussex. It does not appear to have been carried out on so large a scale here. The shoals round the Essex coast would make it tricky. But detection also would be more difficult in Essex than in Kent and Sussex, because there were few conveniently placed eminences above the flat marshes. In the most likely places the preventive men would have to get right up to the sea wall in order to see anything, and they would be lucky indeed if they reached it alive. Such detection as there was would be contrived more easily at the receiving end, either in or nearer London. But the liquor smuggled into the county would never get so far. Most of the inns and ale-houses near the coast, it is said, got their supplies on the spot from smugglers.

For other goods there was a sale held regularly on Tiptree Heath, where again the approaches could be watched.

One good reason for the lack of documentary evidence for smuggling is that every one in the coastal villages was involved. This is not so shocking an admission as it might appear. The law, which was made in the middle of the fifteenth century, requiring that all merchandise leaving or entering England should be forfeited if loaded or landed in creeks or small landing-places was considered by many to be unjust. Most Essex landing-places failed to qualify, and the inhabitants rebelled against a law that took their livelihood away from them. If the parsons were often a party to smuggling, as they undoubtedly were, even to the extent of lending their churches for the hiding of merchandise brought in, it was because they believed they were resisting the oppression of harsh and unjust law-breakers, much as the 'black market' on the Continent during the Second World War was part of a freedom movement and kept the spirit of the people alive.

But if we have few authentic records of goods being brought into the county to the embarrassment of the authorities, we have one of corn being taken out. It is in a letter from Thomas Sackville, the poet Earl of Dorset, to the justices of Essex, and tells its own tale. It is dated 22nd February 1605, and states that: 'Whereas the Lords of the Council have been informed that huge quantities of corn have been transported beyond the seas out of the ports in Essex, and that thereby the price of corn is so enhanced as that it is far above the Statute and likely to grow higher whereby the poor people are ready to mutiny and like to suffer great want and penury, and that a very great quantity of corn has lately by the permission of the Officers of the Ports been transported beyond the seas at a price above the rate limited for transportation by the Statute, wherefore that the truth may be examined and a present remedy given for the stay of further transportation, the Justices are required to call the Officers of the Ports before them, and all such others as can give any good information concerning the transportation of

Leigh-on-Sea

corn since Midsummer last, and by what warrant it was transported, and what is the price of every sort of corn in the
market at present and what store of corn now remains in sur-
plusage in the shire; and in the meanwhile they are to have
vigilant care that neither the Officers by their permission
nor any other by their unlawful transportation, do pass away
any corn, and likewise if the present urgent necessity and
the public good and preservation of the poor from misery
shall so require, even to make stay as well of all corn already
embarked and not yet passed away, as also of all corn from
henceforth to be transplanted, yea though by licence from the
King's Majesty.' [1]

Towns near the coast are always rich in tales of defiance
and adventure. In such places the people know that life is
not spent everywhere in raising crops and tending cattle.
Reports have always come in of mysterious things that
happened in far-off countries, which stimulated the imagination and produced ghost stories, legends, and all manner of
superstitions. There were no more of these in Essex than in
other counties, and most of them were not peculiar to the
one place. The real character of the people on the Essex
coast is not produced by these but by the nature of the land
they live on. Probably the traditional character of the Essex
coast was never described better than by Baring-Gould in
*Mehalah*. Some of his paragraphs become lyrical, as when he
describes the bird life. 'The marshes are alive and wakeful
with countless wild fowl,' he writes. 'At all times they are
haunted with sea mews and Royston crows; in winter they
teem with wild duck and grey geese. The stately heron
loves to wade in the pools; occasionally the whooper swan
sounds his loud trumpet, and flashes a white reflection in
the still blue waters of the fleets. The plaintive pipe of the
curlew is familiar to those who frequent the marshes, and the
barking of the brent geese as they return from their northern
breeding places is heard in November.' Such glory as it had
has gone from most parts of the Essex coast; but the marshes
remain inviolate.

[1] Essex Record Office, Q.S.R. 171/57.

# CHAPTER XIV

## THE PURITANS

Where I saw a Puritane one
Hanging of his Cat on Monday
For killing of a Mouse on Sunday.
*Drunken Barnaby's Journal.*

MOST of the troubles of the seventeenth century had their roots in religion. What are thought of as parsons' quarrels now were people's quarrels then. Politics hung upon theology, and theology seems to have been the most vital thing in life after the permanent biological interests had been provided for. Elizabeth had been far from benevolent towards Roman Catholics. When Thomas More of Leyton was charged at Chelmsford on 24th March 1603 with not attending service at his parish church, he complained that he had already 'forfeited all his goods to the late Queen, and two parts of his lands and tenements to the yearly rent of two hundred pounds, which were seized into the hands of the said late Queen.' This property now remained in the hands of the new king. In 1605 several members of the same family, including Thomas and Mary his wife, were in the list of recusants who had wilfully been absent from church. In the same list the son and daughter-in-law of William Byrd the composer are found under the Stondon Massey heading. Ingatestone and East Tilbury had families of recusants. Elsewhere there was little trouble from papists in the Essex archdeaconry, which did not, however, include Harlow, Hedingham, and Dunmow. These were in the Middlesex archdeaconry.

Throughout the reign papist and Puritan abused each other roundly and more than one divine of distinction joined in the fray. There was the learned rector of Stanford Rivers, Richard Montagu, afterwards Bishop of Chichester, and later again of Norwich, who introduced into England the Arminian doctrine. Montagu, like Arminius, was a man of liberal views, equally opposed to extremists of both the Roman right and the Calvinist left, and he found that the middle course, which was to become characteristically the English course, was so imperfectly understood that at first he got little support. The Roman Catholics in his parish began to make nuisances of themselves—according to the rector's way of thinking—in 1619. In 1623 Montagu was attacked in a pamphlet entitled *The Gagg of the Reformed Doctrine*, to which he replied with *A New Gagg for an Old Goose*. The origin of this lively controversy is explained in a spirited letter written by Montagu from Stanford Rivers to John Cosin, Bishop of Durham, which is preserved in the archives of the Surtees Society. It is dated 12th December 1624, and is worth quoting at length. 'About some twenty months since,' wrote Montagu, 'some of the Romish limitors had come within my pale and had been tampering with some woman at Stanford Rivers. Understanding thereof, I blanched them and settled the partie. But they came again, and she to me. Whereupon after other resolution to her I said that I desired to speak with them, for I was willing to learn and save my soul if I were amiss, as well as they. Wherefore if they would not come to confer with me, I desired resolution in three propositions which I gave her written, promising to subscribe and go to mass if in these things they could persuade me. They went to the quick. She gave them to the parties. I heard no more of them till the 5 of October last. Then she cometh to me and bringeth me from one A. P., who or what I know not, two sheets of paper written in two several hands, often without sense, without true orthography, nothing to my propositions. This missive I answered presently as I thought fit, and left it with her that brought me the paper, who said the partie promised to come again within four days. But he is not yet come, I understand. He also sent me a little whipjack in a blue jacket, called *A Gagg for the Newe Gospell*, that either I should be converted by it or answer it. This choice I was put to. It was not like to convert me. Had

H

I not been settled, it would have fastened me, I have seen many foolish things in that kind, but never saw more; therefore answer it I must . . . and answer it I have—bitterly and tartly, I confess, which I did purposely, because the ass deserved so to be rubbed.'

But the real trouble came after Laud's visitation as Bishop of London in 1636, and it came from the Puritans, not from the Roman Catholics, who by that time were powerless. Laud's proposals for the more dignified and orderly conduct of services were acceptable to most of the clergy. The protests were usually from the pew rather than from the pulpit, though obviously the refractory congregations had been incited to rebellion by Puritan or Calvinist lecturers, usually maintained by voluntary subscriptions. Often these lecturers were a blessing at first and a curse afterwards. The inflammatory and disruptive power of pulpit eloquence was not recognized at the beginning of its vogue, and many of the rectors in their innocence believed that nothing but good would come from having full churches, even though unsuspected passions did appear to be roused by this new kind of preaching. Probably they expected the intemperate phase to pass. What is specially to be observed in these outbreaks of fanaticism is that emotion usually fastened on an apparently irrelevant object which served as a symbol. In most cases it was the surplice worn by the priest that stirred the furies most, and the people had ways of protesting against its use that no self-respecting clergyman could counter. For example, John Newton, vicar of Little Baddow, after dutifully wearing his surplice on the Sunday, as his bishop required, went into church during the week and found that a woman named Susan Cooke had hung out her linen there. When the vicar asked what she meant by it, she replied that as the surplice was hanging in church she did not see why she should not 'hang *her* rags there as well.' Her daughter Ann came forward with the impudent remark: 'It were a good turn if *he* were hanging up there.'

There were shocking scenes in every part of the county. In 1642 a Colchester mob rifled the house at Ardleigh of

Gabriel Honifold, the vicar, who was then seventy years of age. He went straight to the mayor, but could get no redress. On leaving the mayor's house he was followed by a rabble of mud-slinging, stone-throwing townsfolk, who, when at last he found refuge in a kinsman's house, became so violent that he was glad to take cover in the common jail. Robert Cotesford, vicar of Canewdon, believed to have been the son of Laud's half-sister, on Christmas Day, 1641, having heard that the rails round the communion table were to be torn out that day, entered the sanctuary, and, drawing out a stiletto, threatened to stab any man who dared to set hands on them. No one came forward then, but the next day they had gone.

Most of the charges brought by the Puritans against the orthodox ministers were petty and malicious. The Rev. John Jegon, vicar of Sible Hedingham, was presented because he allowed his wife and servants to bag hops on the sabbath, and had even conducted an afternoon service while hops were being bagged. After the Parochial Inquisition of 1640 action against the orthodox divines was intensified. In 1643 many lost their livings. The exact number of sequestrations is not known, nor is it always possible to discover the date of an ejection, but the available facts are given by Dr. Harold Smith in his *Ecclesiastical History of Essex*. Some of the depositions against ministers alleged to be of scandalous life are extremely foolish. Thomas Darnell was ejected from Thorpe-le-Soken for having cleaned out his cow shed on the Lord's Day. The Rev. Ambrose Westrop of Great Totham was in trouble because he did 'commonly prophane the ordinance of preaching by mentioning in the pulpit matters to stir up his people to laughter.' One of the stories told against him by his scandalized parishioners was that he had alluded in the pulpit to a man in the village named Kent. 'They say the Devil is in Harwich,' the parson had said; 'but I am sure he is in Kent.' Walker, in reporting Westrop's case in his *Sufferings of the Clergy*, says of the charges against him: 'Nothing serious; but a talkative, maggoty person, especially about women.' Westrop, indeed, would have been regarded as a treasure in a more enlightened age. Major Ayloffe, an Essex justice of the peace and a sensible man, wrote to Walker that he had heard many pleasant stories about Westrop, but never that he vented immodesties in the pulpit or was in any way vicious. He was known to be a woman-hater, and Ayloffe had heard that he had a rhyme on his door, ending:

... into this house
No female creature enter, rat or mouse.

What is most curious about sequestrations in Essex is that they so seldom had any connection with the Covenant. Indeed, it was hardly ever mentioned in the depositions.

One of the commonest charges was drunkenness, or 'tippling' as it was called. Lawrence Washington, rector of Purleigh, the great-great-grandfather of George Washington, had to answer this charge, and was unsuccessful in his defence. His case is typical. He was removed from his living, we read, 'for that he is a common frequenter of alehouses, not only himself sitting daily tippling there, but also encouraging others in that beastly vice, and hath been often drunk, and hath said that the Parliament have more Baptists belonging to them in their armies than the King hath about him in his army, and that the Parliament army did more hurt than the Cavaliers, and that they did none at all; and hath published them traitors that did lend to or assist the Parliament.' The charge of tippling was obviously a cover for the real reason for sequestration, namely, Parson Washington's dislike of Cromwell and his friends. Let us again look what the sensible Major Ayloffe has to say about him. He did not believe that Washington had been either drunken or malignant. On the contrary, he believed him a 'very worthy, pious man; so often as he was in his company, he always appeared a very modest sober person, and he was recommended as such by several gentlemen who were acquainted with him before he himself was. He was a loyal person, and had one of the best benefices in these parts, and this was the only cause of his expulsion, as I verily believe.' How right the major was!

One of the saddest cases is that of Dr. Michaelson of Chelmsford, who became rector in 1623, and according to Sir John Bramston was 'a very learned man and an excellent preacher, bating but his Scotch tone and pronunciation of our language.' Three years after his appointment the people of Chelmsford, 'wanting one to break the bread of life unto them,' invited Thomas Hooker, famous as the inspirer of many emigrants to New England, to become their lecturer. Dr. Michaelson welcomed Hooker and made him his assistant curate. Hooker was a man of tremendous personality, and the parish church, to-day the cathedral church, was packed whenever he preached. The new curate and lecturer soon became an established favourite. He was a product of Emmanuel College and therefore acceptable to the Mildmays of Chelmsford and to the Earl of Warwick. The Chelmsford constables found him useful because he drew the people away from the ale-houses, which were apt to get rowdy. Chelmsford overflowed with the Word.

Dr. Michaelson cannot be blamed for not seeing that this new preaching was a more dangerous intoxicant than anything sold in the 'Dolphin' or the 'Spotted Dog.' Nor could the constables be expected to know at the time that a sermon-drunk man can be a more deadly disturber of the public peace than a man drunk with any of the liquors then being brewed in the town. Hooker himself was an honest man. After four years with Dr. Michaelson, conscientious scruples compelled him to sever his connection with the Established Church, so he left Chelmsford to start a school in the adjoining village of Little Baddow, where John Eliot, the Apostle to the Indians, was at one time employed as usher. Hooker continued, according to his lights, to be an influence for good among the ministers in the neighbourhood, and he was doubtless unaware of the sad harvest Dr. Michaelson would reap from the seed he had sown. That these two did for a time agree speaks well for both, for it is as difficult for two parsons to agree in one parish as it is for two women to agree in one kitchen. Hooker was the first to fall from popular favour. He was officially silenced in 1630, and later was obliged to leave the country, the Earl of Warwick, always generous to Puritan ministers in distress, providing 'a courteous and private recess' in Holland.

The first load of Dr. Michaelson's harvest of troubles was carried home ten years later, in August 1641, when Parliament ordered all 'scandalous pictures' to be removed from churches. The east window at St. Mary's was then full of original glass depicting the life of Christ from the Conception to the Ascension, along with the arms of the Essex nobility who had been benefactors of the church. The churchwardens at once removed the glass depicting the Blessed Virgin and the Crucifixion. But this was not enough for the nonconformists trained by Mr. Hooker. On 5th November these vandals went into the churchyard with pockets full of stones and broke every fragment of that beautiful window. The following Sunday Dr. Michaelson preached against this crazy conduct, which he described as casting out one devil by another and substituting sedition for superstition. This so infuriated his congregation that they threatened to ruin him if he preached again on the subject. One wild sectary actually fired a carbine through the window of the rector's room, and a fortnight later a young clothier entered the church at the close of the service, seized the rector by the throat, and tried to tear the surplice off his back. There was the usual frenzied nonsense about the 'rags of Rome' and 'Baal's priest,' and the good doctor, who was far from being unsympathetic towards the Reformation, had to flee for his life. His wife and eight children were reduced to poverty. On one occasion when he ventured to visit them he was seen and thrown into the 'house of correction.' Later he was able to rejoin his family, and they lived together quietly in a small house at Writtle, supported by the Bramstons of Roxwell and other friends until the rector was restored to his living under Charles II. It is worthy of note that during his absence the dominant figure in the 'religious' life of the town was 'Parson Oates,' leader of the local Anabaptists, who came before the judge of assize on one occasion charged with the murder of a convert, who apparently had died while being dipped by Oates. 'Parson Oates,' incidentally, was the father of the notorious Titus Oates.

As an illustration of the bitterness between neighbours, even though gentlemen of standing, at this time, we have the report of a conversation between Sir John Bramston of Skreens and Henry Mildmay, son of Sir Henry of Graces. In the course of a lawsuit over the responsibility for repairing the bridge at Chelmsford, Henry Mildmay referred disrespectfully to the rector, alleging that he owed money. In doing so he called him Michaelson. 'Michaelson?' asked Sir John, 'What Michaelson?'

'Dr. Michaelson,' said Mildmay.

'Why cannot you give him his title—doctor?' rejoined Sir John.

'What is that?' retorted Mildmay. 'A feather in his cap?'

'By your leave,' said Sir John with dignity, 'the title is great and good. I do not know but it is as good as colonel, at least an apocryphal colonel.'

Mildmay, cut by the thrust, threatened revenge. He had been bred a Puritan and was colonel of horse in the Parliamentary army. He was also governor of Cambridge Castle, to which Dr. Michaelson had been carried as a prisoner and where he had been harshly treated Sir John had this in mind.

Mildmay did, in fact, take revenge almost immediately. He informed against Sir John, alleging that he was a papist, who with twenty-five others had taken an oath to advance popery. He alleged further that Sir John enjoyed a pension from 'the Roman Congregation and received a dispensation from the Pope, as he was informed.' In support of this allegation against his neighbour he made use of one Ferdinando de Macedo, who signed a statement implicating Sir John in subversive activity. Subsequently this was found to have been drawn up by Mildmay himself. When the truth was out, Ferdinando fell on his knees before the king in council, in Mildmay's presence, and confessed his guilt, imploring the king to pardon him. He said that he had neither seen nor heard of Sir John until Mildmay drew him into the conspiracy.

These tales of Dr. Michaelson's afflictions come from Walker's *Sufferings of the Clergy* and Sir John Bramston's autobiography. Of the afflictions of another clergyman who reared a cuckoo in his nest, William Drake of Radwinter, we have a detailed record written by himself. Drake was an intelligent Laudian, and the first editor of Lancelot Andrewes's *Private Devotions*. He was educated at Abraham Puller's school at Epping while Jeremy Dyke was vicar, and afterwards at Pembroke Hall, Cambridge, which he entered in 1624. In 1631 he was elected a fellow of his college, and four years later ordained priest by the Bishop of Ely. He came to Radwinter in 1638, and at once set about repairing and improving the church, already dear to us as the place where William Harrison ministered so long. He levelled and repaired the chancel floor, blocked up a doorway, and set up a new screen richly carved with figures of cherubim, which the Puritans of Radwinter swore were images, and accused Drake of worshipping. This screen was broken down in 1640 by soldiers billeted in the neighbourhood, who carried the offending figures to Saffron Walden and burned them in the market-place. Drake, fortunately, was in Cambridge at the time, or he might have suffered personal injury. Two months later, when he preached at the bishop's triennial visitation at Dunmow he had to be given protection. Dr. Harold Smith, in *The Ecclesiastical History of Essex*, gives many pages to Drake, with extracts from his diary, together with a report of his examination by the Grand Committee on Religion in February 1641 and the Plundered Ministers Committee in October 1643. The reports of these examinations are of exceptional value because they include Drake's answers to the charges brought against him.

The diary is full of the petty annoyances endured while ministering to the disaffected and churlish people of Radwinter. The Traps family in particular seem to have taken every opportunity to make themselves offensive:

'21st Feb. 1642. John Traps, a tailor, came insolently into church in time of divine service and with his hat on his head confronted the curate with these words: "Are you at Mass again? I 'll have one to fetch you down presently." He also contemptuously said that those books which Chapman took away were mass-books, and that the bell tolled twice a day to mass.

'March 1. The said Traps did and said again to the same purpose . . .

'March 17. George Traps in service time came up to the reading desk and threw to the curate a base pamphlet (called an Answer of the Roundheads to the Rattleheads), saying, "There is reading work for you, read you that." . . .

'April 8. At the christening of Alice, daughter of Richard Clark, John Traps confronting the curate by coming up close and standing in a daring manner by him, told him that he should not have her out of the godmother's arms, nor sign her with the sign of the cross; and to that end flung the cloth over the face of the child, keeping his hand upon it and saying, "It is the mark of the Beast."'

Others were little better, and we are not surprised to find the comment: 'The insolences were so many that they seemed to tire a greater patience than mortality can attain unto. These are more than enough to show the disposition and temper of Radwinter.'

Durden, the rector's churchwarden, refused to allow him to have bread and wine for monthly communion, which he wished to introduce instead of the established quarterly celebration, and when William Voyle was chosen by the people to be their lecturer, Drake's position became intolerable. On Palm Sunday, 1643, Voyle, who was afterwards lecturer in Hereford, said that Palm Sunday and Easter Day were and had been two most bloody days in England in regard of many souls damned by unworthy receiving. This was the kind of language those of the now fanatically reformed religion in England liked, and in consequence not ten people were present to receive communion on Easter Day in Radwinter church. That very same afternoon Voyle actually gave public thanks to God for blessing his pains in keeping the people from profaning the Lord's Table.

On 15th January 1643 matters came to a head, and

* H

here we must take a report attested by witnesses of what happened:

'William Voyle, pretending authority to be the lecturer of the aforesaid parish, whence or how we know not, coming into the church in the time of divine service with a great cudgel in his hand, came directly to the reading desk where the aforesaid Richard Drake was performing his duty; and in a violent manner pulled open the door, crowded in, laid both his hands upon the said Richard Drake, endeavouring to thrust him out of the desk. Richard Drake thereupon labouring to go into the pulpit to preach, was violently pulled down by the said William Voyle. But the said Richard Drake, recovering himself and taking hold with both hands on the pulpit door and rail, was again pulled down by the said William Voyle, John Smith, Richard Smith, Matthew Spicer, and Stephen Sellon, and thrown down in the desk, and from thence haled on his back on the church floor, and getting on his legs again was punched on his back, tugged by his gown, and violently thrust out of the church by Matthew Spicer, Richard Smith, and John Hawkins, a stranger.' Six people signed this statement, one of them the parish clerk. Three people swore that they heard Augustine Hawkins of Sampford Magna say: 'Let us have him out of the church and knock out his brains.' And if others in the congregation had not protected the poor man they might easily have done so.

Drake could bear no more. He left the parish. But that also was an offence. These unreasonable people thereupon accused him of deserting his cure and got an order of sequestration against him. He was restored to his living in 1660 and stayed seven years. When he died in 1681 he was chancellor of Salisbury and was buried in the cathedral.

Another clerical diarist of the day, Ralph Josselin, was vicar of Earls Colne from 1640 to 1683. He was an Essex man, born at Writtle of good yeoman stock, and throughout his life a Puritan. He was by no means the scholar that Drake was, and his diary is less concerned than Drake's with theology and the troubles that sprang from that harassing science. As his principal parishioner, Colonel Harlackenden, was on the Parliament side and a man of influence, Josselin got through these troubled times more comfortably than most. In 1645 we find him attending the colonel's regiment as chaplain, and the following year, the colonel being sheriff, he preached the assize sermon. Alas, there are one or two sadly revealing entries. On Christmas Day, 1647, he noted that 'People hanker after sports and pastimes which they were wonted to enjoy,' and at Easter, 1665, he noted that there had been an administration of the Lord's Supper, the first for twenty-two or twenty-three years.

Josselin's reflection for Christmas Day, 1647, reminds us of that forthright Royalist, Dr. William Osbaldston, parson of Great Parndon. Of all this Puritan preaching he said that 'it was never a merry world since there was so much of it . . . and that once hearing of common prayer is better than ten sermons.' He went even further and said of one of his Puritan parishioners that he 'stanke of two sermons a day.' Dr. Osbaldston was, as we should expect, ejected from his living. Why, he even encouraged games after service on Sundays, and in a prayer for a sick child of two years old said that 'actual sin it had committed none, and as for original it was washed away at baptism.'

Man is by nature a contentious beast, and these rival ministers may have got some kind of crude satisfaction from their quarrels; but these disputes and ejections must have been hard on their dependants, especially on their wives, who have so often been impoverished by this pig-headed masculine addiction to principles and theories, which normally count for little with women. But there is the inspiring story of Mrs. Wiborow of Pebmarsh, a most courageous creature. On 10th June 1643, after her husband had been ejected by the Puritans, a rebellious crowd hammered on the parsonage door demanding to be admitted. Mistress Wiborow secured the doors and windows as best she could and retired with her children to an upper room reached through a trap-door. In time the rebels broke through the boards and climbed up after her. Three of them took out pistols and threatened to shoot her if she refused to leave the house and allow the new minister to move in. Mistress Wiborow said she would rather die indoors than out, but entreated them to leave part of the house in her possession, as a shelter for herself and her poor family. Her entreaties were useless. She and her children were thrust into the yard, where she found the sequestrators looking on. She implored them for a habitation of some kind to be provided; but the only answer she got was that she could have a dung cart to carry her from constable to constable till she found her husband.

The most popular preacher of the seventeenth century in Essex was John Rogers of Dedham, who held enormous congregations spellbound by his dramatic descriptions of the wrath and love of God, as he conceived them. He stirred his hearers to such a pitch of excitement that they sobbed out their repentance in public and implored forgiveness. To any sane and healthy man to-day the scene in the great church at Dedham with Rogers in the pulpit would be revolting, but in those days even a man like Ralph Brownrig, afterwards Bishop of Exeter, could say: 'John Rogers will do more good with his wild notes than we shall with our set music.' Dr. Thomas Goodwin, afterwards president of Magdalen College, Oxford, while a student at Cambridge heard so much about Rogers that he rode over to Dedham on purpose to hear him. Happily he remained sufficiently in possession of his senses to record not only the gist of the sermon, but also the absurd tricks used by Rogers to ensnare his victims. On this occasion these included a ridiculous dialogue purporting to be between a penitent sinner and an offended God. Though Goodwin kept his head, his nerves were so strained that when at last he got out of the bedlam and was preparing to mount his horse and ride away he broke down, and for fifteen minutes hung on the animal's neck weeping, before he could pull himself together.

It is a relief to turn from the passionate and incoherent Rogers to the calm and tolerant Joseph Hall, who for many years was incumbent of Waltham Abbey. On the second Sunday in Lent, 1641, Hall, at this time Bishop of Exeter, preached before Charles at Whitehall on 'The Mischief of Faction and the Remedy of it.' He lamented the divisions in the Church: '"This man is right," ye say, "that man is not right: this sound; that rotten." And how so, dear Christians? What! for ceremonies and circumstances, for rochets, or rounds, or squares? Let me tell you, he is right, that hath a right heart to his God, what forms soever he is for. The Kingdom of God does not stand in meats, and drinks; in stuffs, or colours, or fashions; in noises, or gestures: it stands in holiness and righteousness; in godliness and charity; in peace and obedience: and if we have happily attained unto these, God doth not stand upon trifles and niceties of indifferences; and why should we?'

It was too late for such counsels. It had already been too late in the January of that same year, when Hall published his *Humble Remonstrance*, a defence of Episcopacy and the liturgy, for in the last month of the previous year Laud had been arrested and sent to the Tower. In March 1641 the Puritan answer to Hall appeared, signed Smectymnuus, a name as knotty as its logic. The satirist Cleveland on seeing it exclaimed:

> Smectymnuus! The goblin makes me start,
> I' the name of Rabbi Abraham, what art?

The Puritans bestowed on each other some odd names, but this is surely the oddest. It is not, however, as senseless as it appears. It is merely a Puritan conundrum. The solution is to be found in the initials of the authors, two of whom were Stephen Marshall, whose acquaintance we have already made, and Edmund Calamy, minister of Moreton, near Ongar, who caught a quartan ague in Essex, which so affected his head that he could never bring himself to preach from a pulpit and used the reading desk instead. He was evidently more conscious than most of his brethren of the lamentable effect the pulpit had on men of his calling! The third part-author was Thomas Young, minister of Stowmarket in Suffolk, and Milton's old tutor. He is pleasantly remembered in connection with a mulberry-tree planted in the vicarage garden at Stowmarket by Milton on one of his visits there. The fourth part-author was Matthew Newcomen, who succeeded Rogers at Dedham, and seems to have been a sensible, scholarly man; and the fifth and last of this contentious quintet was William Spurstow of Hampden in Buckinghamshire. On discovering the answer to his question, Cleveland continued:

> Next Sturbridge fair is Smec's, for lo! his side
> Into a five-fold Lazar's multiplied:
> Under each arm there's tucked a double gizzard;
> Five faces lurk under a single vizard.

There is a reason for so many of the best Essex livings being held by distinguished Puritans at this time. A large proportion of them were in the gift of the Earl of Warwick, who is the figure behind the scenes in Essex Puritanism as in so many other branches of Essex life. In the Rochford hundred alone he was patron of Hadleigh, Leigh, Ashingdon, South Shoebury, Prittlewell, Rochford, Foulness, Hawkwell, Southchurch, Shopland, and perhaps others. In the centre of the county, where he lived, he held most of the livings, in particular the influential one of Bocking. But in nothing did he make his influence in the religious sphere more lasting than in his patronage of Felsted School, founded by the first Lord Rich in 1564. When the headship became vacant in 1627 the earl invited John Preston, of Queens' College, Cambridge, the most eminent Puritan of the day, to nominate a successor, and he named Martin Holbeach, who was appointed and remained for twenty-two years. Under his headship Felsted became the most renowned Puritan school in England, especially when Cromwell sent his own boys to it. Many of the boys educated at Felsted became Puritan ministers themselves and slipped into Essex livings, so that by the middle of the century Essex was overrun by these Puritan ministers, who were, in effect, so many political agents for the Earl of Warwick.

In 1649 Holbeach left Felsted to become vicar of High Easter, but his influence continued. He acted as ordaining presbyter and as one of the commissioners for the removal of scandalous and inefficient ministers. Throughout the Cromwellian period he was regarded as 'a very godly and learned divine,' but these estimable qualities were subjected to political reconsideration at the Restoration and they proved to be of no avail to the Rev. Mr. Holbeach. He was ejected under the Act of Uniformity and retired to Dunmow, where he lived quietly until his death in 1670.

The Puritans got their own way practically everywhere in Essex during the Cromwellian period. There was one courageous lady, however, who defied them. She was the dowager Lady Maynard, widow of the first Lord Maynard and the noble and gracious lady who used that expressive word 'curdled' in describing the effect of the barbarous soldiers on the liquid circulating in her husband's veins.[1] Lady Maynard had the gift of the Thaxted living, and in 1647 tried to exercise her right. The previous vicar, Newman Leader, had been sequestrated and one of the usual 'godly learned ministers' set up in his stead. While away from his living, Leader died, and the valiant Lady Maynard, considering the living now vacant in spite of the usurper in possession, forthwith announced her intention to nominate a successor. The committee respectfully begged her to consider the claims of the present occupant, but she scorned all things Puritanical and nominated Edward Croxon. Certain people who described themselves as 'well affected parishioners' of Thaxted objected that Mr. Croxon was 'a soul-starving pastor' whom 'the whole country could not parallel . . . for swearing, cursing, drunkennesse,' and the various other indecencies that it takes a Puritan to think of. The committee again acted, and Mr. Croxon was declared a sequestrated minister. The stout-hearted lady thereupon proceeded to nominate another vicar, the first not having been instituted. Again the 'well affected' protested, but the committee gave way to the lady, and the Rev. Samuel Hall was nominated. But when this gentleman's record was examined it was found that he had preached 'a malignant sermon in Cambridge against the

1 See p. 32.

Parliament,' and he was then sent back to Lady Maynard
with a note that he was 'found unfit.' But still Lady Maynard and her obedient Mr. Hall were undaunted, and Hall
actually submitted himself five times to the examiners for
trial, until these divines lost their patience and declared him
'discharged from inter-meddling with Thaxted any more.'

But that was not the end. Mr. Hall, supported by Lady
Maynard, next addressed himself to the House of Lords, who
looked favourably on his case and ordered yet another
examination. This had the same result as the previous five.
The Lords then requested the examiners 'to make good their
charges,' and a committee of them, with Stephen Marshall as
spokesman, attended at the bar of the House of Lords, where
they gave their reasons for rejecting Mr. Hall, and flatly
refused to reconsider them. The Lords found this unsatisfactory and appointed a new committee to consider the case of
Mr. Hall. This was in June 1647, just before both Houses
broke up. When they reassembled in July they were without
their Speakers. Fairfax's army was marching upon London,
and the Speakers were with it. Hall seized his opportunity.
In the general confusion he obtained an order from the House
of Lords for 'institution and induction' to the living of
Thaxted. Alas, Lady Maynard did not live to see it. She
died two days after the order was made.

Still Mr. Hall was not at the end of his troubles. When
the Houses reassembled with their Speakers they passed a
measure rendering all ordinances carried in their absence null
and void. Hall was again shut out; but he determined to try
to gain admittance on the strength of the order he had. With
the mayor, Mr. Nightingale, and the town clerk, Mr. Jebb, he
presented himself at the door of the church the following
Sunday morning, and succeeded in gaining possession of the
pulpit. He officiated all that day. But again the 'well
affected' appealed to the House of Lords, and Samuel Hall
was ordered to vacate the living, while the town clerk was
sent to the Fleet for using contemptuous words.

The Rev. Samuel Hall preached for the last time in the
pulpit to which he so ardently aspired on 24th September.

In the morning the 'well affected' stepped forward and asked
for his authority. He said it was not for them to question it
and began the service. In the afternoon, however, they were
in church before him and took possession of the pulpit. Hall
was now obliged to ask for their authority. The mayor came
to the support of the vicar, but the 'well affected' were
kings of the castle. Then the churchwardens, Christopher
Tanner and Edward Muntford, told them that if they did not
come out they would be pulled out. Presently passions were
roused and the nave of the church became the scene of a disgraceful fight, led, it is amusing to note, by the women of
the congregation. The men do not appear to have done more
than shout them forward. Indeed, when some of the men
seemed inclined to interfere, the mayor from his pew called
out: 'Let them alone; let the women settle the case.' The
Royalist dowager was not the only Amazon in Thaxted, and
as usual the women won.

## CHAPTER XV

# WHEN BAN-DOGS HOWL

The time when screech-owls cry, and ban-dogs howl,
And spirits walk, and ghosts break up their graves.
SHAKESPEARE.—2 *Henry VI*.

THE alleged connection between Puritanism and witchcraft in the sixteenth and seventeenth centuries may be debatable for the country as a whole. We cannot doubt that they were connected in Essex. The blackest page in the story of the Essex witch hunt has upon it the signature of the Earl of Warwick, who on 29th July 1645, after listening to a sermon by one of his Puritan preachers, proceeded to the trial at Chelmsford assizes of twenty-nine women charged with this crime, and in the faith and fear of his narrow creed condemned nineteen of them to death. They had been caught in the trap by Matthew Hopkins, the Manningtree lawyer who called himself the Witchfinder General. Hopkins was the son of a Suffolk minister. Both the man who caught and the man who condemned were fired by Puritan fervour, and as in the last chapter we had to turn to honest English gentlemen for sanity and tolerance in judging the ejected ministers, in this we have to turn to them for a just verdict on these women accused of being witches. Professor Trevelyan, in *English Social History* (pp. 258–9), says: 'it was lucky for the witches that England was still aristocratically governed. In many rural parts the populace, if it had not been restrained by the gentry, would have continued to drown or burn witches down to the nineteenth century.'

In view of this, it is sad to reflect that our noble earl should have allowed himself to be influenced by brooding parsons until he was incapable of sifting the evidence of such a scoundrel as Hopkins. Arthur Wilson, his steward, a scholar and a gentleman, sat in court throughout the trial, weighing the evidence in his quiet mind, untroubled by the zeal that had clouded the mind of his master, and after his death it was found that he had left a record of the trial.

'About this time in Essex,' he had written, 'there being a great many arraigned, I was at Chelmsford at the trial and execution of eighteen women. But could see nothing in the evidence which did persuade me to think them other than poor, melancholy, envious, mischievous, ill-disposed, ill-dieted, atrabilious constitutions, whose fancies working by gross fumes and vapours, might make the imagination ready to take any impression, and they themselves by the strength of fancy, may think they bring such things to pass which many times, unhappily they wish for and rejoice in when done, out of the malevolent humour which is in them: which passes with them as if they had really acted it. And if there be an opinion in the people that such a body is a witch, their own fears (coming where they are) resulting from such dreadful apprehensions, do make every shadow an apparition; and every rat or cat an imp or spirit, which make so many tales and stories in the world, which have no shadow of truth.'

Such sanity is refreshing, for the abnormal and sensational character of witchcraft so often seems to have acted like a drug on those who wrote about it. We may say, perhaps, that it affected seventeenth-century writers much as spiritualism affects modern writers. Facts are grossly distorted. In Robert Steele's *Social England*, edited by H. D. Traill in 1903, the number of witches hanged in the reign of James I is given as seventy thousand. We do not know the correct figure; but unless the unknown is far greater than the known, which is unlikely, the number must have been considerably less than one thousand. Then there are the lurid descriptions of witches being burned to death, as indeed they were; but not for witchcraft. Mother Jourdain of Eye and Mother Lakeland of Ipswich were burned to death, but for treason not witchcraft. Mother Lakeland was alleged to have murdered her husband, which was held to be petty treason, a crime punishable by death at the stake. In every case where a witch has been burned to death the nature of the charge will be found to be such as to involve heresy, poisoning, or treason.

An examination of court proceedings will show that most of the accused not only escaped the death penalty, but suffered only light punishment. In C. L'Estrange Ewen's *Witch Hunting and Witch Trials*,[1] a valuable book on the subject, the indictments for witchcraft found in the records of 1,373 assizes held for the Home Circuit between 1559 and 1736 are examined. These show that out of 513 persons indicted in that long period only 112 were hanged. This list could not be made complete, but it represents 77 per cent of the whole, and there is no reason to suspect that the remaining 23 per cent had a greater proportion of either hangings or convictions. Almost certainly it had less.

But it is disconcerting to find that Essex provided far more indictments and hangings than all the other counties in the Home Circuit put together. Sussex had only seventeen persons indicted, and of these only one was hanged. Surrey hanged only five out of fifty-four. Essex, alas, had 473 indictments relating to 299 persons, and hanged eighty-two of those accused. They were all put to death between 1558 and 1648. After a bad outbreak of witch hunting in Elizabeth's reign, the county seems to have developed a more or less rational attitude towards the end of the sixteenth century, and to have maintained it until the disgraceful trial presided over by the earl in 1645. We can even claim a few cases of quite creditable leniency. At the Lent Sessions held at Chelmsford in 1592, Agnes Hales of Stebbing, a spinster, was accused of having bewitched Elizabeth Pyper on 23rd February, and Mabel Scott three and a half years earlier. Both had languished for a few days after the alleged bewitching and had then died. Agnes was found not guilty of felony and murder, but guilty of witchcraft and sentenced to one year's imprisonment. A typical presentment may be useful. It comes from the record of sessions held at Chelmsford on 5th May 1614:

'Alice Battie of Toppesfield, widow, not having God before

[1] Kegan Paul, 1929.

her own eyes, but being a common enchantress and witch, seduced by an evil spirit, 17 Sept., with malice aforethought exercised certain evil and devilish arts called "witchcraftes inchantments charmes and sorceries" upon Thomas Perrie aged 3 years, son of John Perrie of Toppesfield, by reason whereof the said Thomas languished from 17 Sept. to 3 Oct., on which day he died.' She was 'transmitted to the Assizes and there she was acquitted.'

In 1598 Robert Browning of Aldham in Essex, a labourer, was charged with defrauding the king's subjects by 'persuading them that by conjuration and invocation of evil spirits they might discover hidden hoards of gold and silver, and regain lost goods.' It was a capital crime, yet he was merely sentenced to the pillory.

This pretence of being able to detect a thief was not uncommon, and these reputed wizards, or 'cunning men' as they were sometimes called, probably supplemented their incomes quite considerably from the practice, just as fortune-tellers do still. Literature has many instances of this. John Aubrey gives accounts of the practice under Thomas Allen and John Dee in his *Brief Lives*. Perhaps the best known instance is that in the thirteenth chapter of Scott's *Waverley*. In Loughton we have the case of John Munday, who was charged by the churchwardens of going 'to a connyng man to learne of goods that were stolen or gon.' He was charged with his offence at a court of the Archdeacon of Essex held in Romford chapel, 3rd February 1592.

One of the difficulties in compiling statistics about witchcraft is that they came before so many different courts. The cases that came before the assizes have just been cited, but as witchcraft was against the canon law, cases were constantly brought before ecclesiastical courts as well. There are many of them to be found in the proceedings of the courts of the archdeaconry of Essex. Two widows of Woodford, Widow May and Widow Coppres, came before a court held in West Ham church on 12th July 1591. And before we turn to the popular ideas about the trials of witches it is worth recording that it was not infrequent for an accused person to be discharged simply by producing written testimony of good character. Here are two cases from consecutive days:

2nd May, 1592, in a court of the Archdeacon of Essex, held in Romford chapel, Alice, wife of William Foster of Barking, suspected by common fame to be a witch, brought a certificate of her innocency under the hands of the church-wardens there. The case was dismissed, but the accused had to pay the court fee (12d.) and the apparitor's fee (4d.), as well as the expenses of the journey to Romford.

3rd May, 1592, in a court of the Archdeacon of Essex, held in Ingatestone church, it was reported that one Whaple of Fobbing did make complaint against Joan Bell, of Fobbing, of suspicion of witchcraft. She appeared in court, and 'utterly denieth' the suspicion to be true. She was ordered to bring to a later court a certificate from four of her honest neighbours that she was reputed to be an honest woman and not at all thought to be a witch. On 2nd June she brought this reassurance and was acquitted.

Another method by which women suspected of witchcraft cleared themselves was called compurgation. It began by an announcement in church that at a court to be held at a given place and date the person accused intended to take an oath of innocence. Those who objected to this purgation were requested to attend the court and give evidence. The procedure was similar to that of publishing banns of marriage. When the court assembled the accused, supported by her compurgatrices, took the required oaths and received a certificate of acquittal. Here is a report of such a case:

'5th May, 1592. In a Court of the Archdeacon of Essex, held in All Saints Church, Maldon, Margaret Wiseman (wife of John Wiseman of Maldon) was presented by the church-wardens, for that she is suspected by common fame of witch-craft. She claimed and was allowed purgation.

'5th July, 1592, she appeared in Court with her compurga-trices (Judith wife of John Cowrtnol, Margaret wife of Thomas Carter, Agnes wife of George Warner, Agnes wife of Robert Brierly, Agnes wife of Richard Flude, and Elizabeth wife of John Pratt—all of Maldon). Margaret Wiseman then took oath that she is "altogether guiltless of the fact of witchcraft and also of all occasion of suspicion of witchcraft." Her six compurgatrices then took oath that Margaret Wiseman hath sworn a just and true oath, and that she "hath not given any cause of suspicion of witchcraft." Her purgation was then admitted, and the testimonial of its acceptance was signed; but the Judge of the Court solemnly admonished her to be most careful in future to give no cause, in any way, for like suspicion.'

John Wiseman probably belonged to the famous Roman Catholic family of that name, and it is more than likely that Margaret's religion had brought her under suspicion.

These three cases of witchcraft, it will be seen, all came from different parts of the county within four days. There can be no doubt that the charge was extremely common, and it says much for those who tried the persons suspected, whether clerics or justices, that they treated them with such clemency. Matthew Hopkins, however, soon altered the averages,

> Fully empowered to treat about
> Finding revolted witches out.

In 1644 Hopkins visited every town and village in the east of the county, and if any woman was suspected by her neighbours of being a witch he could be relied upon by hook or by crook to extract a confession of guilt from her. Of the thirty-three accused brought before the Earl of Warwick in July 1645, twenty-nine came from the Tendring hundred, in which Hopkins's own town of Manningtree stood. Of the nature of his 'call' to this evil ministry we get an account in his book, *The Discovery of Witches*, which is something of an apologia. He says that in March 1644 he discovered that there were 'some seven or eight of that horrible sect of witches living . . . in Manningtree, with diverse other adjacent witches of other towns, who every six weeks in the night (being always on the Friday night) had their meeting close to his house, and had their several solemn sacrifices there offered to the Devil.'

Elizabeth Clarke of Manningtree, the first in the list of

those hanged after the 1645 trial, was alleged to have confessed that the devil visited her dressed like 'a proper gentleman with a laced band.' She was supposed to have four
evil spirits to do her bidding, one in the likeness of a white
cat called Holt, another in the likeness of a black rabbit
called Sack-and-Sugar, a third in the likeness of a greyhound
called Vinegar Tom, and the fourth in the likeness of a sandy
spaniel called Jeremiah. She was charged with having
desired of her spirit that a Mr. Edwards should be met at the
middle bridge as he was riding home to Manningtree across
the Stour from East Bergholt, and that his horse should be
startled, thrown down, and killed. Mr. Edwards deposed
that 'his horse started and stumbled at the bridge, but that
he kept his seat, whereupon he heard something about his
horse cry "Ah! Ah!" much like the shriek of a polecat.'

On that evidence Elizabeth Clarke was hanged. It seems
flimsy enough. But what shall we say when we discover how
it was obtained? This woman was kept awake for three
consecutive days and nights and given no peace until on the
fourth night, completely exhausted, she 'confessed' to ten
people then in the room with her that she entertained and
employed familar spirits, and that she had had carnal inter-
course with the Devil.

Rebecca Jones, another of the nineteen, a servant in the
house of John Bishop of Clacton, confessed that she had been
visited by 'a very handsome young man, as she then thought
him; but now she thinks it was the Devil.' He inquired about
her health, she said, and then asked to see her left wrist.
Taking a pin from her sleeve he pricked her wrist twice, and
'there came out a drop of blood, which he took off with his
finger, and so departed.' Three months later she was carrying a basket of butter to St. Osyth when she met a ragged man
who terrified her with his fearsome glaring eyes. He gave
her three black creatures with four legs and no tail, like
moles, and bade her nurse them and feed them with milk.
If she did this, he promised, they would avenge her on her
enemies. These became her imps, which she called Margaret,
Annie, and Susan. She confessed that she had sent one to

kill a sow at Clacton; another with the help of Joyce Bone, also among the nineteen, had been sent to kill Thomas Bumpstead, who had beaten her boy. Three weeks later Thomas died, and then she sent her imp to kill his wife, who also died. That was quite sufficient evidence to hang Rebecca Jones.

Another of the nineteen, Elizabeth Gooding, had tried to get half a pound of cheese on credit from Robert Taylor. When the credit was refused she went away mumbling and muttering to herself, and shortly afterwards Taylor's horse fell sick, Its belly would rumble and make a noise like a chimney on fire. Margaret Moone, or Moore, was alleged to have as many as twelve imps working for her. They killed children, it was said, as well as cattle; they spoiled bread for the baker, and vats of beer for the brewer; they made verminous the houses of clean and decent women. Margaret, on the strength of this idle gossip, was sentenced to death. And so we might go through the entire list.

By 17th July 1645, thirty-three women had been imprisoned pending trial, but between 27th May and 29th July four of them—Rose Hollybread of St. Osyth, aged about sixty-five; Elizabeth Gibson of Thorpe-le-Soken, aged about forty; Joan Cooper of Clacton, aged eighty; and Mary Cooke of Langham, aged sixty—had died 'by the visitation of God.' Shortly before the trial others had been brought in, most of whom were alleged to have employed evil spirits in the form of natural creatures, or 'familiars' as they were called, adopting the word used in 1 Samuel, xxviii. 3: 'And Saul had put away those that had familiar spirits, and the wizards, out of the land.' There was Margery Grew of Walton. She had an evil spirit in the likeness of a bird called a jay. Mary Johnson carried a rat about with her, which she was alleged to have sent through a hole in a door to rock a cradle. She had even been seen to kiss a child and give it an apple. Soon after this it had died, and the kiss and apple were held responsible. The mother of the child had suffered pains, but she had attacked Mary Johnson with her nails and had drawn blood from her. To make a witch bleed and touch the blood was believed to destroy the enchantment. Shakespeare, in *Henry VI*, alludes to this belief. Others had rats, mice, moles, squirrels, and 'kitlings.' Rebecca West of Lawford was actually accused of having an evil spirit in the likeness of a young man called 'her husband.' So when the Earl of Warwick, Sir John Barrington, Sir Martin Lumley, Sir Henry Holcroft, Sir Henry Mildmay, and William Conyers, Esq., had ridden or driven into Chelmsford for that historic trial they had found an alarming array of half-witted women awaiting their pleasure.

Of the nineteen sentenced to be hanged, one, Margaret Moone, died on the way, which accounts for eighteen being given in Arthur Wilson's account as the number hanged. In addition, five men and eight women were sentenced to imprisonment. Six men were acquitted; three men who claimed benefit of clergy were ordered to be branded in the hand; three women were required to 'find good sureties to appeare att the next gaole deliverye & in the meantime to bee of good behaviour.'[1] Nearly three years later four of the women included in the list of those under sentence to be kept in jail until delivered by due course of law, together with one other, were still held according to the jail delivery roll of 1648.

Other charges followed regularly during the next ten years or so, and show how dazed by superstition the common people were. In 1651, Joan Wayte of Great Barnston, the wife of a labourer, was charged with not having God before her eyes at Audley End on 29th August 1650, when she did entertain, employ, and feed an evil spirit called a butterfly. There were six witnesses.

Hopkins never had another year like 1645, during which sixty persons were hanged for witchcraft in Essex and nearly forty at Bury St. Edmunds, besides others in Norfolk and Huntingdonshire. Town after town invited him to come and discover its witches, paying his fee of twenty shillings for a search. Some, it must be said, refused to have him. One of these was Great Staughton, where John Gaule, the parson,

[1] P.R.O. Assizes, 35/86. Essex file.

denounced the self-styled Witchfinder General, and in 1646 published a work entitled *Select Cases of Conscience touching Witches and Witchcraft*, which proved to be a most effective exposure of Hopkins and his friends, and a useful account of their methods. Of the starving and watching process that Hopkins found so successful, Gaule says: 'Having taken the suspected witch, she is placed in the middle of a room upon a stool or table, cross-legged, or in some other uneasy posture, to which if she submits not, she is then bound with cords; there is she watched and kept without meat or sleep for the space of twenty-four hours, for (they say) within that time they shall see her imp come and suck. A little hole is likewise made in the door for the imp to come in at; and lest it should come in some less discernible shape, they that watch are taught to be ever and anon sweeping the room, and if they see any spiders, or flies, to kill them. And if they cannot kill them, then they may be sure they are her imps.'

Witches were alleged to suckle their familiars or imps at teats discovered in different parts of the body. A mere mole or spot of any kind would be sworn to be used for this purpose, and Hopkins actually took his own searcher, a woman named Goody Phillips, about with him. But the chief end of the watching was not to catch the imp but to weary the witch until at last, out of sheer exhaustion, she was ready to admit anything if only she could be left alone and allowed to sleep. This particular method was forbidden by the justices soon after the Chelmsford trial, and Hopkins had to resort to the trial by swimming, which he disliked. He said that though he had practised it, it was 'a trial not allowed by law or conscience,' two subjects on which he considered himself an expert. For this method of discovery, the victim, wearing a single under-garment, was supposed to be thrown into a river or pond with her right thumb tied to her left toe. If she sank she was declared innocent, irrespective of whether she drowned or not; if she floated she was declared a witch and might live to be hanged. In spite of popular belief, the plain truth is that it is very doubtful whether any witch was, in fact, hanged on the strength of this particular evidence, though it was a test that had the approval of James I, who came from the land of witches, and was no mean authority on them. It was a method employed by the village folk themselves rather than one used officially. One might almost say that it was a village sport more than anything else.

In the diary of John Bufton of Coggeshall[1] there is a case of this trial by water:

'July 13, 1699. The widow Comon was put into the river to see if she would sink, because she was suspected to be a witch—and she did not sink, but swim.

'And she was tried again on July 19th, and then she swam again, and did not sink.

'July 24, 1699. The widow Comon was tryed a third time by putting her into the river, and she swam and did not sink.

'Dec. 27, 1699. The widow Comon, that was counted a witch, was buried.'

Widow Comon was examined for witchcraft by the rector of the parish, the Rev. James Boys, who wrote a long report of his conversations with her in the summer of 1699. She was old, and had recently lost her husband. Her mind was obviously disordered. When Mr. Boys asked her if she believed in God, she replied that she did; but when he asked if she believed in ' Jesus, the Son of the Living God,' she replied that she did not know him. Did she know the Devil? asked Mr. Boys. She did: he had big goggle eyes and very rough hands, and had gone away because he knew the minister was coming. This reply gave great satisfaction to the reverend gentleman. His own words are: 'Whereupon I informed the standers by that it was worth their observation that if this woman spake advisedly the Devil was forced to shun the presence of a servant of Jesus upon his own confession.'

When Mr. Boys asked if she was baptized, she said she was and gave her Christian name. But when he told her that this meant there was a covenant between God and her soul she only looked confused. When he asked if she had been guilty of making another covenant with the Devil, she said that butter was eightpence a pound and cheese a groat. Mr.

Boys was determined to have his answer, and repeated the question over and over again until at last she agreed that she had sold her soul to the Devil and must go to hell. There was no help for it. She was reminded of what God had done for her, creating and preserving her. 'Ay,' said she, 'above sixty years.'

There seemed little harm in this. But later she became talkative and confessed that she had struck Mr. Cox on the knee and made him lame. She had made a hen in wax and stuck pins in it, and had afterwards hidden it in Bundock's Croft. When asked to produce the hen she said again that butter was eightpence a pound and cheese a groat, and when asked to pray, confessing her sins and pleading for pardon, she babbled about pretty women. It was all very sad for a minister of the Gospel, and after evensong he returned to her. This time he found her eye very sharp and her pulse uneven, and decided that she needed sleep. So he prayed for her, and gave her relations instructions to get a sleeping draught from Mr. White the apothecary. The next day she seemed better, and surmised that she had talked a lot of nonsense the previous day, 'and said abundance of things which were not true.' Mr. Cox was present on this occasion, and poor old Widow Comon was reminded of what she had said about making him lame. She denied everything. As for the hen, her husband had killed a hen belonging to her neighbour Pemberton once, and she suggested that very likely that was what she had been thinking of. Again she was tried with the Lord's Prayer, which no witch, it was believed, could ever repeat in full; and again she broke down over it at the point where forgiveness is asked. Then to the amazement of every one in the room she said of her own accord: 'O Lord God Almighty have mercy upon my soul. Create in me a clean heart and renew a right spirit, that I may speak no evil and do no evil actions; but may live in Thy fear and keep Thy commandments all my life in Jesus Christ.' This should have satisfied the parson, but he was still worried about the hen, and asked for it to be sent to him next morning.

Mr. Boys, to give him his due, was half inclined to be her friend; but three Coggeshall gossips sat up with her all night, and afterwards reported that she had got very hot and had confessed that she was suckling her imps. She denied this to Mr. Boys. The house was packed with townspeople for this examination, as it had probably been for the others. The whole affair is horrible.

The examination of Widow Comon, we see, follows the usual lines, and the examiners found exactly what they wanted to find. The practice of making images in wax and melting them was a favourite method of destroying enemies. Shakespeare mentions it in *Henry IV*, and James I says: 'The Devil teacheth how to make pictures of wax or clay that by roasting thereof, the persons that they bear the name of, may be continually melted, or dried away, by continual sickness.' It is also to be observed that before Mr. Cox would be satisfied that Widow Comon had no power over him he insisted on having a drop of her blood. Perhaps this poor old woman caught a chill in one of the swimmings and died in consequence. She was obviously ill when first examined. Such stories make sad reading, and Essex had no occasion for pride in its record. 'It is setting a high value on our conjectures,' said Montaigne, 'to roast a man alive on account of them.' The 29th of July 1645 was a black day in Essex history; but it had one bright moment. Five Essex magistrates at once petitioned the House of Lords to pardon the prisoners convicted, because, they said, they were 'not fully satisfied with the evidence given.'

## CHAPTER XVI

## PARLIAMENT AND PEOPLE

Treason doth never prosper: what's the reason?
Why, if it prosper, none dare call it treason.
                                        SIR JOHN HARINGTON.

No one could doubt which side Essex would take when war came in 1642. Anger against the king had been roused first in 1626, when the people were horrified to find two such loyal landowners as Sir Francis Barrington and Sir William Masham committed to prison. They had not been alone in resisting the demands of the council, which at the king's behest had tried to levy a forced loan, or in being punished for their resistance. Thirteen poorer men in the county who refused to pay money on such terms were pressed as sailors at Portsmouth. The following February martial law was declared and fifty Essex objectors were ordered to enter the service of the King of Denmark. On refusing press money they came near to being hanged. When this loan failed, Essex men remembered with pride the part they had taken in defending their rights as a free people. The forced loan was the first trial between a hard-pressed king and a spirited people, and as the reign continued it became increasingly clear how greatly its failure had strengthened the champions of democracy. When the next Parliament of Charles I was elected in March 1628 the men who had been imprisoned for their stand were returned with large majorities everywhere.

Then there was trouble with ship money. In 1634 the people of Colchester made it clear that they were paying their share—£6,615—under protest. In the following year they refused to pay anything at first, and later grudgingly paid part only. In 1640, immediately after the dismissal of the Short Parliament, the sheriff of Essex was called upon to explain why he had collected so little ship money in the county, and Samuel Sherman of Dedham, with two others, to explain why they had refused to attempt to collect the tax in their own respective parishes. Sherman was imprisoned for three weeks in the Fleet, and on returning home found that some of his household silver had been taken to settle his personal account.

But while the differences between king and people touched only the pocket, peace continued; it was when the Puritans brought the differences round to the Prayer Book that a fight to the death became certain, and Essex was well prepared for this. So in 1641 Sir John Bramston of Skreens and Mr. Grimston, afterwards the redoubtable Sir Harbottle, looked grave as they sat on the bench at Chelmsford hearing the case of soldiers who had broken into the church at Kelvedon, torn down and burnt the rails in front of the altar, and carried away the surplice and some of the church plate. They saw in the case an indication of the coming clash. Mr. Grimston had in fact just returned from a visit to the North of England with Sir John Barrington. They had gone with other worthy gentlemen to present a petition to the king begging him to recall Parliament. After their failure events were bound to move quickly to a crisis. The nation, it was all too clear, had made up its mind to

> Decide all controversy by
> Infallible artillery,
> And prove their doctrine orthodox
> By apostolic blows and knocks.
>
> *Hudibras.*

Much damage was done in Essex before the outbreak of civil war by troops raised by Charles to enforce episcopacy upon the Scots. These were billeted in the county and had no stomach for the northward journey. The pressed men of Essex, who were to be carried to Scotland by ship, refused to go on board. Lord Maynard, the Royalist lord lieutenant of the county, reported in July 1640 that 'the insolencies of the soldiers billeted in Essex are every day increased by new attempts, insomuch as they have now within these few

Felsted School

The Essex Procession from Chelmsford to St. J—s's Market, for the good of the Common Veal

days taken upon them to reform churches; and even in the time of divine service to pull down the rails about the communion tables, and in Icklinton, in Cambridgeshire, to force the minister to run over the river, and the minister of Panfield near Braintree to forsake his charge and family to save his life.' On the same day the Earl of Warwick, as leader of the opposite party, wrote: 'The soldiers have been reasonably quiet till this last occasion, caused by a barrel of beer and fifty shillings money sent them by Dr. Barkham, parson of Bocking, of whose kindness it seems they took too much, for I found them much disordered by drink that day, and in that distemper they went to his church and pulled up the rails about the Communion Table in the Chancel, and brought them before their captain's Lodging and there burnt them; the like they did in another town near. The ringleaders I have sent to the House of Correction at Chelmsford.' [1]

A third account of the same day's escapade comes from Dr. Robert Aylett, the writer of religious verse, a godly and learned man who was the commissary of the Bishop of London and judge of the commissary court. He lived at Feeringbury, a house that belonged for hundreds of years to successive bishops of London. Tudor arms are still to be seen in its windows. Dr. Aylett wrote that the troops billeted in the Braintree district were given permission to ring the church bells, and that afterwards these tipsy soldiers reeled up to the rails and agreed that it was not fitting that the communion table should be 'impounded,' so they tore them down and set them on fire. Laud added his testimony,[2] which makes four reports by eminent men of this escapade of a few drunken soldiers. We get some idea from that how seriously the matter was regarded. The people of Braintree, we may be sure, would be on the side of the soldiers here, just as they were in the similar escapade at Radwinter.

Small disturbances occured in various parts of the county during the next two years, until in June 1642 the sheriff, who had received a royal proclamation forbidding the trained

---

[1] *State Papers, Domestic*, 461, 24.
[2] Ninth Report Hist. MSS. Comm., ii. 342.

I

bands in the county to muster for exercise, received also a
'Petition and Resolution of the Captains of Hundreds and
other inhabitants of the County of Essex,' which declared:

'Thus, with our hands upon our swords, we stand ready at
your command to perform our vows to God and oaths of
fidelity to His Majesty, in taking up arms against these false
flatterers and traitors who abuse his Royal favour, intending
under the glorious title of his name and standard to fight
against the peace and honour of their Sovereign, against
religion and the laws, and to make a prey and spoil of three
flourishing kingdoms at once; and so spend our dearest
blood in the defence of the lives and liberties of our country-
men; the laws which are the life of our liberty and peace,
religion more precious than both; and the King and Parliament in whose rights lieth bound up the life of all the rest,'[1]
It was signed by ten thousand hands.

Two months later, news reached Colchester that the royal
standard had been raised at Nottingham to the shout of
'God save King Charles and hang up the Roundheads.'
There were few in Essex with any desire to join the king; one,
however, Sir John Lucas of Colchester, had assembled in his
house the small company of Essex cavaliers, numbering about
two hundred, and was ready to march at once. But they
were too late. When Sir John rode out through his back
gate he found the townsfolk lying in wait. An agreed signal
was given, and directly the whole town seemed to have been
raised against him. There were two thousand people, drawn,
it was learned, from Colchester, Coggeshall, Braintree,
Bocking, and Halstead, led by Captain John Langley of the
Colchester trainband, a grocer of the town, and Henry
Barrington, a brewer and alderman, clamouring outside the
house. Sir John and his followers withdrew, but the mob
were not long in forcing an entrance. When inside, the first
person they seized was the Royalist parson of Holy Trinity,
Thomas Newcomen, whom they took prisoner and cast into
the common jail. Sir John Lucas was handed over to the
mayor, who took him to his own house, thinking he would be

[1] Journals of the House of Lords.

safe there.   But the people demanded that he should be given
up to them, shouting that they would have him out if they
had to pull the house down to get him, and the mayor was
obliged to send him to the common jail, the only place
where he could have adequate protection.   By this time the
town was completely out of control, and the mayor dispatched a post to London with an appeal for help in
restoring order.

Each hour brought news of fresh disturbances.   Lady Lucas
and Sir John's sister had been thrown into jail.   His mother,
faint and breathless, had escaped from the street into a shop
for shelter, until again the rabble threatened to pull down
the building if she did not come out.   When the poor old
lady was at last dragged into the street again one of the mob
struck at her with his sword and would have killed her if
a halberd had not crossed the blow.   Meanwhile Sir John
Lucas's house was plundered.   Everthing—furniture, money,
plate, jewels, brass, pewter, household linen, and all that on
the previous day had gone to compose the home of a cultured
gentleman—was carried away and gloated over by the lawless
mob.   Most of the servants were sent to the jail; but one,
John Brown, a loyal old man who had been with the family
since the time of Sir John's grandfather, was tied to a tree, a
musket set to his breast and a sword to his throat, lighted
matches tied to his fingers, while an insolent young puppy
named Furley taunted and questioned him.   What was he
going to get out of his loyalty to his master? he was asked.
Did he expect to ride on a fine horse?   Was he to wear a buff
jerkin and a scarlet coat?

Early in the afternoon a new alarm was raised.   Two
hundred horsemen were alleged to have been discovered in a
vault at Sir John Lucas's.   These were said to have killed
nine men and to be planning to destroy the town.   All the
shops were shuttered and the rabble again set out to wreak
their fury upon these reported Cavaliers.   The mayor tried
to pacify them, but, as he sadly confessed in the letter he
dispatched by post to Parliament, he 'could do no more than
a child among them.'   They found the house deserted, and

as there was now nothing inside for them to steal they spent their rage on breaking windows, battering down doors, pulling up the palings of the park, killing deer and driving away cattle, until nothing seemed left for them to violate and destroy. But their passion had not yet spent itself, and as the day wore on the last gruesome act was conceived. 'To St. Giles!' yelled the ghoulish leader, and his drunken followers broke into the family vault of the Lucases in St. Giles's Church and violated the coffins of the dead.

When Parliament, on 26th August 1642, received news of the affair, Sir Thomas Barrington and Sir Harbottle Grimston, the member and recorder for Colchester, were sent down to quell the riot and bring Sir John Lucas back with them. Standing in the market-place in front of the prison door these two stout-hearted gentlemen received reports of what had happened and dealt at once with the offenders of both parties with pacification as their prime objective. They declared Sir John Lucas and his followers guilty of high treason for their intention to assist the king against Parliament and the will of the people, and gave thanks to the people for the good service they had done in obstructing their disloyal neighbours. But they pointed out that it was unlawful for the people to plunder and destroy any man's property as the people of Colchester had done. This criticism was resented. One of their ringleaders produced what he held to be a printed Order of Parliament, which he claimed justified all their actions. Sir Thomas Barrington replied that it was not a true order, and that it had never before been heard of among honest men. Such an order, he said, would render the House odious, and as gently as he could he begged the people to refrain from such conduct in future.

The following day the ladies of the Lucas household were set free, and Sir John and the parson were carried to London. Once more the most violent demonstration was against the parson, who would certainly have suffered injury if he had not been taken away unexpectedly in Sir Thomas Barrington's coach. When he was recognized, the people did not dare to strike or stone him lest in doing so they injured Sir

Thomas, who had won their confidence by his courteous and restrained bearing, and who was, they remembered, the son of Sir Francis, who had given his life in resisting the king.

As the coach that carried Sir Thomas Barrington, Sir Harbottle Grimston, and their prisoners, with the captured horses behind, drove through Chelmsford and Romford, the people came out to cheer and curse. The following Monday the prisoners were tried. Sir John was committed to the Gatehouse, Newcomen to the Fleet. A public proclamation followed, addressed to the whole kingdom, but particularly to the county of Essex. It was ordered to be read in all churches, 'for the better encouragement of good people,' informing the nation of the fate that had befallen the treacherous Sir John and his chaplain. Actually, Newcomen was kept in the Fleet for rather less than a month, and was then discharged, while Sir John was released on bail of forty thousand pounds, and an undertaking not to leave London without permission.

Sir Thomas Barrington's handling of the Colchester mob had shown him to be a fine diplomat; but, after all, he had been able to ride off next day. Much as the mayor may have been relieved by the arrival of Sir Thomas and Sir Harbottle, and much as he may have admired their ability to pacify his unruly townspeople, he must have had misgivings as to what would happen when they left. If he had, they were not ill founded. The rabble, having enriched themselves by plundering the home of one Royalist, now looked round for another. They had got away with the first, why should they not try a second? There was the wealthy Countess Rivers, a well-known Roman Catholic, who besides a town house in Colchester had mansions at St. Osyth and Long Melford in Suffolk. When a call on the countess was suggested it was received with enthusiasm, and away these Essex malcontents went to St. Osyth. The countess, hearing that they were heading in her direction, fled to Long Melford and sent an urgent message to the Earl of Warwick, craving his protection. The earl was at sea. Colonel Rich, who succeeded as third earl, to his father's great distress was on the Royalist side and had gone to join the king; Charles Rich, the second son, who became the fourth earl, was hunting the stag at Rochford. But the doughty Arthur Wilson was at Leighs and loyally took the matter in hand. He set out in the earl's great coach, which was drawn by six horses, and with a few retainers in attendance drove through Braintree and Hedingham as though making for Haverhill. As he passed through Essex towns and villages, from which many of the poor had gone to join the Colchester rebels, he could see that the people were in a dangerous mood; but as he and the coach were known, and the earl's allegiance honoured, he reached the Stour without incident, and turned east to Sudbury. His intention, if accosted, was to say that he was making for Bury St. Edmunds. On reaching Long Melford he intended to pull up and, without rousing suspicion, make a few tactful inquiries—perhaps at the 'Bull'—about the countess's whereabouts, realizing that she might have to flee again before he could reach her.

As the coach entered Sudbury there was not a man to be seen, but by the time it reached the market-place the streets were swarming with people. A few men rushed forward and seized the reins, bringing the horses to a standstill. Wilson got out quietly and asked for the mayor or one of the magistrates. He protested that he had offended nobody and demanded to know why he had been stopped. The people cried out that they knew whose coach they had seized—it was Lady Rivers's. Some even pretended to recognize Wilson as Lord Rivers. He replied that he was steward to the Earl of Warwick, a servant of the Parliament, and that he had letters in his pocket to prove it. At this point the mayor presented himself and was shown the letters, which Wilson had prudently brought with him. The mayor said that he did not know the earl's hand. It might be his or it might not. Wilson feared the townspeople had taken a fancy to his horses, the town having been required to furnish a number for the Parliamentary service. No one seemed willing to believe his story until Mr. Man, the town clerk, whose father was in the earl's service, came up to see what had caused the commotion, and readily assured the mayor that Wilson was speaking the truth. He had often seen him at Leighs when visiting his father. This relieved Wilson of the attentions of the mayor and citizens of Sudbury, and when they had gone he took Mr. Man into his confidence. After some little discussion they decided that it would be foolish to venture into Long Melford with the coach, so they left it at Sudbury, and the two of them, along with Lady Rivers's messenger, then proceeded to Sir Robert Crane's house, Chilton, near Melford, where they learned that Lady Rivers had gone to London.

The Essex rebels, by this time so greatly reinforced that they numbered many thousands, followed to Long Melford, vowing that if they found the countess there they would 'try what flesh she had.' Fortunately, she had escaped in time. But the house was rifled as the others had been, and the deer park despoiled. Her losses at the two houses was valued at a hundred thousand pounds. On 9th September 1642 an 'Order of the Lords and Commons in Parliament' was issued for the finding out and regaining the goods of the Countess Rivers taken from her houses in Essex and Suffolk: and for encouraging her tenants to pay her rents. It read:

*'Die Veneris, 9 September, 1642*

'Upon the Humble Petition of Elizabeth Countess Rivers *Dowager*, who hath been in an unlawful and disorderly manner despoiled of all her Goods, to a very great value, from her Houses at *St. Osyth's* in *Essex*, and *Melford* in the County of *Suffolk*, herself put in fear of her life, and her servants damnified; it is ordered by the Lords and Commons in Parliament, That strict and narrow search shall be made by all Sheriffs, Deputy-Lieutenants, Mayors, Justices of Peace, Customers, Searchers, High-Constables, Petty-Constables, and other His Majesty's Officers, for the Goods of the said Countess *Rivers* so taken away, in all and every place and places, and in such Creeks, Vessels, Waggons, and Carts, as the Servants or Agents of the said Countess, or any other person or persons shall give notice of, as justly to be suspected to harbour the same; and the said Goods, or any

part thereof being found, and appearing to be the Goods of
the said Countess, shall be forthwith redelivered unto her,
her said servants or Agents, who by virtue and authority
of this Order are to be permitted without interruption to
repair to any of the Houses of the said Countess, or any other
place or places, and with the assistance of some of the Officers
aforesaid, to employ themselves in the searching for the said
Goods, and discovery of all places, and persons suspected,
and to give information thereof to all Mayors, Justices of
Peace, and other His Majesty's Officers aforesaid, and to
cause wait to be laid with the Tradesmen in London, and elsewhere, as they shall think fit, for the finding out and making
stay of the said Goods so taken away as aforesaid.   And it
is ordered, that this business be by the Lords and Commons
in an especial manner recommended to the care of *Harbottle
Grimston*, Esquire, Recorder of the Town of *Colchester*, and
other Justices of the Peace of the Counties of *Essex* and
*Suffolk*, for the finding out of the said Goods, and for the
deterring of all persons from committing the like offences
hereafter.   And lastly, the Lords and Commons do likewise
recommend to the said Mr. *Grimston*, and other the Justices
of Peace near adjoining, to give such encouragement to the
Tenants of the said Lady Rivers, for payment of their rents
to her, notwithstanding the discouragement (mentioned in
her petition) by reason of the disorder and spoil aforesaid,
that there be no cause of her Ladyship's further complaint
in that behalf.

'JOHN BROWN.   Clerk Parliamentorum.'

This seems fair enough.   But what, in fact, happened?
One of the plunderers was actually caught in London trying
to sell some of the precious things he had stolen at Long
Melford.   His name was Bowyer, and he was committed to
Newgate for felony.   But here again Parliament showed itself
afraid of taking a strong line with the rebellious people, whose
service they knew they would need.   Bowyer petitioned the
House of Commons, and was not only released but thanked
for his zeal in the people's cause.   Lady Rivers, having lost

her property, and believing her life to be in danger, obtained a pass to go abroad; but when she was about to start a certain Mr. Martin, who became known as the Roundhead Plunder Master General, seized her carriage horses and prevented the journey. The unhappy countess, though at the beginning of the wars an extremely wealthy woman, was obliged to sell such of her Essex estates as had not been seized in order to pay her debts. Yet even after she had done this she was unable to clear herself. After suffering countless humiliations she was arrested for debt, and though she pleaded privilege as a peeress was imprisoned. She died on 9th March in the same year.

Though the county was so strongly Parliamentarian, there were several prominent Royalists to be found besides the Lucases and Lady Rivers. Lord Petre joined the king early. His estates were seized, but as a descendant of Sir William Petre he was much too astute to rest content with the one-third of his rents allowed him by Parliament. In 1647 complaints came before the justices that Lord Petre held private courts at Ingatestone, and made many thousands of pounds by them. At home, Lord Maynard was the Royalist leader.

The Wiseman family, long extinct in Essex, were so prosperous in the seventeenth century that their rentals were said to bring in about seven thousand pounds a year. At the Michaelmas sessions, 1644, several witnesses informed against Ralph Wiseman of Rivenhall. One deposed that Wiseman had said that the Parliament had done Sir Thomas Wiseman grave injustice in branding him a papist and sequestering his estates, and that he hoped the king would come and make them pay for it all. He had further expressed the opinion that there could be no Parliament without the king, and that the present government was made up of 'tradesmen and such kind of fellows.' There were no gentlemen left, he said. Worse still, Wiseman was said to have referred to his excellency the Earl of Essex as 'cuckold, rebel, and traitor.' The earl's wife, it will be remembered, was the Earl of Suffolk's daughter who married Carr and was responsible for the

*I

murder of Overbury. Other Royalists of standing in the county were Sir Thomas Bendysh of Steeple Bumpstead, Sir Henry Audley of Berechurch, Sir John Tyrrell of East Horndon, Sir Dennis Strutt of Little Warley, Sir John Bramston of Skreens, John Aylett of Magdalen Laver, the Maxeys of Bradwell, the Lynnes of Horkesley, the Nevilles of Cressing Temple, Sir Humphrey Mildmay of Danbury, and the Fanshawe family. In 1655 many of the Cavaliers were imprisoned by Cromwell. Among them were Lords Maynard and Petre, both of whom were referred to in verses ascribed to Sir John Denham:

> Lord Petre we wonder what crime he falls under
> Unless it be 'legem pone'?
> He has ended the strife between him and his wife,
> But now the state wants alimonie.

> Since the Whip's in the hand of another command,
> Lord Maynard must have a smart jerk,
> For the love that he bears to the new cavaliers,
> The Presbytery and the Kirk.

But Royalists were not confined to the gently born. There is a reference in the quarter sessions roll for 1644 to an Epping man who would not pay his Parliamentary rates and jeered in church when the ordinances were read out, and one of the brightest documents at the Essex Record Office is the information of Robert White of the parish of Barking, yeoman, taken upon oath the 28th day of June, 1645, before Sir Henry Mildmay, Knight, & William Toppesfield, Esquire, two of His Majesty's justices of the peace for the said county:

'The Informant saith that two Months since or thereabouts going along Fishers street in the town of Barking upon his occasions, Margaret, the wife of Thomas Edwards of the same, fisherman, in a violent and outrageous manner called him roundheaded rogue, and said it was long of such roundheaded rogues as he was that they were brought into such a condition, using many other reviling words whereby a great tumult was raised in the said town insomuch that this

Informant was constrained to take a Marsh fork from a Marshman to defend himself from hurt & violence, which was like to be offered to this Informant by reason of the said uproar and tumult.

'(Signed) WILLIAM TOPPESFEILDE.'[1]

What the royalists lacked in confidence they were obliged to make up in zeal, for it was obvious from the start that numbers would be against them. After the battle of Edge hill on 23rd October 1642 fear spread that the king might march on London. The gentlemen of the county assembled at Chelmsford and resolved to place themselves and twelve thousand men at the service of the Earl of Essex, who was in command of the Parliamentary forces, attaching to their offer a request that the Earl of Warwick should be their general, to which Parliament agreed. The twelve thousand were duly raised, and on 1st November marched into London under the command of the Earl of Warwick, prepared 'to join with his Excellency for the preservation of the peace of the Kingdom, and suppressing of the malignant party, God prosper their designs and good endeavours.'[2]

At the end of that eventful year the seven counties of Huntingdon, Hertford, Cambridge, Lincoln, Norfolk, Suffolk, and Essex, combined to form the Eastern Association, and it was this united front, together with its favourable geographical position, that preserved the county from bloodshed during the first civil war.

[1] Essex Record Office, Q/SBa, 2/57.
[2] *A True Relation*, King's Pamphlets, Brit. Mus. Lib., E126, 16

## CHAPTER XVII

## TO THIS END

The soldier in the assault of famine falls,
And ghosts, not men, are watching at the walls.

AFTER the disturbances at Colchester in August 1642, Essex had no further alarms of any consequence until the autumn of 1643, when a rumour spread quickly that the king had commissioned Sir John and Sir Charles Lucas 'to go into Essex with eight thousand foot, ten troops of horse, and twelve hundred dragoons.' A captured scout was said to have disclosed that the Royalists had been assured that ten thousand Essex men were ready to join them if they came into the county, and that every week new recruits came to the king's standard from Essex with heartening promises of loyal support. One, he said, had come in the guise of a pedlar, with bundles of horse-hair and tobacco on his back. When, in October, the Earl of Warwick was told that the Royalists were already in Huntingdon, and were expected to advance east, he drew up his Essex forces of six thousand foot and nine hundred horse alongside the Suffolk forces of four thousand foot and five hundred horse, and prepared for the defence of Cambridge and the Isle of Ely. When that stage was reached, the people of Essex felt that in a few weeks, if not days they might be fighting for their own homes. But the tide of battle turned and the county again felt secure. Life fell back into its normal course.

Behind this untroubled face, however, there was always the anxiety of not knowing how the struggle would end. There was also the practical problem of finding the money for its continuance. When the original funds provided by voluntary contributions were exhausted a war tax had to be imposed. It was not a light one. In the spring of 1644 the

associated counties agreed to contribute to the war chest
these sums weekly:

|  | £ | s. | d. |
|---|---|---|---|
| Norfolk | 1,875 | 0 | 0 |
| Suffolk | 1,875 | 0 | 0 |
| Essex | 1,687 | 0 | 0 |
| Lincolnshire | 1,218 | 15 | 0 |
| Hertfordshire | 675 | 0 | 0 |
| Cambridgeshire | 562 | 0 | 0 |
| Huntingdonshire | 330 | 0 | 0 |
| The Isle of Ely | 221 | 5 | 0 |

For the whole of that year, according to the Duke of
Manchester's papers in the Public Record Office, Essex contributed £60,664 6s. 10d. The assessments of the various
counties provide some indication of their relative prosperity
at the time, though other factors were taken into account.
Cromwell, with so many Essex connections, looked to the
county from the start for generous financial aid. In 1642 he
wrote to the mayor of Colchester for men and money to be
sent to him at Cambridge. In the following year he made a
similar appeal, but this time added generously: 'Lay not too
much upon the back of a poor gentleman who desires without
much noise to lay down his life and bleed the last drop to serve
the cause and you.'

The cost of clothing alone was far beyond anything thought
of in the first flush of the quarrel. In 1643 the committee
of the Eastern Association complained to Sir Thomas Barrington that the Essex recruits were 'in so naked a posture that
to employ them were to murder them.' They needed clothes
now even more desperately than arms. If these did not come
quickly a mutiny could be expected. It was the same everywhere. Sir Samuel Luke, said to be the original of Butler's
Hudibras, who at the beginning of the war helped to raise
forces in Essex for the Parliament army, wrote from Newport
Pagnell: 'There were two in my Company that had but one
payre of britches betweene them, soe that when one was up
the other must upon necessity be in his bed.' The war was
never popular. Clarendon said truly 'that the number of

those who desired to sit still was greater than of those who desired to engage with either party,' and if it had not been for the fanaticism engendered by the Puritan clergy on the one side and king-worshippers on the other, the men would have been back at their ploughs and benches within a year. But the Puritans and the Cavaliers continued to believe in their causes. As an example of the view-point of a moderate Puritan take this typical entry from Parson Josselin's diary, 29th March 1644: 'Keeping a day of humiliation at my Lady Honywood's; while we were praying, God was making Waller victorious over Hopton near Alsford, and turned back the forces of Rupert that we feared would have come on after they had routed our forces at Newark; oh, the sons of Jacob never seek the Lord in vain!' It was one thing for Josselin to feel assured about the Almighty's concern for the sons of Jacob on this occasion; but Hopton's chaplain, the great Tom Fuller, cannot have interpreted the divine pleasure in quite the same way.

Josselin, good honest man, was at the centre of things in the one dramatic encounter in the entire course of the civil wars that had its scene in Essex, the siege of Colchester. The events leading up to this fearful and heroic end are worth tracing. In the spring of 1648 Essex gave angry expression to its weariness with the struggle. From the spring assizes at Chelmsford a petition was sent to Parliament demanding a treaty with the king and the disbanding of the army. Parliament did not receive it favourably. But the men of Essex were not to be silenced. Two thousand of them, representing, they said, 'thirty thousand inhabitants of the county,' marched to Westminster in support of the petition. This time Parliament went further than merely to reject the plea, it threatened reprisals. The Earl of Warwick was warned that if he did not prevent such assemblies in future the peace of the county might be endangered.

The army was fully as tired and rebellious as the people. Forces under Fairfax, quartered at Saffron Walden, had asked some time ago why they had no voice. They had alleged that 'while petitions from Essex and other places were openly

encouraged against the army, their mouths were stopped.'
It was to inquire into 'the causes of these distempers' that
Cromwell visited Saffron Walden, staying with Fairfax at the
Sun Inn, now the elaborately pargeted houses in Church
Street, and making his 'long grave speech' in the church to
a council of forty-three of his officers.

There wore similar demands for peace in Kent.  There the
grand jury assembled at Canterbury as the Essex grand
jury assembled at Chelmsford, and drew up a petition against
alleged grievances, which Parliament denounced as seditious.
There also the supporters of those who framed the petition
resolved to march into London bearing, they vowed, the
petition in one hand and the sword in the other.  Parliament
could not allow these riotous assemblies to continue, so when
news reached London that several regiments had mustered,
that magazines had been seized, and later that seven thousand foot with a large force of horse had assembled on
Barham Downs and placed themselves under the command
of the old Earl of Norwich, there was no time to lose.
Fairfax was rushed off with six thousand foot and two
thousand horse, and the upshot of it was that Parson
Josselin was again able to assure his flock at Earls Colne
that the sons of Jacob never seek the Lord in vain.  The
following week even he may have had doubts.

The Kentish Royalists had been kept informed of parallel
movements in Essex, and after their defeat saw a union of
forces as the one hope of continuing their cause.  Fairfax,
or Old Gouty Legs, as they called him, had scattered them, so
they were obliged to cross the Thames as best they could,
assembling near Stratford and joining the Essex Royalists
under Sir Charles Lucas at Shenfield, his brother's seat, on
8th June.  Meanwhile Parliament, having news of this
intended uniting of forces, had warned the Essex committee
on the 3rd that unless they gave up the men of Kent 'as a
well pleasing sacrifice' war would lay waste their own fair
county.  If they did give up the men of Kent they would be
granted indemnity.  Some of the Essex committee, whose
opposition to Parliament had been designed only to bring

peace, were frightened by this. It was in no way what they had intended when they first made overtures to the men of Kent. Nor had they any love for the king. Sir Charles Lucas, on the other hand, was a Royalist first and last. With him it was not a question of being on the winning side at the end, or of bargaining for peace. So when others hesitated he came forward to rally the people, and though not an eloquent man, and certainly not a diplomat, his forthright manner gave those who heard him confidence. At once they chose him to lead them.

The vacillating committee were surprised to see how quickly the boldness of Sir Charles had reconciled the people to the prospect of war. They were more surprised when the fury of these newly converted Cavaliers was turned upon themselves. When they met at Chelmsford to consider means of pacifying the people without further offence to Parliament they were mobbed and taken prisoner. Two of them, Charles Rich, the Earl of Warwick's second son, and Sir Harbottle Grimston, were then forced to visit London again, escorted by representatives of the rebel forces, and petition once more for peace, at the same time demanding for the Kentish rebels the indemnity that had been offered to themselves if they would betray their neighbours. A large number of freeholders and men of substance in the county went so far at this juncture as to declare publicly that they would not pay 'any more excise or other taxes till,' as they put it, 'all the desires expressed in our said petition have been fully obtained by us.'

On 9th June the Royalist forces reached Chelmsford, where they were joined by Hertfordshire men under the command of Lord Capel, reinforced by a body of about fifty from London—young men of good family, 'those gallant youths the apprentices of London'—who had wandered out to Epping, and after a skirmish there had joined Lord Capel's company. The Chelmsford rendezvous was the park at New Hall, Boreham, the Duke of Buckingham's seat. On the 10th, news reached them that Fairfax was in pursuit, so they marched northward towards Braintree, calling on the way at

Leighs, the Earl of Warwick's seat, in the hope of finding a large supply of arms. Here we again meet Arthur Wilson, and with him Mary, the wife of Charles Rich, whose acquaintance we made in more peaceful conditions. Both left accounts of the call.

Mary informs us in her report of that unwelcome visit that the Earl of Norwich, whom she calls Goring, was one of her best friends, 'and upon that account' she says, 'I was used so well that, bating some arms they took, there was not anything touched; and they stayed only a dinnering time with me, and so marched on to Colchester.' To what extent this self-congratulation was justified we cannot know. The soldiers had come in search of arms, not to pay a social call, and they were not likely to be greatly affected by the presence of the earl's daughter-in-law. Yet she, apparently, thought differently. 'For possibly,' she says, 'if there had been none but servants, the house would not have been secured, as by my being there it was.' Perhaps so; but the lady's own word for it is hardly sufficient.

The shrewd old steward, Arthur Wilson, has the better story. It begins some days before the call. He tells us that as soon as the Earl of Warwick heard that the Earl of Norwich, or Goring, as he also calls him, had crossed the Thames from Kent into Essex, he was sent to Leighs to secure it as best he could against attack. On the way he met Mr. Charles Rich (Mary's husband), Sir Harbottle Grimston, and Sir Martin Lumley leaving Chelmsford after their effort to pacify the tumultuous people by telling them that Parliament had granted them indemnity, and by assuring them—without full conviction—that all would be well if only they would return to their homes. Wilson told these anxious gentlemen how decisive the victory over the Royalist forces at Maidstone had been, and they asked him to find Sir William Hickes in Chelmsford and tell him the news, because he had been extremely depressed when they left him. Wilson did this, but found Sir William and his friends hard to convince. They asked if there were no uproars in London like those at Chelmsford, and when told that London was quiet were surprised. Wilson tried to advise them how to handle the people. 'But there was too much noise,' he says, and also 'too many commanders and too few obeyers to listen to any good advice.' He gathered that the members of the committee expected a general insurrection such as had just occurred in Chelmsford. In fact, while he was talking to them an alarming rumour came in. He did not stay to hear the end of it. In the general confusion he slipped away lest he should be caught in a trap. It was lucky he did, otherwise he also might have been taken prisoner.

From Leighs, scouts were sent out daily to learn the movements of the Royalists. Little appears to have escaped them. Wilson knew at once when Lord Capel and Lord Loughborough joined the others at New Hall, and he knew that Sir Charles Lucas had been elected to act as their general. He was inclined to think that at New Hall as at Chelmsford there must be too many commanders, and smiled when told that some had deserted because they were of the same opinion. The next important news that reached him was that Fairfax had sent Colonel Whalley, with a party of fifteen horse and some foot, 'to follow these roysterers and amuse them till he could bring up more forces.' Then he heard that the Cavaliers were preparing to march, and soon afterwards a message was received from the Earl of Norwich to say that he would dine at Leighs on Saturday, 10th June, and 'borrow' the earl's arms.

Wilson saw at once that it would be impossible to hold Leighs against an army with ordnance, so he merely asked for an assurance that arms only would be taken. While this message was being carried to the Earl of Norwich he called his men into the armoury and ordered them to take down a large proportion of the weapons and hide them in different parts of the house. No sooner had this been done than thirty or forty officers arrived, saying they had come from the Earl of Norwich and Sir Charles Lucas to protect the house from the violence of the soldiers. Their real mission, we cannot doubt, was to keep an eye on the inmates, particularly on Wilson. There were several Essex men among these officers, so conversation was easy and they and the steward conducted themselves as though they were the best of friends. In due course the Earl of Norwich arrived, and after dining with the family left, bearing away all the arms his men had been able to find.

When the Earl of Warwick's carts came into the Royalist camp Sir Charles rode over to inspect them. Were those, he asked, all that the Earl of Warwick possessed? He could not believe it. His men had allowed themselves to be hood-winked. In his usual impulsive way he set spurs to his horse and rode up to Leighs himself. Wilson assured him, and indeed showed him, that the armoury had been emptied. He then demanded permission to search the house. Wilson suspected that one of the servants had been disloyal. He called ostentatiously for the housekeeper, to whom he had previously handed the keys with orders to keep out of sight. When the housekeeper failed to answer the summons Wilson, pretended to be angry, and commanded the servants to search until they found him, remarking to Sir Charles that he could not be far away. All this caused delay, which Sir Charles could not afford, so in extreme annoyance he was obliged to leave.

From Leighs the Royalists went on to Braintree, where they heard that Sir Thomas Honywood had garrisoned Marks Hall and was prepared to fight. They heard also that Fairfax was at Billericay. After holding a council of war they decided to turn east again and try to take Colchester. On the Sunday they assembled for prayers in the morning, and later divided themselves up into four troops under the commands of Lords Norwich, Capel, Loughborough, and Sir Charles Lucas respectively, agreeing how to dispose themselves in case of alarm. By this time they were four thousand strong, including six hundred horse.

Parson Josselin was unable to hold services at Earls Colne that day. His men were in arms, ready to defend the village, and the parson himself was with Sir Thomas Hony-wood at Marks Hall. At nine in the evening the Royalists advanced to Halstead, and the following morning they were at Earls Colne. Josselin proudly noted: 'No part of Essex gave them so much opposition as we did; they plundered us, and me in particular, of all that was portable, except brass, pewter, and bedding. I made away to Coggeshall, and avoided their scouts through Providence.' He and his family remained with the Honywoods for ten days. A local tradition holds that the artificial lake in the grounds at Marks Hall was made by the soldiers while waiting for Colchester to fall.

When the Royalists were at Halstead, Fairfax was at Brentwood. Colchester was clearly the objective of the Cavaliers, and Fairfax pressed forward. He could not be there first, but he could be there before the town's defences had been strengthened and provisions brought in.

The Royalists reached Colchester in the early afternoon of Monday the 12th, and about 4 p.m. were about to enter the town when they learned the inhabitants were prepared to resist. On hearing this, Sir Charles Lucas and one or two others set spurs to their horses and rode to the outer defences, where they met about sixty horsemen, well armed and ready for battle. At the almshouses Sir Charles drew rein and sent back a messenger to call the army forward, while four or five of the gentlemen with him charged the outposts and drove them inside the turnpike, from which they retreated quickly to Head Gate. The people of Colchester, now they had seen the size of the army before them, and had good reason to believe that Sir Charles intended to attack at once with all the strength at his disposal, sent out a messenger to say they would treat with him. On receiving assurances that the town would not be plundered, and that the people would not be punished for having planned to resist him, they submitted and agreed to deliver up their horses and arms forthwith. So the Royalist army was able to enter and quarter in Colchester that same night.

There had been no time to spare. The following day, Tuesday the 13th, intelligence came in that Fairfax had advanced to within a mile of the town, where he had been joined by Sir Thomas Honywood with two thousand horse and foot, Colonel Henry Mildmay with a regiment of horse and two troops of dragoons, and part of a regiment from Colonel Carew Mildmay. Confirmation of this report came to hand directly in the form of a curt note from Fairfax demanding immediate surrender. The Earl of Norwich, to whom the demand was addressed, replied that he had heard that the general suffered from gout, but that he intended to cure him of all his diseases. It may have been this personal insult that stung Fairfax into a ferocious and costly attack at once. It came from the Lexden side, and though the defenders, under Colonel Fane, who had been governor of Landguard Fort but had come over to the Royalist side, were able to repulse it three times, finally their line was turned and they were compelled to retreat in confusion through Head Gate. Lord Capel was with them, and when he saw how hard pressed they were, and that there was danger of the attackers entering the town with the defenders, he stood at the gate and with his pike held off the enemy with all his strength. Later he was joined by Sir Charles Lucas and Sir George Lisle, and these three fought a rearguard action with their pikes until the last Royalist who could reach the gates was through. Their gallantry went far to inspire the defenders in the terrible weeks that followed, and theirs was to be the glory in the last act of all.

When the gates had been closed the defenders were ranged along the walls, which the attackers were now attempting to scale. Some of the Parliament's soldiers found a way into the town through the houses built against the churchyard of St. Mary-at-the-Walls. They were killed in the churchyard. Fairfax again demanded surrender, and when a second scornful reply was given he brought up artillery to try to force the gates. It was unsuccessful. The carriage horses were killed by the first volley from the defending musketeers. He then ordered the houses against the walls to be fired, hoping that flying sparks would soon set fire to the whole town. Again his design was frustrated.

For between seven and eight hours the ruthless fight continued, and the following morning's review of it gave little satisfaction to either side. Fairfax had lost close on a

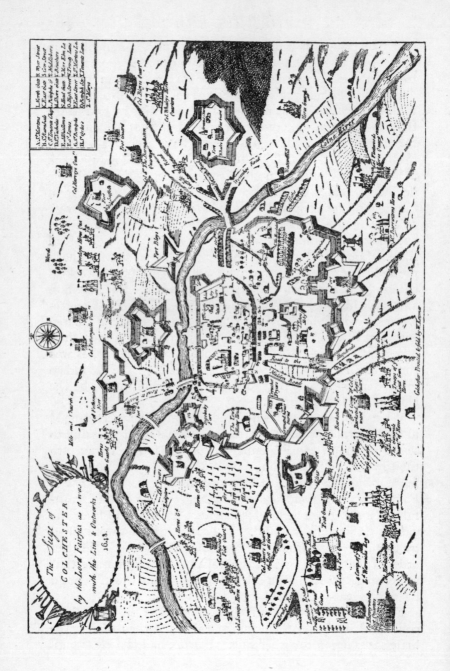

The Siege of COLCHESTER by the Lord Fairfax as it was with the Line & Outworks. 1648.

thousand men, and had alienated many poor weavers who had previously been for him, but whose houses, outside the gates, had been burnt in the last attack of the day. One poor weaver's tale is told by Quartermaster Carter, who left an eye-witness record of the siege. On the morning following that tragic night he found an old woman crying bitterly, and when he asked her the cause of her grief she told him that the previous night some of Fairfax's soldiers broke into her house and pillaged it. Soon after they left another party broke in, and when they found nothing worth taking demanded money of her husband, who was quietly working at his loom. The old man answered that he had but little—nothing, in fact, except a few coins in his purse, which they might have if they would leave him in peace. The soldiers, instead of pitying him, called him a Cavalier rogue, and swore that he had a bag of gold hidden somewhere. They would have it or kill him, they said. When the old man repeated that he had only the purse, they shot him dead. Their son, hearing the shot, came to his father's aid. He, too, was attacked and now lay dying.

Similar tales could be heard in every street. Fairfax received reports of them. He saw also the hundreds of dead and dying men in his own army and decided against further attack for the present. The Royalists were strong in both men and arms. But they were in a trap. Unless they could get provisions they must starve. It was impossible for them to have enough food in the town to feed so large an army for more than a few days. So he decided to blockade the town and disposed his forces to that purpose. The main force he set at Lexden in order to cut off both retreat and succour on the west. He blocked the way to Cambridge and the north, and he seized and occupied the fort at Mersea Island in case the navy proved treacherous—part of it had already shown itself favourably inclined towards the king. Nor was he altogether sure of the lord high admiral, the Earl of Warwick, after the strange tales he had heard about the way the Cavaliers had been feasted and given arms at Leighs. The earl's carts had been seen in the Royalist train.

The Earl of Norwich and his friends inside the town held

their council of war. The earl was made governor of the town, Lord Capel director of the council of war, Sir Charles Lucas commander-in-chief of the horse, and Sir George Lisle of the foot. They also saw that provisions would be their greatest problem, so to avoid any waste they gave orders for the town to be searched and everything placed in the charge of Lord Loughborough. To their surprise and joy a store of wheat, barley, pease, and rye, with large supplies of salt fish, oil, spice, as well as gunpowder was discovered at the Hythe, a suburb in the east with access to the sea. Supplies of wine and salt were found in the same place. The discovery of these gave as much satisfaction to the townspeople as to the soldiers, because for some time they had been unable to buy corn, which the merchants had evidently engrossed in the hope of a rise in price. It seemed to this religious-minded people 'a providence as great as that of the manna to the Israelites in the wilderness.' But it was not enough. Parties were sent into the east of the county in search of further provisions. To the north there was little. The Stour was only five or six miles away, and the bridges at Cattawade, Stratford, and Nayland were already held for Parliament by four Suffolk colonels, Moody, Fothergill, Gurdon, and Barnardiston. Their best hope was of relief coming by water; but when on 18th June two frigates bearing supplies to them were seized at Harwich the prospect became grave. About the same time a relief force under Major Muschamp was met and routed at Linton near Saffron Walden, and all the time there was fear of betrayal by the townspeople. It could not be forgotten that Colchester had contributed £30,000 to the cause of Parliament during the last six years. Indeed, it must have seemed strangely ironic to many that after starting the war by a savage attack on one Lucas the town should now be in control of another, and that the committee men whom they had regarded as their leaders should be within their walls as prisoners while the Parliament army they had supported had pillaged and burnt the cottages of the very weavers who had so savagely attacked the Royalists six years earlier.

The day after the seizure of relief ships at Harwich the Chelmsford committee men held prisoner were allowed to send a message to Fairfax requesting a treaty between the two armies. Fairfax refused this request, but offered terms for surrender, which included permission for the common soldiers to return to their homes and the officers to 'go beyond the seas with equipage befitting their qualities, engaging themselves not to return unto this kingdom without leave from the Parliament.' This was unacceptable to the Royalist officers and the siege continued.

After this an attempt was made by the beleaguered garrison to send out messengers with commissions to try to raise supplies in Norfolk, Suffolk, and Cambridgeshire; but when they reached the Stour bridges they found them broken. The Suffolk forces had mustered at Nayland, and Lord Norwich tried in vain to win them over to his side. On the 24th they joined Fairfax and were placed outside the north and east gates. There was now no means of escape left open to the Royalists, and they could only trust that sympathetic forces— perhaps from as far away as Scotland—would come to their rescue. Each night parties were sent out into the Tendring hundred, the only part of the county open to them, in search of food. One morning they brought in about a hundred sheep and sixty oxen. Another night they returned with fifty oxen and cows, many sheep, and the ever welcome corn. They might have gained more on these expeditions if Sir Charles Lucas had not insisted that cattle should only be stolen from those who were known to sympathize with Parliament.

All this time sporadic attacks continued to be made and the pincers to close on them. Almost daily the weavers of Colchester were alarmed by what Byron described as

> The death shot hissing from afar,
> The shock, the shout, the groan of war.

The forts at St. Mary's Church and the North Bridge were the Royalist strong-points throughout. The fame of a one-eyed gunner named Thompson, who had his stand among the bells in St. Mary's steeple, still lives. He had a brass saker on the belfry platform, and annoyed the Parliament soldiers so much that they brought up artillery to destroy the steeple, but were attacked with such force that they were obliged to withdraw. It is worth recording that when on Sunday, 25th June, the Rev. John Owen, Puritan parson of Coggeshall, preached before Fairfax he was bold enough to declare: 'Fire and fagggots are no good reformers.' Later he became Cromwell's chaplain.

Towards the end of the first week in July the enemy crept up into East Street and seized the mill, placing a strong guard there. The Royalists held a council of war and decided to make a grand sally through the East Gate, with Sir Charles Lucas in command of the horse and Sir George Lisle in command of the foot. In all there were about six hundred foot and four hundred horse, and the only passage was across a narrow bridge with one end within five feet of the Parliament barricade. Nevertheless they went boldly over it 'as if it had been a sporting skirmish amongst soldiers at a general muster,' and got past the guard houses. The attack was a brilliant success, and the Cavaliers returned with a captain, lieutenant, and about eighty private soldiers as captives. But they did not all return. In one place twenty Royalists were killed, 'mostly gentlemen; they could be none else, from their white skins and goodly apparel.'

The advantage thus gained could not be held. The Parliament army came up and set fire to any houses that might provide cover for another sally, and when they had burnt the houses they burnt also all the windmills surrounding the town so that the besieged should not be able to grind their corn. This, however, was not entirely effective. Millstones were found at the Hythe which could be worked daily to provide bread for as long as the corn lasted. But the nightly sallies for food became increasingly costly as the enemy grip tightened.

On 14th July the Hythe church was taken. Then Lord Lucas's house, St. John's, fell. Here about a hundred men were killed at once when soldiers who had scaled the gatehouse threw in grenades from the battlements and exploded a magazine. They next set the streets on both sides of the Head Gate on fire, and all that night the sky was black with smoke from the burning houses, and streaked with the lurid glow of flames that leapt up afresh whenever the wind veered to fan the smouldering embers.

Next morning the one-eyed gunner was found to be within range. A heavy cannon was placed on St. John's Green, and to the cheers of the Parliamentarians one side of the steeple and a great part of the church crashed in ruins about the dead gunner. Still the gallant defence continued. But as news of the suppression of Royalist risings in other parts of the kingdom continued to come in despondency closed on the besieged. When the condition of the townspeople was at last seen to be desperate, the commanders resolved to make another effort to cut their way through the enemy's lines after nightfall and escape through Nayland into Suffolk. On the night of the 17th, twelve hundred men under Sir Charles Lucas sallied out and crossed the Colne near the Middle Mill. They were making their way towards Boxted when they took a wrong turn and lost so much time that retreat seemed the safest course. The countryside was now aware of their movements and the Parliamentary army might soon overtake and rout them. But retreat was not easy. The enemy had again fired property across their route in the neighbourhood of the North Bridge. They did, however, get back, and in so dejected a state that all hope of escape was finally abandoned. The horses had shown themselves unfit for service through lack of provender. A few days later they had to be killed for food. In order to raise the spirits of the soldiers a sort of festival was made of the slaughter. The horses were driven into the castle yard and the fattest selected. On 22nd July it was roasted whole near the North Gate 'to make the soldiers merry at the entrance into such diet.'

Four days after this killing of the horses Fairfax again attacked near St. Mary's Church. But the defenders still fought back with incredible fury and the attacking forces had to withdraw. When, at the end of the month, tidings of new Royalist risings came in, spirits again revived; but from the beginning of August the misery became indescribable. The horses that were left had by this time eaten all the thatch off the houses. Every leaf had been eaten off the trees, and when the last horses were killed they were so diseased that those who ate them died. On 19th August the mayor, with the consent of the Royalist commander, begged Fairfax to allow the inhabitants to leave the town. A reply came back that the request would be granted if the Parliament's committee came with them. The earl would not agree to this, but tried to send the women and children through the gates, thinking the soldiers would be so moved by their plight that they would allow them to pass. Fairfax ordered them to be driven back. On the 25th a last desperate attack was decided upon by the Royalist officers, but the men mutinied, and when news came through that Preston had fallen to Cromwell the last hope went. Colonel Samuel Tuke was sent out to make the best terms he could with Fairfax. The deed of capitulation was signed on the 27th, and the following day Fairfax entered the town in triumph.

Sir Charles Lucas and Sir George Lisle, along with Sir Bernard Gascoigne, who was afterwards found to be an Italian and pardoned, were brought before Ireton on the day of the triumphal entry and all three condemned to be shot to death the same evening.

'By what law are we to die?' asked Sir Charles. 'By an ordinance of Parliament, by the council of war, or by the command of the general?'

Ireton replied that it was by vote of the council of war, and also according to an Order of Parliament, by which all who were found in arms were to be proceeded against as traitors.

To this Sir Charles replied: 'Alas, you deceive yourselves. Me you cannot. We are conquered, and must be what you please to make us.'

His words were spoken without fear. His countenance was said by a witness to be as cheerful as that of one going to a banquet. He asked to be given until the following morning to settle his affairs in this world and make seemly preparation for the next. When this was denied him he said:

'Sir, do not think I make this request out of any desire I have to live, or escape the death you have sentenced me to, for I scorn to ask life at your hand, but that I might have time to make some addresses to God above, and settle some things below, that I might not be hurried out of this world with all my sins about me; but since your charity will not grant it, I must submit to the mercy of God, whose holy will be done. Do your worst. I shall be ready for execution.'

Sir George Lisle said little. All he asked for was a little time in which to write to his father and mother. This also was refused. The two then went to prayers, which they were scarcely allowed to finish before being hurried away to the north side of the castle, a few paces from the wall, to face the musketeers. Sir Charles Lucas was the first to fall. Still in the same high spirits he said: 'I have often looked death in the face in the field of battle, and you shall now see I dare die.'

Again he knelt in prayer. Then rose and opened his doublet, exposing his breast. This done he stood at attention and called out:

'See, I am ready for you. And now, rebels, do your worst.'

Sir George Lisle was then brought forward. He knelt and kissed the body of his dead friend, and spoke a few words as though reciting an elegy in his honour. Then he, too, faced the musketeers, first distributing among them one of the five pieces of gold he had in his pocket. The other four he gave to an old servant, asking him to bear them to his friends in London as his last legacy. Turning to the spectators he said:

'Oh, how many of your lives, who are now present here, have I saved in hot blood, and must now myself be most barbarously murdered in cold. But what wicked act dare they not do, who do willingly cut the throat of my dear king, whom they have already imprisoned: for whose deliverance and the peace of this miserable and unhappy nation I shall dedicate these my last prayers to heaven.'

He then called the musketeers nearer. One of them

answered: 'I'll warrant ye, sir, we'll hit you.' To which, with a smile, Sir George replied:

'I have been nearer you when you have missed me.'

After a short prayer he called out: 'I am ready. Traitors, do your worst.'

These two gallant gentlemen were buried in the Lucas family vault in St. Giles's Church. At the Restoration, Lord Lucas, Sir Charles's brother, erected in their honour a monument bearing this inscription:

UNDER THIS MARBLE LIE THE BODIES OF
THE TWO MOST VALIANT CAPTAINS
### SIR CHARLES LUCAS
AND
### SIR GEORGE LISLE,
Knights,
WHO FOR THEIR EMINENT LOYALTY
TO THEIR SOVEREIGN,
were, on the 28th of August, 1648,
by the command of
### SIR THOMAS FAIRFAX,
then General of the Parliamentary Army,
### IN COLD BLOOD
barbarously murdered.

The three peers, Lords Norwich, Loughborough, and Capel, were carried to London for trial. Lord Loughborough, who was not a professional soldier, was allowed to compound with Parliament and retire to his own estate. The old earl was sentenced to the scaffold, but appealed to Parliament, and, 'being a man of jovial and hearty temperament, with few, if any, personal enemies, and, above all, having shown much reverence and submission before his judges,' he was reprieved by the one casting vote of the Speaker. Lord Capel made a daring escape from the Tower on 27th January 1649, two days before the king's execution, but was recognized the following night by the wherryman whom he asked to row him to Lambeth. The captain of the guard in charge of the House of Commons was informed of his whereabouts and he was recaptured. Feeling that further attempts at escape would be in vain, he occupied himself in writing those meditations in both prose and verse, first published with some of his letters in 1654, which bear such moving testimony to the courage and equanimity of this gallant English gentleman:

> That which the world miscalls a jayl,
>     A private closet is to me;
> Whilst a good conscience is my bail,
>     And innocence my liberty.
> Locks, bars, and solitude together met,
> Make me no prisoner, but an anchoret.
>
> The cynic hugs his poverty,
>     The pelican her wilderness;
> And 'tis the Indian's pride to be
>     Naked on frozen Caucasus.
> Contentment feels no smart; Stoics we see
> Make torments easy by their apathy.
>
> My soul is free as is th'ambient air,
>     Which doth my outward parts include;
> Whilst loyal thoughts do still repair,
>     To company my solitude.
> What tho'·they do with chains my body bind,
> My king can only captivate my mind.

'God's secret will is unknown. Whatever it be, His name be magnified. My duty is to walk by the revealed and acknowledged rules of His truth, and the received precepts of virtue, which through my frailty I have not practised so well as I should, and as I wish I had; yet never shall the fear of death (by His divine and gracious assistance), no, not in the ugliest shape attired, daunt me from asserting them.'

'I know my cause is good, and that my sufferings answer not the value and worthiness of it. I know that my Redeemer liveth, that died for me. Most willingly I die for His truth, and for acting my duty to His servant the King, whom He hath placed here upon his terrestrial throne amongst us. I know and believe that to die is gain, the gaining of an immortal and incorruptible life, with eternal felicity in the sight of God our Saviour, and His blessed angels.

> My Saviour the Cross sanctified;
> My King the block hath dignified.
> Crosses nor blocks I do not fear;
> Sanctified, dignified, they are.
> *Gloria Deo in excelsis.*'

Such were Lord Capel's last thoughts. He was beheaded on 9th March 1649 and buried at Little Hadham.

High Street, Colchester

New Hall, Boreham

## CHAPTER XVIII

# THE CAPTAINS AND THE KINGS DEPART

. . . by Time's fell hand defaced,
The rich-proud cost of outworn buried age.

BEFORE the end of the century the passion and fury that disfigured the middle years had gone from Essex. But the glory also had gone. The Commonwealth had banished it. Fuller's 'fair county, plentifully affording all things necessary for man's subsistence,' was never again to be the favourite resort of princes or the pleasance of their courtiers. The old palace at Havering-atte-Bower, the country house of successive sovereigns for more than five hundred years, was bought and dismantled by Richard Deane, one of the judges who signed the king's death warrant. The great trees in as much of the park as went with the palace were cut down and sold. Their destruction was symbolic. The royal forest of Waltham, now Epping Forest, suffered a like depredation. All the best trees were felled and used to build ships to protect the trade routes in a new and different age.

Havering's glories had in fact been waning when the seventeenth century opened. It had served Elizabeth as a hunting lodge and a place to rest in at the beginning and end of her progresses; but in her day the palace was falling into decay. James saw no cause to repair it. He had Theobalds on the western edge of the forest, and for a time Wanstead. Charles I was the last king to use Havering, and the last occasion of a royal visit was when he spent a night there on coming into Essex to meet his mother-in-law, the insufferable Maria de' Medici, who was received at Gidea Hall and was to cause such trouble in the country until she and her retinue were safely shipped out again.

The palace that had enjoyed more recent fame was New Hall, Boreham, which had been rebuilt by Henry VIII and

K

given the proud name of Beaulieu. The royal Tudor arms, carved in freestone, formerly on the gatehouse, are now above the principal door, though only the dignified north wing remains of the house that for more than a hundred years was the scene of such splendour. When Cromwell acquired it on the attainder of the son of George Villiers, first Duke of Buckingham, who had bought it in 1620, it looked for a short time as though Essex would continue in favour, but Cromwell found it inconvenient and used Hampton Court instead.

Anne Boleyn, from whose father Henry had acquired New Hall, had given a magnificent ball there in 1533 to celebrate the birth of Elizabeth; Henry had kept the feast of St. George there in royal style in 1524. But its memories were not all so lively. It was at New Hall that Mary, afterwards queen, received from the hand of her chamberlain a message informing her that she was no longer to bear the title of princess. She replied haughtily—and with good reason—that 'she was not a little marvelled at his undertaking such a matter of high emprise as minishing from her state and dignity, she not doubting that she was the King's true daughter, born in good and lawful matrimony.' Under the Duke of Buckingham it had flourished again, and when the first hearth tax was imposed in 1662, New Hall headed the list for the whole kingdom with a hundred and seventeen hearths. It had then come into the possession of George Monk, Duke of Albemarle, who received it as a gift from the nation, and lived there in proud style on his pension of £7,000 a year. He died while sitting in his chair at New Hall in 1670.

The second Duke of Albemarle, son of the first duke and Anne his wife—a farrier's daughter who was said to have consoled him while he was a prisoner in the Tower—was lord lieutenant of Essex from 1675 to 1685. Sir John Bramston has an account of James II revelling in two days' hunting while the guest of the second Duke of Albemarle at New Hall in 1681. On the first day the stag ran from Chelmsford almost to Wanstead, then turned and was killed near Romford. On the second day a stag that lay in New Hall park was hunted across the Roothings and killed in Hatfield.

'His Majesty kept pretty near the dogs, tho' the ditches were broad and deep, the hedges high, and the way and fields dirty and deep.' Riding home to London, he called unexpectedly on the Dorsets at Copt Hall. The earl was dining with Sir William Hickes at Ruckholts, the cook and butler had gone to Waltham fair; but the countess did her best to entertain His Majesty. On leaving he met the earl returning from Ruckholts, and was evidently in good humour, for when the earl began to apologize the king cut him short with:

'Make no excuses; it was exceeding well, and very handsome.'

Essex lost what might have been another historic association with Cromwell by the death in youth of the second Earl of Warwick's grandson, the heir to the earldom, who had married Frances Cromwell, the Protector's youngest daughter. Had he lived we might have had an Essex line of Earls of Warwick descended from Cromwell. As it was, the association was brief and not entirely happy. Cromwell had heard some unfortunate tales about the youth, and for a time opposed the match. He had heard that young Rich was 'a vicious young man, given to play and such like things.' But he must have been reassured on this point, or possibly on another that he considered adequate compensation, for he gave the couple his blessing, and the wedding, which was celebrated at Whitehall, was a grand affair, with all the nobles of the land lavishing gifts upon the newly exalted bride and her groom. The Countess of Devonshire, it is recorded, sent two thousand pounds' worth of plate. New Hall might have become their residence, for in 1659 we find Richard Cromwell speaking of it as 'a portion for my sister Frances.' It seems unlikely, however, that New Hall was ever lived in by either Cromwell or any member of his family—according to Carlyle, Morant was mistaken here. After less than four months of married life, Robert Rich died and Frances was a widow. The old Earl of Warwick, who had carried the sword of state when Cromwell had been made Lord Protector, received from him a letter of condolence, and replied to it in his best Puritan style:

'Others' goodness is their own; yours is the whole country's —yea, three kingdoms', for which you justly possess interest and renown with wise and good men. Virtue is a thousand escutcheons. Go on, my lord; go on happily to love religion, to exemplify it. May your lordship long continue an instrument of use, a pattern of virtue, and a precedent of glory.'

It would be interesting to know what the young man's father, who became third earl, said in reply to his father-in-law's condolences, if indeed he ever received them. He had joined the king at Oxford at the beginning of the civil wars, though he had not taken up arms, and when called to answer for his 'delinquency,' according to the Royalist Composition Papers, his case presented 'a remarkable complication of royalism, money-lending, imprisonments for debt, and curious turns in the wheel of fortune.' He had evidently mortgaged his allowance from his father, the second earl, before the war, and was deeply involved with a money-lender named Gosse. This man Gosse, unable to collect interest, had one of the two friends of Rich who had guaranteed the interest arrested. Rich and his brother officers, however, were able to obtain his release. The money-lender then had Rich himself arrested, apparently unaware that he enjoyed the privileges of a peer. The House of Lords at once ordered his release, and Gosse, along with four of the sheriff's officers responsible for the arrest, found himself in Newgate. He was detained for a fortnight only; but either the confinement or the fright seems to have upset him, for he died soon after his release, though not before he had cast up his accounts. In them, Rich appears as owing £6,300, though apparently he had borrowed only £600. In addition to the money owing to Gosse, he was embarrassed by a fine of £2,000, by that time imposed for having joined the king at Oxford. In pleading with the committee appointed to deal with delinquents, the old earl was frank about his son's debts and had a sympathetic hearing. The fine was remitted, but the committee were of the opinion that part of his allowance from the earl, his father, should be paid by Rich to the money-lender's widow.

Short memories, often an advantage, became a necessity at this time. As Cromwell's daughter married the son of one part-time Royalist, Fairfax's daughter married another, and again with New Hall in the picture. The second Duke of Buckingham, who was with Charles II at Worcester in 1651 and had to flee for his life, returned to England in 1657 and married Mary, the daughter of Lord Fairfax. He must have had the family good looks and audacity in love, for his bride had been on the point of marrying the Earl of Chesterfield when he came between them. The arrangements for the Chesterfield marriage were in fact so far advanced that the banns had been published twice.

There was an excellent reason for this timely and dramatic intervention. At the Commonwealth most of Buckingham's property was awarded to Fairfax, and the wedding served to keep it in the family. The arrangement was no less convenient at the Restoration when the boot again changed legs. Buckingham met Charles II at Dover, and lost no time in insinuating himself into royal favour again. Most of his estates were restored to him, and within a few years he was reputed to be the richest subject in the land. He did not, however, regain New Hall.

Buckingham's name lives now in the songs and legends of Yorkshire, where his favourite property was at Helmsley, instead of in those of Essex. He would have been a brilliant figure to have had in the county at the Restoration, though a highly disreputable one. He was one of the most licentious men of his day; but withal a poet, a wit, and something of a philosopher. Dryden immortalized him as Zimri in his *Absalom and Achitophel*:

> A man so various, that he seemed to be
> Not one, but all mankind's epitome;
> Stiff in opinions, always in the wrong,
> Was everything by starts and nothing long;
> But in the course of one revolving moon,
> Was chymist, fiddler, statesman, and buffoon . . .
> Beggar'd by fools, whom still he found too late,
> He had his jest, and they had his estate.

When he died in 1687 there was no legitimate heir to inherit the title borne by these two flamboyant figures, the first and second Dukes of Buckingham; estate there was none to inherit. It had been completely dissipated.

As for Fairfax, his estates were in Yorkshire, his native county; but he belongs to Essex history by virtue of his part in the siege of Colchester, and also because, like his daughter, he married into an Essex family. What is so curious is that both father and daughter married Royalists. Fairfax was so typical a Parliamentarian and Puritan, even to the extent of translating psalms and writing poems on Christian warfare and the shortness of life, which, as a soldier, he did so much to promote. His wife was a de Vere, and a lady worthy of her name. She was the fourth daughter of Horace de Vere, Baron of Tilbury, and Clarendon tells us that at the trial of Charles I she caused a most embarrassing interruption in the court's proceedings. When the crier called out the name of the Lord Fairfax, as one of the king's judges, no one answered. The name was called again, and still no one answered. Then a woman's voice muttered audibly: 'He had more wit than to be there.' The speaker was asked to show herself. No one moved. So there was nothing to be done but resume the business of the court. But when the president had read the impeachment, and proceeded in his speech to refer to the will of 'all the people of England,' the same voice called out: 'No, not the hundredth part of them.' An order was thereupon given for soldiers on guard to fire into the box from which the interruptions had come, and it was then discovered that the lady who had twice disturbed the court was the general's wife.

Like the Earl of Warwick and many others, Fairfax was against taking the king's life, and consequently refused to have any part in a trial which he knew could only have that end. He was a man of honour, and must have been saddened by the Commonwealth. His last ten or eleven years were spent in retirement on his Yorkshire estate, where he must have reflected often on the lines that Milton had addressed to him while the Parliament army was besieging Colchester. They had ended:

O yet a nobler task awaits thy hand
(For what can war but endless war still breed?)
Till truth and right from violence be freed,
And public faith cleared from the shameful brand
    Of public fraud.  In vain doth Valour bleed
    While Avarice and Rapine share the land.

After the muddled years that followed the victories of
Cromwell and Fairfax, the cynicism of Charles II at the
Restoration is hardly surprising.  He was generous with his
grants of pardon; but he at least found it an advantage to
remember.  When Sir Henry Mildmay and Sir Francis
Masham, who at the time represented Essex divisions in
Parliament, along with other gentlemen, presented a petition
to the king concerning the rights of Parliament, Charles
remarked that there were some who 'would do well to remember the Act of Oblivion and to take such courses as might not
need another.'  Then glancing towards Mildmay he said:
'Mr. Mildmay, I would you would remember forty,' a
reminder of Sir Henry's betrayal of his neighbour Sir John
Bramston.

'Sir,' answered Mildmay, 'I remember sixty.'

Most people, except the nonconformist ministers, had
reason to remember sixty with gratitude.  Ten years of
Cromwell and Tumble-down Dick had been more than
enough; but Sir Harbottle Grimston, who, as Speaker of the
Convention Parliament, was given the honour of delivering
the speech of welcome when the new king received his faithful Commons at Whitehall, went further than was either
prudent or seemly when, after stating that the restitution
had been 'brought to pass by a miraculous way of Divine
Providence beyond and above the reach of our understanding,' made so bold as to say: 'We doubt not but that
your name is registered in the records of heaven, to have a
glorious place in the highest form among those glorious
martyrs of whom it is reported that through faith in Christ
and patience in their sufferings they converted their very
tormentors. . . .'  Broad-minded and adaptable as Charles
was, the prospect of sharing eternity with the glorious martyrs

Sir Harbottle had in mind cannot have appealed to him very strongly. The truth was that everybody had got into the habit of talking in that fulsome, quasi-religious fashion through listening to so many sermons, and it was difficult to get out of it. But there was a more serious Puritan legacy. The people had been so well trained in the cult of the superman that they were a long time learning that the new king was a mortal, and an erring one at that.

The old Earl of Warwick, the gay old sea-dog with a curious weakness for Puritan preachers, the man who had dominated the politics of the county for more than thirty years, was no longer there to defend the ministers disturbed by the Act of Uniformity. No one had done more than he to proselytize Essex for Puritanism. Whenever a living had fallen vacant he had done his utmost to get a nonconformist appointed, and as patron himself of so many key livings he had often succeeded. He had taken no part in national affairs during the Commonwealth, though Cromwell had esteemed him highly. When Parliament resolved to take the king's life, Warwick withdrew his support and retired from public life. From 1649 to 1653 he was so completely out of sympathy with those in control of the cause to which he had given his life that he left Essex, where his counsel would constantly have been sought, and lived in Surrey. Cromwell and he remained on good terms. They had been of one mind in many things; they died in the same year—the earl in April, Cromwell in September. With their deaths the systems they had fostered broke. The feelings in Essex when the old Earl of Warwick died were the same as those in England at large when the Lord Protector died. He had been the great man. He had also been loved for his genial personality. Even his pious daughter-in-law said approvingly: 'He was one of the most best-natured and cheerfullest persons I have in my time met with.'

But though its heyday as a little kingdom was over, and its kings and their nobles had gone—for the brief spell of royal favour at Saffron Walden in the extreme north-west had no effect on the society of the county—the social changes at the end of the century brought new life to Essex. For the second time in the grand sweep of its entire history its power centre moved. It had first been Colchester, the glory of Essex in ancient times, and still the only large town in the county that knows how to bear itself with dignity in the modern world of commercialism and hustle. It had next been Chelmsford, still the county town, the administrative centre, and the seat of the bishop; but which, though pleasant enough, cannot compete with Colchester. It was now, towards the end of the seventeenth century, to move nearer London into the towns that sprang up in the old royal forest of Waltham.

As Havering had been the great house of one age, New Hall, Boreham, and Leighs Priory the great houses of the next, the great houses of the third were Copt Hall and Wanstead House, both in Epping Forest. The most celebrated house at Wanstead belongs to the eighteenth century, not the seventeenth. But it was Sir Josiah Child, the father of the man who built it, who made it possible, and was the spectacular figure of the redistributed Essex. The house, or its site, had a long and distinguished history. To go back no further than the beginning of our period, it had been the home of Elizabeth's Leicester. We have seen it in association with Mountjoy, or Devonshire, as he had become, and the unhappy Penelope. At his death in 1606 it reverted to the Crown, and James, untroubled by the fate to which he had consigned these too venturesome lovers, made use of it almost at once. Later, he granted it to his beloved Duke of Buckingham. When a medicinal spring was discovered there early in the seventeenth century, Wanstead became a fashionable spa, the resort of the rich and noble. In 1619 its great house became the property of Sir Henry Mildmay, Master of the Jewel Office, who had inherited in full measure the Mildmay gift for obtaining profitable appointments. Clarendon says of him that he was 'a great flatterer of all persons in authority and a spy in all places for them,' which may have been even more profitable than his official employment. He was one of the judges who condemned Charles I. At the Restoration

*K

he was attainted of high treason and Wanstead again reverted to the Crown along with his other estates. One part of his punishment was to be drawn on a hurdle to Tyburn, and under the gallows with a rope round his neck, each year on 30th January.

Charles II bestowed Wanstead on his brother James, who sold it to Sir Robert Brookes. It was in his day that Pepys visited it on 14th May 1665, and wrote:

'I took a coach, and to Wanstead, the house where Sir H. Mildmay died, and now Sir Robert Brookes lives, having bought it off the Duke of York, it being forfeited to him. A fine seat, but an old-fashioned house; and being not full of people looks flatly.'

After the death of Sir Robert Brookes in 1667 the estate was sold to Sir Josiah Child, who made the old house, with all its proud associations, serve, but spent great sums of money in laying out the grounds. Evelyn, who visited him there in 1683, says:

'March 16th. I went to see Sir Josiah Child's prodigious cost in planting walnut trees about his seate, and making fish-ponds, many miles in circuit, in Epping Forest, in a barren spot, as oftentimes these suddainly moneyed men for the most part seate themselves.'

There may have been a reason for these 'suddainly moneyed men,' as Evelyn calls them, seating themselves outside the city. Most of them were of country stock, and were cramped in the narrow confines of streets, to which their descendants were to become so sadly accustomed. So the old Essex, the Essex of the Roothings, the Lavers, the Theydons, and the Colnes, was to find in its south-west corner another life in the new age of capitalized industry and mercantile enterprise. The life of the county seemed to have been shot into the extremities. The king at Audley End in the north-west tip; Sir Josiah Child at Wanstead in the south-west—the one the last great figure of the old, the other the first great figure of the new, the two periods overlapping as to some extent they had done all through the century.

Elizabeth had been the first great patron of mercantile

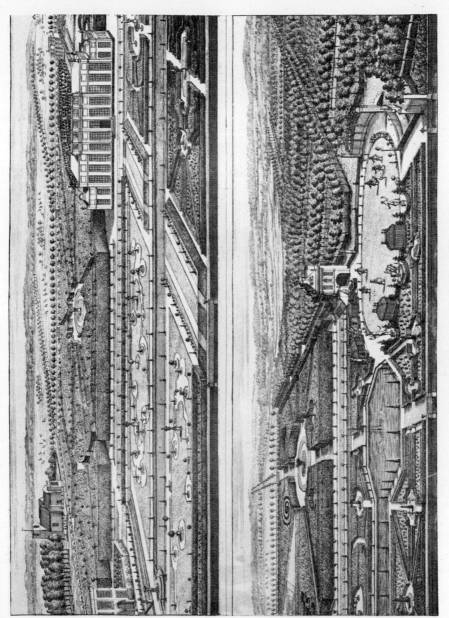

The Gardens at Wanstead House

Sir Thomas Roe

ambition. She had desired to rival and eventually to surpass the Dutch and Portuguese, and had given every encouragement to those who thought it could be done by instituting direct trade with the East, the glorious place of promise. At the outset the idea had been the dream of poets and adventurers. Sir Walter Raleigh had had a vision of a golden city and country called Eldorado, and those nearest her at court had told the queen tales of the legendary wealth of India. In such an atmosphere was trade discussed at the beginning of the century. At the end it had taken a more practical form. And at both ends we find Essex men, the first, Sir Thomas Roe of Woodford, the second, Sir Josiah Child.

When Sir Thomas Smythe proposed the employment of Sir Thomas Roe to the East India Company, he described him as 'a gentleman of pregnant understanding, well spoken, learned, industrious, of comely personage and one of whom they are in great hopes that he may work much good for the Company.' Sir Thomas was engaged, and sailed in the *Lion* under commission to inquire into allegations of wrongs and violences done to the English, who had established a trading post at Surat in 1612. After ineffectual attempts to gain satisfaction from the offending Nawab, Roe declared his intention to visit the Great Mogul, with whom the original terms for direct trade had been negotiated. He conducted himself with dignity upon this enterprise, and is held to have laid the foundations of British India in the treaty he was able to arrange.

Sir Thomas Roe belonged to a Walthamstow family. At his death in 1644 he was buried in the chancel of Woodford parish church.

It is a far cry from this distinguished and honourable knight, of whom it was reported that 'Those who knew him well have said that there was nothing wanting in him towards the accomplishment of a scholar, gentleman or courtier,' to Sir Josiah Child, a brilliant but an utterly unscrupulous merchant. One of the surprising things about Sir Josiah is that he should have known all the tricks of successful, unprincipled enterprise at so early a date, apparently by instinct.

There had, it is true, been a great number of unprincipled men in England before him; but they had worked either by secret diplomacy or by aggressive exercise of power. Sir Josiah was averse to both. His strength was in being the first person in England to see the immense potentialities of directed public opinion. We may call him the Father of Propaganda, as the word is now used, for under the pseudonym 'Philopatris' he wrote tracts and had them sown broadcast over the kingdom.

Besides knowing the value of words, he knew the value of money—the new value of money, for it had not previously had anything like the value that the new trading enterprises were giving it. Sir Josiah saw that a world was being born in which money was going to talk even more effectively than the law had talked for a century, and than the Church had talked for many centuries before that. Money had talked with the Mildmays, and it was in Sir Henry Mildmay's old house at Wanstead that Sir Josiah was to disport himself, and which his son was to replace with a house bigger than Buckingham Palace; but money had never talked in the Mildmays' world as it was to talk in Sir Josiah's.

He was pointed out on the Royal Exchange, Macaulay tells us, as the man who had speculated so successfully that in a short time he had gained for himself an income of twenty thousand pounds a year. Evelyn says that in 1683 his fortune was estimated at two hundred thousand pounds. He reached the summit of his power by his unscrupulous management of the affairs of the East India Company, which Sir Thomas Roe had founded in the manner of an English gentleman, and of which Sir Josiah, to whom the English gentleman was a figure of ridicule, had become the despotic governor. In his initial and experimental stages he copied the 'wise Dutch' as he called them, from whom he learnt the value of using political power for mercantile advancement. To this end Sir Josiah had his brother, Sir John Child, made military governor of the British Indian settlements, an office he filled to Sir Josiah's complete satisfaction. When Sir John died in Bombay and a successor had to be appointed the situation became complicated. The man who gained the appointment actually talked of governing according to law. On hearing this heretical doctrine propounded Sir Josiah is said to have blurted out that in his view the laws of England were 'a heap of nonsense, compiled by a few ignorant country gentlemen, who hardly knew how to make laws for the good government of their own families, much less for the regulating of companies and foreign commerce.' He cared nothing for the old traditions of the land, and had very little respect for anything that interfered with the commercial progress that alone made sense to him. 'To improve and advance trade,' he said, we must 'begin the right way, casting off some of our old mistaken principles in trade, which we inherit from our ancestors.'

Such a man was bound to have many enemies, but again he used money to buy off all opposition. He used also his daughters, marrying them into influential families, again with the help of money. When one daughter married the eldest son of the Duke of Beaufort, Macaulay says, Sir Josiah paid down fifty thousand pounds with her. All the affairs of the company were worked in this private and personal way. The most important papers were not kept in the muniment room of the offices in Leadenhall Street, but in Sir Josiah's desk at Wanstead.

Charles II was so gracious as to accept from him a gift of ten thousand guineas; James did him the honour of accepting the same sum. And courtiers, their mistresses, ministers of the Crown, dignitaries of the Church, and public functionaries of every kind sang his praises in acknowledgment of—to use Macaulay's list—presents of 'shawls and silks, birds' nests and atar of roses, bulses of diamonds and bags of guineas.' When he died he, like Sir Thomas Roe, was buried in his parish church. But he had a much more sumptuous memorial. Perhaps the most fitting touch on the monument of this merchant adventurer who had proclaimed his perfidious ideas so shamelessly, is a pair of angels, brazenly blowing trumpets.

# CHAPTER XIX

## A GREEN RETREAT

How vainly men themselves amaze
To win the palm, the oak, or bays . . .
While all the flowers and trees do close,
To weave the garlands of Repose!

ANDREW MARVELL.—*The Garden.*

It had been a restless and disturbing age. In the seventeenth more than in most centuries there had been 'A time to kill, and a time to heal; a time to break down, and a time to build up,' and at the end of it the question must often have been asked, 'What profit hath he that worketh in that wherein he laboureth?' There were a few wise men in Essex as elsewhere who gave answers similar to that given by the son of David: 'I know that there is no good in them, but for a man to rejoice, and to do good in his life.' Simon Lynch of North Weald was an Essex parson of the day who understood this aspect of wisdom better than most. When Bishop Aylmer, a kinsman, bestowed on him the North Weald living, then of small value, he said:

'Play, cousin, with this awhile, till a better comes.' But Simon Lynch stayed at North Weald for sixty-four years. When the bishop, remembering his promise, offered him 'Brentwood-Weald' some years later, a living worth three times as much as the one he held, he replied that he 'preferred the *weal* of his parishioners' souls before any othere *Weale* whatsoever.'

But it must not be assumed that all who lived quiet, undemonstrative lives were devoid of ambition. There were those whom the age rejected but posterity honoured—who arrived, as it were, along a byway and entered through a wicket. Essex had such a man in John Ray, one of a temper unacceptable to his own generation, who found in his native village a place of retreat from its vain, distracting trends. Ray, whom Gilbert White of Selborne called 'the excellent Mr. Ray . . . the only describer that conveys some precise idea in every term or word,' and whom all men now regard as the father of English natural history, lived at Dewlands, Black Notley, for the last twenty-five years of his life. He was the son of the village blacksmith, and received his early education at Braintree grammar school. From there he went to Cambridge, to become a fellow of Trinity and live an uneventful academic life until deprived of his fellowship by the Bartholomew Act of 1662. After settling in Black Notley again in 1679 he wrote to John Aubrey: 'To tell you the truth this country wherein I live is barren of wits; here being but few either of the gentry or clergy who mind anything that is ingenious.' But he had two or three friends, and they were probably as many as he desired. One of them was Samuel Dale, the learned Braintree doctor who produced the standard history of Harwich; another was Nicholas Jekyll of Sible Hedingham, grandson of William Jekyll, the antiquary, who died at Bocking in 1653, leaving forty volumes in manuscript of notes on the history of Essex and East Anglia.

There is surprisingly little about Essex in Ray's work. He lived happily at Dewlands, which, by the way, was destroyed by fire in 1900, but he was not a demonstrative man, On 13th August 1684 he wrote to a friend: 'I have also lately been a little disturbed and interrupted by the indisposition of my wife, who was yesterday delivered of two children at a birth, both females,' which, to say the least of it, is a mild way of announcing twins, however commendable as a statement of fact. But if there is little in his writings about either his home or his county we know that he was happy in both. Much of his best work was done at Black Notley. Not only were his books written at Dewlands, it was from the rivulet that crosses the road there—'the little brook that runs near my dwelling'—that he worked out a theory of springs, and in an Essex lane that he found field garlic, then an unrecorded plant. Such trifles are like feathers that show the strength and direction of the wind.

John Ray was a good man and a great scholar; but I have to confess that in going through his voluminous correspondence for any reference to Essex that might bring light to these pages I became wearied by dull recitals of learning until I found among his friends that crony of cronies, John Aubrey. Many rude and disparaging things have been said about Aubrey. Anthony Wood said that he was 'a shiftless person, roving and magotie-headed, and sometimes little better than crazed.' But as one who suffers from Aubrey's weaknesses I never see his name without feeling my spirits rise in anticipation of the fun to be provided by the good things he invariably tumbles out of his intellectual pockets, with the zest of a schoolboy displaying his latest finds. He may have been something of an intellectual poacher; but then poachers' pockets always yield far more trove than the pockets of mere gamekeeper scholars. This is the sort of letter he wrote to Ray at Black Notley:

'Honoured Sir . . . I do think there is a greater variety of Withys than you mention; a bencher of the Middle Temple is very curious in them, but he prefers the red withy. King James II sent, by Sir —— Garden, to the Royal Society, a plant called Star of the Earth, with a receipt made of it to cure the biting of mad dogs, which is in Transact., No. 187. By the salt-pits at Lymington, Hampshire, grows a plant called Squatmore, of wonderful effect for bruises, not in any herbal. . . . My old friend, Mr. Fr. Potter (author of the Interpretation 666), told me that a neighbour of his who had the gout many years, an ancient man, was cured by an old woman with the leaf of the wild vine. . . . E. W. Esq. tells me of a woman in Bedfordshire who doth great cures for agues and fevers with meadowsweet, to which she adds some green wheat. . . . Sir Chr. Wren told me once (eating of strawberries) that if one that has a wound in the head eats them it is mortal.' All that in one letter! And what is still more remarkable, useful copy being passed from one author to another. What, we wonder, did the scientific Mr. Ray make of it all?

Aubrey visited Ray at Dewlands, and we trust they talked about country proverbs, a subject on which they could start

equal. Ray compiled a *Collection of English Proverbs* while
at Cambridge, and it was perhaps the only indiscreet thing he
ever did. It is a relief to learn that one so circumspect
should have given offence, as he confesses he did with the
book, 'to sober and pious persons, as savouring too much
of obscenity,' and because some of the proverbs included
were apt to suggest impure fancies to corrupt minds. His
comments tend to be prosy enough to suit even his stuffiest
neighbours. On

> Braintree boys, brave boys,
> Bocking boys, rats,
> Church-street, puppy dogs,
> High-garrett, cats,

he comments: 'The tendency of this proverb is to compliment
the inhabitants of Braintree at the expense of the three
other places.'

Ray was a great naturalist and a good man. Indeed, he
was almost too good. One longs for some sign of friendly
weakness in him that would make him seem more human.
But for those who like their virtue neat he leaves nothing to
be desired. A fellow naturalist, Dr. Derham, said of him:
'In his dealings no man was more truly just; in his conversation no man more humble, courteous, and affable; and
towards the poor and distressed, no man more compassionate
according to his abilities.'

This appreciation of virtue seems to have been stronger
among scientists that among churchmen. At the time when
Richard Montagu and the papists in his parish were abusing
each other, and the folk of Newport and Braintree were sling-
ing mud, there was another 'famous gentleman and a great
lover of plants,' William Coys, cultivating the gardens at his
home, Stubbers, North Ockendon, to the admiration, apparently untinged with envy, of his botanical acquaintances.
Dr. Gunther, in *Early British Botanists*, tells us how Coys was
visited in 1617 by John Goodyer, a Hampshire botanist, who
took back with him a list of new plants growing at Stubbers.
This, says Dr. Gunther, is 'the oldest known MS. list of an
English garden, in which the plants are properly distinguished

by their scientific names.' Three hundred and twenty-four plants were attributed to Coys in Goodyer's lists, and it is charming to note how often an entry ends with such an acknowledgment as to his 'singular good friend,' or 'from Mr. William Coys, often remembered,' or even 'my worthie friend, and most diligent observer and preserver of simples, Mr. William Coys of North-ockington in Essex.' This last, it may be noted, was for a gift of tobacco seed sent in 1620. Goodyer first saw the ivy-leaved toadflax growing in the gardens of his 'faithfull good friend,' who in 1622 gave him tomatoes, which were then called apples of love because they were believed to stimulate desire.

To this same charming old house, Stubbers, North Ockendon, came Sir William Russell a few years later. Sir William's is a pleasant figure to see crossing the garden at this point, because he represents the saner, kindlier man in the business world towards the end of the century, and one worth remembering along with the cynical and aggressive Sir Josiah Child. There were scores of Sir Williams to the one Sir Josiah; but again the one is remembered, the twenty forgotten. Yet how worthy of remembrance Sir William was! He bought Stubbers in 1689. By that time he was a well-to-do London draper. He and a partner had started business in 1665 in a shop at the corner of Lombard Street. Their stock was worth £2,000 and 'by the blessing of God,' as they devoutly recorded, they made a profit of £677 3s in the first year of trading, and nearly twice as much in the second, though their first was the worst year of the plague and their second the year of the Great Fire, which cost them £40.

In 1669 William set up in business on his own account, and four years later we find him sporting a coach and three horses. Those were good times in the city, and a tradesman was regarded not only as a gentleman, but if prosperous as a gentleman to be envied. In a short time William Russell had become an alderman and sheriff of the City of London, and on 20th October 1679 he was knighted. This, he records, cost him £81 13s. 4d., and he paid the fees the following morning.

To bright young economists still enjoying the infallibility and self-righteousness of youth, these rising new merchants of the seventeenth century may appear smug. To tradesmen of later and more strenuous days their prosperity can only provoke envy. How good the world must have seemed to the city draper who drove in each day from his fine house at North Ockendon, when each year's annual stock-taking and balancing of accounts showed his estate expanding as comfortably as his waistline! No wonder that in his own hand he wrote with a flourish at the head of each page, 'Laus Deo,' and at the end of each year, after setting out the figures of the balance, 'Soli Deo Gloria.'

For the benefit of his son he compiled a book of maxims, some of which have been printed in the *Transactions of the Essex Archaeological Society* in an article by Miss I. M. Russell. Here are a few:[1]

'Let your expenses be not above half your income.' O happy world!

'Let your love be guided by reason, not fancy; and as the charge & expenses are great & constant that accompany a wife . . . an only child is commonly most advantageous; for she possesses not only all her parents' love, but all their estate.' In choosing a house he recommends 'not above two chambers at most to spare; one for a friend, the other in case of sickness.'

To her extracts from this homily, Miss Russell appends a pleasant story of the good relations that existed between Sir William Russell and Charles II, who was in the habit of borrowing money from the prosperous draper—which may explain the knighthood. On one occasion, Russell was perturbed about a larger than usual sum of money owed by the king, and with characteristic subtlety tried to persuade Nell Gwyn to come to his aid, offering her a hundred guineas if she succeeded in extracting the money from His Majesty. Nell was ready to try. But Charles was too astute for them.

'Tell me, Nell,' he asked, 'how much has he offered you?'

[1] *Transactions of the Essex Archaeological Society*, vol. xxi, part 1, new series.

'Just one hundred guineas,' replied Nell.

'Well,' said the wily Charles, 'I'll give you two hundred to say no more about it.'

We must regret that such men as these are commonly forgotten. Their virtues, as Thucydides observed, are woven into the tapestry of other men's lives. They have few memorials unless they happen to have kept diaries. Here again Essex has been fortunate. It has three of the extremely rare autobiographical works of seventeenth-century gentlemen, a claim which can be made, surely, by no other county. One is from our friend Arthur Wilson, with the title, *Observations of God's Providence in the Tract of my Life*, a vigorous and sensible chronicle; another is Sir Humphrey Mildmay's diary, and the third is Sir John Bramston's autobiography.

One of the characteristics of the age had been its interest in personalities. Pepys and Evelyn bear witness to this. Every great house had its gallery of family portraits, and the same interest found expression in those short essays called 'Characters,' delightful thumb-nail sketches that were then a favourite form of literary composition. They were all brief. Even the biographies of the day did not run to any length. Izaak Walton, for example, wrote the lives of several of the eminent divines of the age, and the whole collection goes conveniently into one small volume. The full-length biography, with every known fact and connection recorded, did not come into vogue until the eighteenth century. The sense of personal achievement was greater in the later age. There was completeness and finish about the full biography beyond the reach of the sketch; but along with its advantages, the professionalism of the long biography involved the loss of the freshness and naïve candour of the amateur's work. Arthur Wilson is an admirable illustration of this seventeenth-century versatility and charm. What fun to find an earl's steward writing a history of his country, an autobiography, and several creditable plays, of which the best known was *The Inconstant Lady*! And he wrote the better for being a man of action. His imagery is the sharper and brighter for his experience, even if his work lacks the polish of the expert's.

Before coming to the Earl of Warwick, Wilson had been gentleman-in-waiting to Robert Devereux, third Earl of Essex, and had travelled with him through France, Germany, Spain, and Italy. He seems to have begun writing while with the Earl of Essex, who, indeed, encouraged him in it; but none of his work was published until after his death. In reading it, as we saw in his notes on the Chelmsford trial of witches, we feel that we are in the company of a remarkably intelligent and fair-minded man—one who is both well informed and charitable in his judgments. From his account of the journey to Long Melford to help Lady Rivers, and that of the Royalists' visit to Leighs, we know that he was a shrewd man. Writing of Essex he says: 'And it is not the least of the blessings that I have cause to be thankful for, that God hath provided for mee (now that almost all the whole kingdom is in a miserable and devastated condition) a beeing in Essex; where by the sense of charitie more than suffring wee participate of the publique affliction.' Obviously these words were written before the war, in its last throes, came to Essex and visited his own sheltered Leighs. Wilson, and probably he alone, was bold enough to stand up to the great Martin Holbeach at Felsted, 'our poore village,' as Wilson calls it, when the famous headmaster of Lord Chancellor Rich's school there was starting many acrimonious disputes by his rabid sectarianism. In a plain-spoken letter Wilson appealed to Holbeach to make an effort to heal the wounds inflicted by his teaching.

At his death in 1652, six years before his master's, Wilson bequeathed 'that little house and land I have in Felsted, called Drinkalls . . . the yearely revenue of itt . . . to be divided weekly everie Lord's Day morninge amonge the poore in bread.'

Arthur Wilson was evidently known to be a writer in his lifetime, though he published nothing. His plays must have given him repute, for he was invited by Benlowes to contribute commendatory verses, in accordance with the pleasant custom of the age, to *Theophila, or Love's Sacrifice.* The other Essex scholars who allowed their names to add lustre to Benlowes's work were Dr. Gauden, Dean of Bocking, and Francis Quarles of Romford. Quarles and Benlowes were the two most gifted poets among the Essex country gentlemen of their day, and they were devoted friends. Wilson would not have been invited to join their company if Benlowes had not thought highly of his gifts as a writer.

The other two gentlemen of the age who have given us the pleasure of their society, the one by his diary, the other by his autobiography, were Royalists. They were gentlemen of moderate estate, and like Wilson represent the middle point of sanity and good humour to which the swinging pendulum of religious and political enthusiasm must ever and anon return.

Sir Humphrey Mildmay, grandson of the Sir Walter who founded Emmanuel College, is an unexpected figure on the king's side. Evidently the more potent strain in his blood came from his mother, who was a Capel. Lord Capel was the son of Sir Humphrey's first cousin, Sir Henry Capel. To strengthen this Royalist strain inherited from his mother he married when he was twenty-four the daughter of Sir John Crofts of Little Saxham, Suffolk, whose fifteen children were noted for their gaiety. If the excessive gravity of the Mildmays had turned Humphrey into a Cavalier, the excessive gaiety of the Croftses might almost have been expected to turn him back to Puritanism. So gay were the girls at Little Saxham that 'going to Saxham' in Charles II's time meant much the same as 'going to Jericho' had meant in Henry VIII's. Endymion Porter, a gentleman of the bedchamber to Charles while prince, had to promise his wife that he would be a 'true loving husband, that will not go to Saxham.' To a husband, it might seem, the charms of a Crofts lady were not what they were to a lover, for Sir Humphrey rarely refers to his wife with anything more affectionate or complimentary than 'my wife,' or 'my old woman.' But it is regrettably clear that he had compliments enough for other ladies of his acquaintance.

Sir Humphrey was as gay as Pepys himself. Such an entry

Braintree

Dewlands, Black Notley

HARWICH

as 'This afternoon I visited pretty Mrs. Oxwick [of Stratford] with much solace, and came home to Jane,' might have come straight from the *Diary*. They belong, however, to the first half of the century, for Sir Humphrey was a Jacobean, rather than a Caroline, gentleman.

Like Pepys in merriment, he was like him also in being a loyal churchman with a critical ear for a sermon. 'Goodcole fooled in the pulpit, for preach he cannot,' reads one entry, and another sermon was set down as 'a pitiful preachment.' Most of these, we find, were delivered by Puritans, whom Sir Humphrey had no cause to love. One of his best parson friends—and he had many—was the Dr. Osbaldston who was turned out of his living at Great Parndon after being so rude about his Puritan neighbours. His own rector at Danbury, Parson Vincent, and the rector of Woodham Ferrers, Parson Webb, were as much members of his household as Parsons Gauden and Walker were members of the Earl of Warwick's; but how these two trios would have detested each other's society! They could not have remained in the same room with each other for more than a few minutes, unless Parson Walker happened to be telling his tale about the cider. The chief interest that Sir Humphrey and his brace of parsons had in common was the love of the bottle. Nothing amused Sir Humphrey more than to get Parson Vincent merry:

'Came to supper Parson Vincent drunk, Alex not much better; Parson Webb to laugh at them. And so I laughed away the time.' Vincent was in fact a genuine case of a 'scandalous liver' and 'common drunkard,' and no credit to his cloth. There is abundant evidence in the diary alone to show that his parishioners were well rid of him when he was turned out of his living, though he could on occasion 'play the brave man' in the pulpit, and 'preach rarely,' to Sir Humphrey's way of thinking. Among the better type of parson whose friendship Sir Humphrey valued was Dr. Brian Walton, rector of Sandon and editor of the Polyglot Bible. With him Sir Humphrey had 'sweet discourse.' As a rule, he found great delight in the company of visiting clergy, and they were numerous, for Parson Vincent was often away

from home.   Sir Humphrey usually entertained them, and
the hospitality was rarely, if ever, begrudged.

He would drive into Chelmsford regularly, either to hear
a sermon by Dr. Michaelson at the parish church, or to dine
with friends at the 'Cock'—Richard Potto's inn.   'To dinner
at the "Cock" in Chelmsford,' reads one entry, 'where was Sir
Henry Mildmay and his company.   The Sergeant Major
paid for all.   I came home late and well potted.'   It was the
custom for knights and their ladies from the surrounding
villages to drive into Chelmsford or Colchester on market day
and dine together at an ordinary, exchanging news and gossip.
Among Sir Humphrey's cronies were the Petres, the Waldegraves, and other Roman Catholic families.   Dearest of all
was Sir John Tyrrell of Springfield, a near neighbour and a rare
companion.   They were fellow justices of the peace, gover-
nors of Chelmsford grammar school, Royalists, and good pot-
fellows.   Sir John was evidently a great talker and well able
to prate with the two parsons.   Sometimes he appears as
Sir John Prattle, a title conferred with entire good humour
and affection:

'To dinner came Parson Webb, Vincent, and Sir John
Prattle, where we were merry until evening.'

Sir Humphrey divided his time between London and
Danbury, usually travelling to and fro on horseback.   Part
of the year he might be in either place; but he was always
at home for harvest.   After harvest he was almost certain to
go up to London for a fling, returning in time for Christmas,
which he preferred to spend at Danbury with his family and
tenants about him.   This balancing of town and country life
seems to have been very happily contrived by most of the Essex
gentlefolk of the day, and made for an admirable combination of
urbanity and wholesome simplicity, though in Sir Humphrey's
case the urbanity was more pronounced than the rusticity.

He looked after his tenants, and seems to have been a good
and considerate master.   He attended the village weddings—
tempted, perhaps, by the promise of conviviality rather than
by a sense of duty, and he might even honour a christening
with his presence, though not always approvingly:

'To church again, where was such a racket with women at a christening of a child as I never saw and desire to see no more such. God make them wiser.' At all events it is clear that he mixed very freely with his tenants.

In 1636 Sir Humphrey had the honour, and as it proved, the misfortune, to serve as high sheriff for Essex. It cost him a pretty penny and many a headache. Like every good autobiographer he had an eye for trifling details, and viewed them as matters of importance. He tells us that when he became sheriff his gilded sword had to be burnished, and that he had to carry his beard to a more fashionable barber. From Mr. Lee, the haberdasher, he informs us, he thought it necessary to buy 'twenty livery hats and bands at £10 and fair, and band of gold for myself at £4 12s.' At the same time he added to his establishment Tegg, an Irish footman, who stayed for more than twelve years and got one of the maids into trouble. But the worry of his office was the collecting of ship money. The people of Chingford were among the more troublesome. They came 'in heaps about their rate for the ship.' Hatfield Broad Oak still remembered Sir Francis Barrington's stand in 1626 and opposed the tax to a man. Even more powerful than the dead hand of Sir Francis Barrington was the living hand of the Earl of Warwick, the most eminent among those who refused to pay during Sir Humphrey's term of office. The money was paid eventually; but something must have remained in dispute until 1638, for in April of that year Sir Humphrey noted: 'Before my Lords Marshal and Chamberlain at Whitehall . . . was concluded the quarrel between the Earl of Warwick and me.' The conclusion of the quarrel, however, cannot have been more than a brief armistice, for the Earl of Warwick was already stirring up trouble for the Puritan cause by the agency of his ministers, who were exceptionally prone to poach for souls in other men's parishes, and were the great subversive force in the county in the years immediately before the civil war. On 25th October 1642 Sir Humphrey wrote: 'To Chelmsford in coach to see the foolery and impiety of the Earl of Warwick and his rabble.'

The civil wars did not greatly perturb Sir Humphrey. He was one of the thousands of quiet, sensible men who remained in the background while the hotheads were cancelling each other out. He owned property in the Royalist west as well as in the Parliamentary east, so he was able to avoid the worst clashes. While Colchester was being besieged he was in Somerset. Somehow he contrived to keep his estates, though he was duly fined as a delinquent. There was no question of evasion. Both his sons fought with the Cavaliers, and one was inside Colchester when Fairfax marched in. He stood his chance like a gentleman.

The Puritan abolition of Church festivals troubled Sir Humphrey as much as anything in the new way of life. Christmas, Easter, and Whitsuntide were passed over without observance during the Commonwealth, and this grieved him so much that he became most punctilious in his own observances, preparing for them reverently by entering the dates of the Church's calendar in his diary.

The third Essex gentleman to give us the benefit of his day-to-day experiences, this time written up into an autobiography of considerable length, Sir John Bramston of Skreens, Roxwell—a house completely demolished in the twenties of the present century—was more eminent than the other two. Like them, he was a kindly and sensible country gentleman, sufficiently detached from events to see them in perspective, and sufficiently near to be well informed. Like Sir Humphrey, he was a loyal churchman; unlike him, he was a man—apparently—of blameless character. Born in 1611, he was nineteen years younger than Sir Humphrey and sixteen years younger than Arthur Wilson. The civil wars and the Commonwealth must have blighted all the ambitions of his youth; but he seems to have used his disappointments to build character as an athlete might carry burdens to produce muscle. At the Restoration he was knighted and elected to the first Parliament of the new reign. He was then fifty, and might have felt that the best years of his life had been lost; but he lived to his ninetieth year, so for nearly forty years was able to serve his country and enjoy the esteem of his neighbours in a more congenial world.

The election of Edward Turner and Sir John Bramston to Parliament in 1660 infuriated the new Earl of Warwick, Charles Rich, who is said to have fretted himself into a fever over it. What really enraged him was that by refusing to come to terms with Sir John and his friends, the Puritans lost both seats. Sir John Bramston had signified his intention to stand for election, and had offered to support Sir Harbottle Grimston's candidature for the other seat of the Earl of Warwick and his party would accept himself as one member. In view of all that he and his father had suffered at the hands of the Puritans it was a generous offer. The Earl of Warwick, true to the principles of his race, replied that he would have both seats or none. Another Royalist candidate, Edward Turner, afterwards Sir Edward, a gentleman of Great Parndon, was then interviewed and persuaded to stand. At the beginning of the contest Mr. Turner thought so little of his chances that after a very short time he wished to withdraw, and was practically forced back into the field by Sir John, who had his finger on the county pulse by this time, and saw how favours were likely to go. The result was that both were elected, and in sad mood Parson Josselin entered in his diary: 'The godly party lost their choice, but God will not lose his right.' Sir Harbottle Grimston, fortunately, was elected for Colchester. The election had made one thing clear. The sun of the house of Rich in Essex had set.

One of the happiest features of Sir John Bramston's autobiography is that he is as interesting when chatting at his own fireside in slippers as he is when attending his sovereign in court dress. There is the account of his first school, conducted by the Rev. Andrew Walmesley, parson of Blackmore. Walmesley, according to his old pupil, was 'a greatly followed preacher, lecturing at Ongar and other places, a great pretender to sanctity and religion'; but a humbug, and 'a very mean superficial scholar.' He used to send his scholars out into the fields with their lessons in one pocket and their dinners in another, under orders to study hard, learn their piece, and at the same time keep an eye on the parson's cattle. If they failed, they were punished. Walmesley was a hard taskmaster. But there was one way of winning his favour, and that was by bringing in a rabbit, or perhaps a bird, for the parsonage pot. We must not be too hard on him here. It was no easy matter to feed a school of boys in a remote parish. The masterstroke of the boys in Bramston's time was the catching of a neighbour's pigeons during a severe frost. This was done, he tells us, 'by making a trap with corn under a door, which we took off the hinges and propped with a stick, to which we fastened a line which we put through a lattice in a lower room, where one held the line, and we were out of sight; and when the pigeons were under the door, we gave a pull, and, the stick coming away, the door fell on the pigeons, so we culled at a pull a dozen or more at a fall, and so we did often. He at first seemed angry, but the pigeons were baked, and we ate them, and his wife commended us, and we followed the trick until we had destroyed all the pigeons in Smyth's Hall dovehouse.'

Sir John, when the time came, married much more soberly than did Sir Humphrey. His wife was a sister of Sir Thomas Abdy of Albyns, a fine old house still standing at Stapleford Abbots. She was a perfect wife and mother, though few of her ten children lived long. They were all carefully tended, Sir John assures us—taught to read their Bible and prayer-book and kept clean and tidy, though not expensively dressed. The cause of Lady Bramston's death at a compara-tively early age is uncertain. One theory is that it was caused by a fright she had in the shop of Mr. Thorowgood, a Chelmsford linen-draper, where she was hit 'by a foot-ball kickt into the shop, which hit her on her belly, then very bigg, and she neere her tyme.'

It is clear throughout the autobiography that Sir John Bramston was well placed for a clear view of the pageant of his times, and in consequence his comments have been useful to national as well as to local historians. He is able to cover an unusually long period, because in addition to his own life of nearly ninety years he was able to draw on the experiences and wisdom of his father, who had been chief justice of the King's Bench under Charles I. The Earls of Warwick, the Lords Maynard, the Barringtons, the Grimstons, the Petres, and the Mildmays figure in his narrative. He was less self-centred than most autobiographers. Rather was he one of those who in their private lives sustained in this restless age values which, in the course of history, are like a thread on which all the ill-assorted events and personalities hang like beads on a necklace. Without this thread the assertiveness of the so-called strong characters—most of whom are stubborn fools—would produce only chaos. In short, he was a distinguished and enlightened example of the middling people.

He was particularly good on elections. At the beginning of this book we had a note on the election of knights for the first Parliament of James I; now at the end we might do worse than follow Sir John's account of the election of knights for the first Parliament of James II, eighty-two years later. Sir John himself was unwilling to stand for the county again, and the Duke of Albemarle advised the king that Sir William Maynard and Sir Thomas Fanshawe would be put forward, adding that though Sir John Bramston would not be a knight of the shire he would be elected a burgess for Maldon, where the whole town was for him. Sir John says: 'This really grieved me . . . because I really intended to be quiet, and meddle with no more public business . . . but it having been told to the king that I might be chosen if I would, without charge or trouble, I feared his Majesty would be displeased should I refuse.' Sir William Maynard and Sir Thomas Fanshawe were opposed by one of the Mildmays and a Mr. Luther. The inns and streets of Chelmsford must have presented a lively spectacle on election day as Sir John Bramston and his party rode in from Roxwell; Lord Maynard, and the gentlemen of Dunmow and the Roothings, from Little Easton; Lord Petré, at the head of a procession of his kinsmen and neighbours to the number of three hundred, from Thorndon. The Wisemans, the Tyrrells, and all the old Catholic and

Royalist families were there, looking as optimistically towards the second James as the Howards, the Riches, the Petres, the Dennys, and the Barringtons had looked towards the first. Most of them were disappointed; but the Petres were still socially and politically resilient.

The common people were on the other side. Sir John tells us how, as the Royalist procession approached Chelmsford, 'the company would needs have me ride into the town before them, as their conductor.' In the main street they met the opposing procession. 'I kept my path,' says Sir John, 'and so did those that followed me, falling a little nearer the wall, and he and his company from it, so we passed by and had full view of our companies.' The climax was reached when the Duke of Albemarle rode in from New Hall, and was received by Sir John Bramston, who gave orders for his procession to divide and make a lane through which the duke could ride to the head. Then his grace, with Sir William Maynard on one hand and Sir Thomas Fanshawe on the other, rode forward to the court house, with the others following five abreast in splendid cavalcade. When the writ had been read and the candidates named, Mr. Mildmay demanded a poll. Clerks were then appointed to count the votes, and every freeholder had to be sworn. As it happened, there were fewer than expected with the necessary qualification of having a forty-shilling freehold who wished to support the opposition, so half an hour later the sheriff, Joseph Smart, a London draper living at Theydon Bois, went up to Mr. Mildmay and asked whether he desired further delay.

'Make three proclamations,' said Mr. Mildmay, 'and if nobody comes I will acquiesce.'

The proclamations were made and more voters came forward to support Sir William and Sir Thomas. No more could be found for Messrs. Mildmay and Luther, so the Royalist knights were declared elected. A curious feature is that the poll was declared before the votes had been counted, which Sir John thought wrong, but both Mr. Mildmay and Mr. Luther were evidently satisfied that the majority were against them. When the clerks had finished counting, the figures were found to be 1,843 for Maynard and Fanshawe, 1,324 for Mildmay and Luther.

So, with Bramston as with Wilson and Mildmay, we learn of the daily pleasures and anxieties of life, its high lights, its shadows, and its continuing change. We sense its quality and atmosphere the better for the casual nature of the record. In spite of Mildmay's tippling and such weaknesses as the others may have had, we feel with all three—as with Ray, Coys, and Sir William Russell—that we are in a saner, kinder world than we infer from reading only of the principal figures in seventeenth-century history. To the nation, the second Earl of Warwick and Sir Henry Mildmay were far more important than Arthur Wilson and Sir Humphrey. But both the earl and Sir Henry are seen more clearly for what they were when related to these normal, middling men, who are, we feel, flesh of our flesh and bone of our bone. The more limited field of local or county history leaves room for a greater variety of minor characters than can be accommodated in national history. Without them the great can never be seen in lifelike setting. The seventeenth century seems intolerant and doctrinaire until we see it through families and homes instead of through religious and political assemblies. Only then do we realize that while the Puritans were tearing out communion rails and—in Essex at all events—torturing witches, while demagogues in Parliament were putting gallant and God-fearing men to death, and while the new princes of commerce were feathering their nests by shameless betrayal, there were quiet, honest, and scholarly men living as peaceably as the saints and reformers would let them.

# EPILOGUE

THERE we leave them. The future of what was to be the populous part of Essex, the Essex on the London border, was with men like Sir William Russell: the bankers, brewers, and merchants; and with all the teeming thousands of factory and office. The future of the Essex of the Suffolks, the Warwicks, the Buckinghams, and the rest of them, was with the farmers, those stout yeomen of good stock who were already there when the others came, and remained after they had gone. When John Norden visited the county in 1594 he wrote: 'This shire is most fat, fruitful, and full of profitable things, exceeding (as far as I can find) any other shire.' It seemed to him, 'to deserve the title of the English Goshen, the fattest in the land.' Such it remained. Even though it lost its pre-eminence as a county favoured by courtiers, its villages kept much of the look they had when Warwick or Buckingham rode through them. Much of Essex was enclosed early; but even to-day it has fewer hedges and fences than most counties, so that in some places the view of a village or farmstead from the fields may be almost exactly the same as three centuries ago, with a cluster of low thatched cottages about a tiny church with wooden tower and taper spire, resting on the earth as lightly as a fleet of fishing smacks on a calm sea.

It is a land of long memories. When I told a friend from one of its villages that I had discovered in a seventeenth-century sessions roll an amusing character from his neighbourhood, he replied calmly: 'Ah, yes! His descendants keep a small shop not many yards away from the building you mention.' A matter that in a town would have been obliterated in less than ten years was still fresh in the memory of a village three hundred years later.

This particular difference between town and country is more marked in the Home Counties than elsewhere. The rapid development of London has produced towns without roots. But is it not true in every part of the kingdom that the real two Englands are not the England of the rich and the England of the poor, but the England of the town and the England of the country? The town did its best to kill the village—draining away its best blood and reducing its farmers to bankruptcy—until the need for home-grown food in war-time reminded the nation of its physical dependence upon the countryman. Its spiritual dependence also has been pointed out. Its cultural dependence is less obvious; but it is none the less real. The characteristic sanity of English art and literature in its best periods was due to a fine balancing of rural and urban interests, depending upon values preserved through the centuries by the country gentlefolk who are now being taxed out of existence. The extravagantly rich, as we saw with the Suffolks, the Warwicks, the Buckinghams, and a few others, were of little use to any one. But we owe more than we can estimate to those trusty knights of the shire, the Barringtons, the Bramstons, the Mildmays, and the Maynards. Essex, at all events, has reason to remember its grand old families.

And why should we divest ourselves of all joy in the pride and splendour of even the discredited members of a broken aristocracy? Think of the de Veres, whose glory as a family had already passed when the seventeenth century opened, though their fame has been so startlingly revived of late by the claim that Edward de Vere, the seventeenth Earl of Oxford, had at least a hand in Shakespeare's plays. What-ever he did for literature, the seventeenth earl wasted his inheritance, and none of his three successors in the title was able to maintain the state that Stow, in his *Survey of London*, and again in his *Annals*, described in a record of the sixteenth earl riding into London 'with eighty gentlemen, in livery, of Reading tawny, and chains of gold about their necks, before him; and one hundred tall yeomen in the same livery to follow him, without chains, but all having his cognizance of the blue boar, embroidered on their left shoulder.' When the line became extinct in 1703 with the death of the last Aubrey de Vere to hold the title, there had been twenty Earls

L

of Oxford. Words can be a more enduring monument than stone, and where shall we find a nobler memorial to a family than the words spoken by Lord Chief Justice Crewe in 1625, after the death of the eighteenth earl?

'No King in Christendom hath such a subject as Oxford. He came in with the Conqueror, Earl of Guynes; shortly after the Conquest made great chamberlain, above five hundred years ago by Henry I, the Conqueror's son, brother to Rufus . . . no other Kingdom can produce such a peer in one and the self-same name and person. . . . I have laboured to make a covenant with myself that affection may not press upon judgment; for I suppose there is no man that hath any apprehension of gentry or nobleness but his affection stands to the continuance of so noble a name and home and would take hold of a twig or twine-thread to uphold it. And yet Time hath its revolutions; there must be a period and an end to all temporal things, *finis rerum*, an end of names and dignities and whatsoever is terrene; and why not of de Vere?—for where is Bohun? Where is Mowbray? Where is Mortimer? Nay, what is more, and most of all, where is Plantagenet? They are entombed in the urns and sepulchres of mortality.'

Now the lesser breeds are failing. Their beautiful homes are going out of use as places where gentlefolk live and bring up their families, where they entertain their friends and sit with them in panelled halls hung with hunting trophies, or in elegantly furnished drawing-rooms, telling the tales their fathers told them, exchanging titbits of gossip, or earnestly discussing political or social manœuvres. They were born, not as their birth certificates would have us believe, in the seventies or eighties of last century, but when the England in which their kind matured first became poised and creative.

We shall not lose all knowledge of the England of our prime while we have Shakespeare and a score of others; but even the greatest literature is tinged with unreality for many. The things we see are the most convincing. And only while families live in these mellow old houses, built by a village master-builder from timber that came from oaks on the estate, and whose craftsmen were his own kinsmen and the tenants of the man whose house he was building, can townsmen passing that way, as they pause for a moment to admire, sense the past, neither coloured by literary genius nor ticketed in museums, but actual and living. The best are being taken over by the well-meaning public bodies for preservation. Is is all that can be done with them; but when the family leaves, the soul goes out of them.

# WHO'S WHO

AUDLEY, THOMAS, BARON AUDLEY OF WALDEN (1488–1544), lord chancellor; born at Earls Colne; town clerk of Colchester, 1516; created peer, 1538; acquired the Benedictine abbey at Walden at the Dissolution and resided there; his only daughter, Margaret, married Thomas, fourth Duke of Norfolk, and their son, Thomas, first Earl of Suffolk, built Audley End; buried in Saffron Walden church.

AYLETT, ROBERT, OF FEERINGBURY (1583–c.1655), religious poet; Laud's agent in Essex; an ecclesiastical lawyer who acted as commissary of the Bishop of London and judge of the commissary court; consequently a man of great power in the county; his letters are preserved with *State Papers : Domestic.*

BARRINGTON, SIR FRANCIS, OF HATFIELD BROAD OAK (1550–1628), country gentleman; married Joan, daughter of Sir Henry Cromwell of Hinchingbrook, grandfather of Oliver Cromwell; represented Essex in Parliament, 1575–1628; knighted, 1603; baronet, twentieth in order of creation, 1611; commanded one of the ten trained bands raised in Essex to meet the Armada, 1588; imprisoned in the Marshalsea on refusing to contribute to the loan demanded by Charles I, 1626; died from the effects of incarceration, 1628.

BARRINGTON, SIR JOHN, OF HATFIELD BROAD OAK (1614–1682), country gentleman; son of Sir Thomas; married Dorothy, daughter of Sir William Lytton of Knebworth.

BARRINGTON, SIR THOMAS, OF HATFIELD BROAD OAK (*d.* 1644), country gentleman; son of Sir Francis; married, first, Frances, daughter and co-heiress of John Gobert; secondly Judith, daughter of Sir Rowland Lytton of Knebworth; represented Essex in Parliament and left an account of debates; served on the first committee of 'The Eastern Association for the Parliament,' 1642.

BENLOWES, EDWARD, OF FINCHINGFIELD (c. 1602-76), poet; inherited Brent Hall; squandered his fortune on friends; published *Theophila, or Love's Sacrifice*, 1652; was wont to style himself 'Turmae equestris in com. Essex praefectus.'

BLOUNT, CHARLES, EARL OF DEVONSHIRE AND EIGHTH BARON MOUNTJOY (1563-1606); member of a family of scholars and patrons of learning; grandson of the fifth baron and great-grandson of the fourth, who brought Erasmus to England; associated in various exploits with Robert Devereux, second Earl of Essex; K.G., 1597; implicated in Essex's conspiracy to remove Elizabeth's counsellors but escaped punishment; lord deputy of Ireland, 1601; styled lord lieutenant under James, 1603; returned to England and was created Earl of Devonshire, 1603; keeper of Portsmouth Castle, 1604; married Penelope (Devereux), sister of Essex and divorced wife of Robert, third Baron Rich, afterwards first Earl of Warwick, 1605; though he had enjoyed the king's favour while living with her unmarried, was dismissed from court and held in public dishonour for having married a divorced woman; lived unhappily at Wanstead until his early death in 1606.

BRAMSTON, SIR JOHN, THE ELDER, OF ROXWELL, NEAR CHELMSFORD (1577-1654), judge; son of Roger Bramston of Maldon; studied at Middle Temple; counsel to Cambridge University, 1623; counsel at law to the City of London, 1628; queen's serjeant, 1632; king's serjeant and knighted, 1634; chief justice of the King's Bench, 1635; impeached by Commons for speaking in favour of ship money, 1641; removed from office after applying for permission to visit the king at York, 1642; restored, 1643; buried in Roxwell church.

BRAMSTON, SIR JOHN, THE YOUNGER, OF ROXWELL, NEAR CHELMSFORD (1611-1700), autobiographer; son of Sir John the elder; married a daughter of Anthony Abdy, alderman of London, whose country seat was at Leytonstone; survived all except one of his ten children; called to the Bar, 1635; knighted, 1660; elected to Parliament for Essex, 1660; represented the county for many years, and afterwards Maldon; frequently acted as chairman of committees; his autobiography published by the Camden Society, 1845.

BRETON, NICHOLAS, OF WALTHAMSTOW (c. 1545-c. 1626), poet; stepson of George Gascoigne, also of Walthamstow; probably in the service of Sir Philip Sidney.

BROOKES, SIR ROBERT, OF WANSTEAD; figures in Pepys's Diary; lord of the manor of Wanstead, 1662-7; retired to France in reduced circumstances, and appears to have been drowned at Lyons.

BUCKINGHAM, DUKES OF. See Villiers.

BYRD, WILLIAM, OF STONDON MASSEY (1543-1623), the greatest English composer of his time, lived at Stondon Place, Stondon Massey, near Ongar, for thirty years, first as tenant and later as owner; with his family, was frequently presented as recusant.

CALAMY, EDMUND, THE ELDER (1600-66), nonconformist divine; Puritan lecturer at Rochford by patronage of Robert Rich, second Earl of Warwick; component of 'Smectymnuus,' an attack on Biship's Hall's defence of episcopacy; opposed the execution of Charles I and favoured the Restoration.

CALAMY, EDMUND, THE YOUNGER (c. 1635-85), ejected minister; son of Edmund Calamy the elder; intruded rector of Moreton, near Ongar, to which he was presented by the Earl of Manchester, son-in-law of Robert Rich, second Earl of Warwick, 1659-62.

CAPEL, ARTHUR, FIRST BARON CAPEL OF HADHAM (c. 1610-1649), Royalist general; son of Sir Henry Capel of Rayne Hall, Essex, and father of Arthur Capel, created Earl of Essex at the Restoration; represented Hertfordshire in the Short and Long Parliaments; raised to peerage, 1641; Royalist lieutenant-general of Shropshire, Cheshire, and North Wales; prominent in the defence of Colchester, 1648; surrendered to Fairfax and was imprisoned in the Tower; after escape and capture was beheaded, March 1649, and buried at Little Hadham.

CARR, OR KER, ROBERT, EARL OF SOMERSET (d. 1645), favourite of James I; involved, though possibly only as accessory after the fact, in the murder by poisoning of his former friend, Sir Thomas Overbury, who tried to save him from marriage with the Countess of Essex; married this lady, a daughter of Thomas Howard, Earl of Suffolk and builder of Audley End, 1613, soon after she had obtained a decree annulling her marriage with the Earl of Essex; created Earl of Somerset, 1613; displaced as king's prime favourite by George Villiers, afterwards first Duke of Buckingham, 1614; accused with countess of poisoning Overbury, 1615; imprisoned in Tower till January 1622; pardoned, 1624; afterwards lived in obscurity.

CHAMBERLEN, HUGH, OF WOODHAM MORTIMER HALL, NEAR MALDON (fl. 1720), physician, eldest son of Peter Chamberlen; court physician, 1673; F.R.S., 1681; prosecuted for practising without proper qualifications, 1688; published details of a scheme for a state medical service, supported by taxation, 1694; settled in Amsterdam late in life and communicated the family midwifery secrets to a Dutch doctor.

CHAMBERLEN, PETER, OF WOODHAM MORTIMER HALL, NEAR MALDON (1601–83), surgeon; pioneer in operative midwifery; grandson of the first Peter Chamberlen to use forceps in midwifery, which remained a family secret through four generations; physician to Charles II; an anabaptist and writer of theological pamphlets.

CHILD, SIR JOSIAH, OF WANSTEAD (1630–99), merchant and writer on trade; son of a London merchant; established a business at Portsmouth; victualler to the navy when about twenty-five; became mayor of Portsmouth, and, 1659, member of Parliament for Petersfield; amassed a fortune and acquired large stock in the East India Company, of which he became chairman and despotic ruler; bought Wanstead, 1673; created baronet, 1678; exercised immense power through bribing courtiers and officials; author of *A New Discourse of Trade*, etc.; father of Richard Child, created Viscount Castlemain, 1718, Earl of Tylney, 1731, builder of the palatial Wanstead House; a sumptuous monument to his memory was erected in Wanstead parish church.

COOKE, SIR ANTHONY, OF GIDEA HALL, ROMFORD (1504–1576), country gentleman; tutor of Edward, Prince of Wales; represented Essex in Parliament, 1559–67; early advocate of education for girls; one of his daughters became the second wife of William Cecil, Baron Burghley, who was lord lieutenant of Essex, 1588–98, and whose first wife was a daughter of Peter Cheke of Pirgo, Romford. His monument is in the north aisle of St. Edward the Confessor's Church, Romford.

DALE, SAMUEL, OF BRAINTREE (c. 1659–1739), botanist and antiquary; physician with large practice in mid Essex; prominent nonconformist; friend of John Ray, the naturalist; author of *Pharmocologia*, 1693; edited and enlarged Taylor's *History and Antiquities of Harwich and Dovercourt*, 1730.

DEANE, SIR ANTHONY, OF HARWICH (c. 1638–1721), master shipwright and friend of Samuel Pepys; mayor of Harwich, 1676 and 1682; knighted and appointed commissioner of the navy, 1675; represented Harwich in Parliament, 1679 and 1685; invented the 'Punchinello' cannon.

DENNY, EDWARD, EARL OF NORWICH (c. 1565–1637); grandson of Sir Anthony Denny, a favourite of Henry VIII who acquired valuable estates at Waltham Abbey at the Dissolution; knighted, 1587; elected to Parliament as member for Essex, 1604; created Baron Denny of Waltham, 1604; Earl of Norwich, 1626.

DRAKE, RIGHARD, OF RADWINTER (1609–81), ejected rector; first editor of Lancelot Andrewes's *Private Devotions*; son of a London mercer; seven years pupil at Abraham Puller's school at Epping; entered Pembroke Hall, Cambridge, 1624; elected fellow, 1631; ordained priest, 1635; presented to the living of Radwinter by his father, 1638; examined by the Grand Committee on Religion, 1641; sequestrated, 1644; restored, 1660; chancellor of Salisbury Cathedral, 1663; his diary, which is in Latin, is MS. Rawlinson, D. 158, in the Bodleian; in shorter form it is MS. Baker, 36 (MM1. 47) in the Cambridge University Library; the most valuable parts are reproduced in *The Ecclesiastical History of Essex*, by Harold Smith, D.D. (Benham & Co., Colchester).

DUDLEY, ROBERT, EARL OF LEICESTER (*c.* 1532–88), favourite of Queen Elizabeth; bought Wanstead House, 1578; married Lettice Knollys, Countess of Essex, 1578; attended the queen at Tilbury when she made her stirring speech to the troops there, 1588; figures in Scott's *Kenilworth* as husband of the unfortunate Amy Robsart.

EVERARD, SIR RICHARD, OF LANGLEYS, GREAT WALTHAM (1624–94), country gentleman; prominent member of an old Essex family first seated at Mashbury; son of Sir Richard Everard, first baronet, and Joan, daughter of Sir Francis Barrington and cousin of Oliver Cromwell; one of the three commissioners for Essex controlling the militia, the other two being Sir William Masham and Sir Thomas Honywood, 1655; *Custos Rotulorum*, 1656.

FAIRFAX, THOMAS, THIRD BARON FAIRFAX OF CAMERON (1612–71), soldier; general in Parliamentary army, 1642; commander-in-chief, 1645; broke the Royalist defence of Colchester by siege, and approved the execution of Sir Charles Lucas and Sir George Lisle, 1648; married Anne, daughter of Sir Horace de Vere, Baron Vere of Tilbury (1565–1635), who was the son of Geoffrey de Vere of Crepping Hall, Essex, and nephew of the sixteenth Earl of Oxford; his only daughter, Mary, married George Villiers, second Duke of Buckingham, whose father, the first duke, bought New Hall, Boreham, in 1620.

FIRMIN, GILES, OF SHALFORD (1614–97), ejected minister; son of a Sudbury apothecary; entered Emmanuel College, Cambridge, 1629; went to New England, 1632; practised medicine there until ordained deacon of the first church at Boston; returned to England after being shipwrecked off the coast of Spain, *c.* 1647; ordained by Stephen Marshall; vicar of Shalford, 1648; ejected, 1662, and again practised medicine; author of *The Real Christian* and other works; devoted friend of Stephen Marshall.

FULLER, THOMAS, OF WALTHAM ABBEY (1608–61), historian; travelled with Royalist forces as chaplain to Sir Ralph Hopton; chaplain to the infant Princess Henrietta at Exeter, 1644–6;

*L

returned to London after surrender of Exeter and became chaplain to James Hay, second Earl of Carlisle, who presented him to the perpetual curacy of Waltham Abbey, 1648 or 1649; lost his library during wars, but received from Lionel, third Earl of Middlesex, who lived at Copt Hall, near Waltham Abbey, the books of the first earl, who had been lord treasurer; was thus enabled to resume his writing; compiled a history of Waltham Abbey from papers left by the last abbot, Robert Fuller, whose *Leidger Book* had come into the possession of the Earl of Carlisle; author of *The Worthies of England* and many other works.

GAUDEN, JOHN, OF BOCKING (1605–62), Bishop of Worcester; son of a vicar of Mayland, Essex; chaplain to Robert Rich, second Earl of Warwick, 1640; Dean of Bocking, 1641; retained his valuable benefice during the Commonwealth by facing both ways, but wrote in defence of the Church of England and against the army; Bishop of Exeter, 1660; edited Hooker's *Ecclesiastical Polity*, 1662; translated to Worcester, 1662; reputed author of the *Eikon Basilike, the Pourtraicture of his sacred Majestie in his Solitudes and Sufferings*, published within a few hours of the death of Charles I, and throughout the Commonwealth almost universally believed to be the work of the king himself.

GRIMSTON, SIR HARBOTTLE, SECOND BARONET, OF COLCHESTER (1603–85), speaker and judge; second son of Sir Harbottle Grimston, first baronet, who died in 1648; born at Bradfield Hall, near Manningtree; educated at Emmanuel College, Cambridge; recorder of Harwich, 1634; recorder of Colchester, 1638–49; member of Parliament for Harwich, 1628, for Colchester, 1640 and in Long Parliament; deputy-lieutenant of Essex after the militia ordinance was passed, January 1642; presided over the committee that inquired into the king's escape from Hampton Court, 1647; prominent in negotiations with the king at Newport, Isle of Wight, 1648; retired from public affairs until 1656, when he was returned to Cromwell's second Parliament as member for Essex, but was not allowed to take his seat; re-entered Parliament, 1660; member of council of state on the abdication of Richard Cromwell, 1659; Speaker of Convention Parliament, 1660; master of the rolls, 1660–85; by his first wife had six sons and two daughters, but only one son survived him, at whose death the baronetcy became extinct; by his second wife, a great-granddaughter of Sir Nicholas Bacon, had one daughter; bought Sir Nicholas Bacon's estate, Gorhambury, St. Albans, where the descendants of his eldest daughter, the Earls of Verulam, still reside.

HADDOCK, SIR RICHARD, OF LEIGH-ON-SEA (1629-1715), admiral; commanded the *Royal James* in the battle of Sole Bay, and later Prince Rupert's flagship, the *Royal Charles*; knighted, 1675; commander of the Nore, 1682; admiral, 1690; also comptroller of the navy.

HALL, JOSEPH, OF WALTHAM ABBEY (1574-1656), Bishop of Exeter and Norwich; educated at Emmanuel College, Cambridge; presented to the living of Waltham Abbey by Lord Denny; frequently invited to preach before James I at Theobalds in the adjoining parish; accompanied James to Scotland to defend the ceremonial proposed for use by the Scots, 1617; one of the English deputies at the Synod of Dort, 1618; refused see of Gloucester, 1624; accepted Exeter, 1627-41; translated to Norwich, 1641; impeached and imprisoned with other bishops, 1642; episcopal revenues sequestrated and cathedral despoiled, 1643; ejected from palace, *c.* 1647; retired to the nearby village of Higham; a voluminous writer in prose and verse; advocated *via media* in religious matters, but strongly defended episcopacy. His *An Humble Remonstrance to the High Court of Parliament*, 1640, provoked five Puritan ministers to reply under the name of 'Smectymnuus'; Milton entered the fray and wrote five pamphlets in the course of the controversy.

HARRISON, WILLIAM, OF RADWINTER (1534-93), topographer and social historian; rector of Radwinter, 1559-93; his *Description of England* was printed with Holinshed's *Chronicles*, 1578, and in Furnivall's edition, 1877.

HARVEY, GABRIEL, OF SAFFRON WALDEN (*c.* 1550-1630), poet and scholar; son of a prosperous rope-maker of Saffron Walden; educated at Christ's College, Cambridge; elected fellow of Pembroke Hall, 1570; friend of Spenser, in whose poem *The Shepheard's Calendar* he appears as Hobbinol; reader in rhetoric, 1576; fellow of Trinity, 1578; D.C.L. Oxford, 1585;

engaged in public dispute at Audley End before Queen Elizabeth when she visited Sir Thomas Smith, 1578; retired to Saffron Walden and was buried there.

HARVEY, RICHARD, OF SAFFRON WALDEN (*d. c.* 1623), astrologer; brother of Gabriel Harvey; fellow of Pembroke Hall, Cambridge, 1581; author of *Plaine Percevall, the Peacemaker of England, Astrological Discourse, Theologicall Discourse of the Lamb of God and his Enemies;* his predictions were savagely ridiculed by Nash.

HOLBEACH, MARTIN, OF FELSTED (*c.* 1600–70), schoolmaster; taught at Braintree and Halstead for a short time; headmaster of Felsted School, 1627–49; with the support of his patron, the second Earl of Warwick, made Felsted the leading Puritan school of the day; extravagantly praised by his own party, violently abused by Royalists; vicar of High Easter, 1649; ordaining presbyter and one of the commissioners for the removal of unsatisfactory ministers; himself ejected under the Act of Uniformity, 1662; died at Great Dunmow, 1670, and was buried at Felsted.

HONYWOOD, SIR THOMAS, OF MARKS HALL, NEAR COGGESHALL (1586–1666), country gentleman; grandson of Dame Mary Honywood of Marks Hall, who at her death had 367 descendants, reaching to the fifth generation; knighted, 1632; raised troops in Essex for Cromwell; commanded the third of three Essex regiments embodied at Saffron Walden, 1643, the first being commanded by the second Earl of Warwick, the second by Sir Thomas Barrington; served under Fairfax at the siege of Colchester, 1648; at its fall was placed in command of the town with orders to dismantle the fortifications; led his Essex regiment at the battle of Worcester, 1651; had LL.D. conferred on him by Oxford University while passing through the town on returning to Essex; knight of the shire for Essex, 1654, 1656; sat in Cromwell's House of Lords, 1657; *Custos Rotulorum*, 1656–9.

HOOKER, THOMAS, OF CHELMSFORD AND LITTLE BADDOW (*c.* 1586–1647), New England divine; fellow of Emmanuel

College, Cambridge; lecturer at Chelmsford, 1626; conducted a school at Little Baddow after being ejected from Chelmsford; provided by second Earl of Warwick with refuge in Holland when Laud's opposition made it advisable for him to leave England; joined his many Essex friends in New England, 1633; pastor of the eighth church in Massachusetts; published theological works.

HOPKINS, MATTHEW, OF MANNINGTREE (d. 1647), witchfinder; son of a Puritan minister; lawyer at Ipswich and Manningtree; toured the eastern counties in search of witches, 1644–1647; responsible for the hanging as witches of sixty women in Essex, nearly forty at Bury St. Edmunds, and others in Norwich and Huntingdonshire, 1645–6; exposed by John Gaule, vicar of Great Staughton, 1646; hanged, 1647.

HOWARD, THOMAS, FIRST EARL OF SUFFOLK AND FIRST BARON HOWARD DE WALDEN (1561–1626); son of the fourth Duke of Norfolk and his second wife, Margaret, daughter and heiress of Thomas, Baron Audley of Walden; behaved gallantly while in command of a ship sent to oppose the Armada, 1588; distinguished himself in attack on Azores fleet, 1591; became admiral, 1596; created Baron Howard de Walden and K.G., 1597; advanced to earldom of Suffolk by James I, 1603; lord chamberlain, 1603–14; lord high treasurer, 1614–18; heavily fined and imprisoned for embezzlement, 1619; Custos Rotulorum of Essex, 1611–25; married, as his second wife, Catherine, widow of Richard Rich, an avaricious woman who seems to have been partly responsible for his downfall; at the cost of £200,000 built Audley End, on the site of the Benedictine abbey acquired at the Dissolution by his grandfather, Lord Chancellor Audley.

JOSSELIN, RALPH, OF EARLS COLNE (1616–83), diarist; born at Chalk End, Roxwell; vicar of Earls Colne, 1641–83; wrote diary, published by the Royal Historical Society in 1908, which records events in Essex during the civil wars from the point of view of a moderate Puritan; gives weekly lists of deaths from the plague, which show that it became worse in Essex after it had abated in London; useful for records of weather, crops, food prices, and other day-to-day interests.

KEN, THOMAS (1637–1711), author of well-known hymns; Bishop of Bath and Wells; rector of Little Easton, 1663–5; friend of the Maynard family.

LISLE, SIR GEORGE (*d.* 1648), soldier; fought for Charles I at Newbury, Cheriton, and Naseby; governor of Farringdon, 1644–5; prominent in the defence of Colchester; shot as a rebel when the town surrendered to Fairfax.

LUCAS, SIR CHARLES, OF COLCHESTER (*d.* 1648), soldier; son of Sir Thomas Lucas of Colchester; knighted, 1639; joined the king at the outbreak of war and was wounded in the first cavalry charge at Powick Bridge; on Prince Rupert's recommendation made lieutenant-general of Newcastle's northern army, 1644; swept Fairfax's cavalry before him at Marston Moor, but was taken prisoner later; exchanged during winter, but again taken prisoner at Stow-on-the-Wold; released on undertaking never again to bear arms against Parliament; as a native of the town and a gallant officer, took foremost part in seizure and defence of Colchester; condemned to death by court-martial at surrender; shot the same evening along with Sir George Lisle.

MARSHALL, STEPHEN, OF FINCHINGFIELD (1594–1655), Puritan divine; born at Godmanchester, Huntingdonshire, the son of a poor glover; educated at Emmanuel College, Cambridge; married Susanna Castell, a wealthy lady of Woodham Walter; had a large family of daughters, only one of whom brought comfort; lecturer at Wethersfield, *c.* 1618; vicar of Finchingfield, 1625; reported for 'want of conformity,' 1636; frequently preached before Parliament, and exerted great influence; advocated liturgical and episcopal reform, even supporting Bill to abolish episcopacy, 1641; component of 'Smectymnuus'; lecturer at St. Margaret's, Westminster, 1642; chaplain to Earl of Essex's regiment, 1642; member of Westminster Assembly, 1643; waited on Archbishop Laud before execution; chaplain to Charles I at Holmby House and Carisbrooke; assisted in preparation of 'shorter catechism'; one of Cromwell's 'triers'; seems to have been reasonable and tolerant in dealing with his neighbours in Essex; a moderate Presbyterian; buried in Westminster Abbey, 1655; exhumed and dishonoured at Restoration.

MASHAM, SIR WILLIAM, OF OTES, HIGH LAVER (*d.* 1705), country gentleman; married Elizabeth, daughter of Sir Francis Barrington; created baronet, 1621; represented Maldon in Parliament, 1623; twice, 1625; member for Colchester, 1640; with Sir Martin Lumley, represented Essex in Long Parliament; member of the council of thirty-two entrusted with powers of government after the death of Charles I; gained prestige among Essex Parliamentarians by refusing to contribute to the forced loan of 1626, suffering imprisonment in consequence; *Custos Rotulorum*, 1654–6.

MAYNARD, SIR HENRY, OF LITTLE EASTON (*d.* 1610), country gentleman; first of family to settle in Essex; built Easton Lodge; secretary to Sir William Cecil, Lord Burghley; represented Essex in Parliament, 1601; sheriff, 1603; knighted, 1603; *Custos Rotulorum*, 1608–10.

MAYNARD, WILLIAM, FIRST BARON MAYNARD OF ESTAINES PARVA (1585–1640), created baronet in first list, 1611; created Baron Maynard of Wicklow in Ireland, 1620; advanced to English barony, 1628; lord lieutenant of Cambridgeshire, 1620; lord lieutenant of Essex, 1635–40; had the difficult task of raising levies, which appears to have caused his premature death; married, first, Frances, daughter of William Cavendish, first Earl of Devonshire, who died in her twentieth year, secondly, Anne (*d.* 1647), only daughter and heiress of Sir Anthony Everard, of Langleys, Great Waltham.

MAYNARD, WILLIAM, SECOND BARON MAYNARD OF ESTAINES PARVA (1622–98), son of the first baron and Anne, his second wife; married, first, Dorothy, daughter and heiress of Robert Banastre, secondly, Margaret, daughter of James Murray, Earl of Dysart; a Royalist, he was impeached for high treason, September 1647, but discharged June 1648; imprisoned with other Royalists by Cromwell, 1655; privy councillor and comptroller of the household to Charles II, 1672; held same position under James II; *Custos Rotulorum* for Essex, 1673–1687; his second wife was a friend of Thomas Ken, rector of Little Easton, 1663–5, afterwards Bishop of Bath and Wells; she was probably the original of Hilda in Ken's epic, *Edmund*.

MICHAELSON, JOHN, OF CHELMSFORD (*d.* 1674), rector of Asheldham, 1615; rector of Chelmsford, 1623; well disposed at first towards Puritans in neighbourhood, particularly towards Thomas Hooker, who had been lecturer and curate at Chelmsford; ejected and barbarously used by soldiers and sectaries, 1642; supplanted in each parish by the man who had been his curate; long account of his persecution in Walker's *Sufferings of the Clergy*; obliged for several years to live away from Chelmsford, then a hotbed of violent dissenters; returned to live quietly at Writtle until reinstated, 1660; resigned Asheldham in favour of his son; accepted living of Orsett, 1660, and held along with Chelmsford until death. The Chelmsford nonconformists did not agree among themselves any better after Dr. Michaelson's removal; the intruded rector, Mark Mott, tried to enforce his own brand of conformity on the local Brownists, and both Brownists and reformed churchpeople, or Presbyterians, were slandered by the Anabaptists under 'Parson Oates,' their local leader, father of Titus Oates.

MILDMAY, SIR HENRY, OF WANSTEAD (*d.* 1664), politician; grandson of Sir Walter and son of the first Sir Humphrey of Danbury and Mary, his wife, who was a cousin of Sir Henry Capel of Rayne Hall, the father of Arthur, first Baron Capel of Hadham; brother of Sir Humphrey, the diarist; enriched himself by unprincipled conduct as master of the king's jewel house; knighted, 1617; member of Parliament for Maldon, 1620, 1625–1660; revenue commissioner, 1645–52; sat as one of the king's 'judges' and made violent speeches against the king, but did not sign the death warrant; member of state councils, 1649–52; called at the Restoration to give account of the Crown jewels; tried to escape from the country; seized at Rye; imprisoned at Dover; carried to London; degraded and sentenced to life imprisonment, with condition that he should be drawn on a hurdle on 27th January each year to the gallows at Tyburn and back to the Tower; appealed against this sentence, 1661, actually stating that his only purpose in attending the king's trial had been to prevent any harm coming to him; ordered to be deported to Tangier, 1664; died at Antwerp.

MILDMAY, SIR HUMPHREY, OF DANBURY (*b.* 1592), diarist and Royalist gentleman; eldest son of the first Sir Humphrey of

Danbury and brother of Sir Henry; knighted, 1616; married Joan, or Jane, daughter of Sir John Crofts of Little Saxham, Suffolk, 1616; took little part in public affairs, but served as sheriff, 1636; his diaries, *Sir Humphrey Mildmay: Royalist Gentleman*, edited and discussed by P. L. Ralph, published by Rutgers University Press, New Brunswick, 1947.

MILDMAY, SIR WALTER, OF MOULSHAM (*c.* 1520–89), statesman; grandfather of Sir Henry and Sir Humphrey; knighted, 1547; chancellor of the exchequer, privy counsellor, and loyal public servant to Elizabeth; founded Emmanuel College, 1584, where the most renowned leaders of public life in seventeenth-century Essex received their training as Puritans; benefactor of many educational institutions, including Christ's Hospital, London; buried in the church of St. Bartholomew the Great, West Smithfield, London.

MONK, CHRISTOPHER, SECOND DUKE OF ALBEMARLE (1653–1688), son of George Monk, first duke, and Anne, daughter of John Clarges, a farrier in the Savoy; K.G., 1670; lord lieutenant of Essex, 1675–85; colonel of the First Horse Guards, 1679; recorder of Colchester, 1681; commanded the Green Regiment of the Essex militia; chancellor at Cambridge University, 1682; died in Jamaica, of which he had been appointed governor, 1687.

MONK, GEORGE, FIRST DUKE OF ALBEMARLE, OF NEW HALL, BOREHAM (1608–70); began his fighting career by thrashing the under-sheriff of his native Devonshire in revenge for a wrong to his father; served at Cadiz and the Isle of Rhé; gained useful experience in the Low Countries; colonel of Leicester's regiment in Irish rebellion; returned to serve Charles I at outbreak of civil war; taken prisoner by Fairfax, 1644; released after two years to serve in Parliament army against Irish rebels; served in Cromwell's army in Scotland; left in command when Cromwell returned to England, 1651; appointed admiral to fight the Dutch, 1652; resumed military command in Scotland, 1654; greatly trusted by Cromwell; put in command of all Parliament's forces, 1659; elected head of new council, 1660, and for a time in complete control; negotiated terms for

Restoration; raised to peerage and granted a pension of £7,000 a year; lived in splendour at New Hall, Boreham, until his death there in 1670.

MONTAGU, RICHARD, OF STANFORD RIVERS (1577–1641), bishop and controversialist; fellow of Eton and rector of Stanford Rivers, 1613; Dean of Hereford, 1616; exchanged deanery for a canonry of Windsor, 1617; chaplain to James I; entered into controversy with Roman Catholics while at Stanford Rivers; angered Puritans also; consecrated Bishop of Chichester, 1628; translated to Norwich, 1638.

MOUNTJOY. *See* Blount.

NEWCOMEN, MATTHEW, OF DEDHAM (*c.* 1610–69), son of Stephen Newcomen, vicar of St. Peter's, Colchester; lecturer at Dedham, 1637–62; component of 'Smectymnuus'; leader of church reform party in Essex; related by marriage to the Calamy family; ejected, 1662; became pastor of English church at Leyden and died there of the plague.

NEWCOMEN, THOMAS, OF COLCHESTER (*c.* 1603–65), Royalist clergyman and chaplain to the Lucas family at Colchester; incumbent of Holy Trinity, 1628; prebendary of Lincoln, 1660.

OSBALDSTON, WILLIAM, OF GREAT PARNDON (1577–1645), divinity professor at Gresham College, London, 1610–15; rector of East Hanningfield, 1616; rector of Great Parndon, 1635; ejected, 1643; did not live to be reinstated at the Restoration, but his son, Robert, was presented to the living, 1662.

PARKER, WILLIAM, FOURTH BARON MONTEAGLE AND ELEVENTH BARON MORLEY (1575–1622); lived at Great Hallingbury Hall; related to many prominent Roman Catholics; involved with Essex in rebellion, 1601; fined £8,000; accepted James I as king of England; became Protestant, 1605; received from his brother-in-law the letter that led to the detection of Gunpowder Plot; accompanied his Essex neighbour, Lord Suffolk, in searching the vault under Parliament House;

received pension of £700 a year in reward; sat in Parliament for many years; summoned to the Lords as Baron Morley and Monteagle, 1621; died at Great Hallingbury, 1622, and was buried there; his baronies fell into abeyance at the death of his grandson, Thomas, in 1686.

PETRE, JOHN, FIRST BARON PETRE OF WRITTLE (1549–1613), son of Sir William Petre of Ingatestone; married Mary, eldest daughter of Sir Edward Waldegrave of Borley; served as sheriff and knighted, 1575; commanded one of the Essex trained bands at Tilbury, 1588; raised to peerage, July 1603.

PETRE, SIR WILLIAM, OF INGATESTONE (c. 1505–72), secretary of state; tutor at Oxford to Anne Boleyn's brother, George Boleyn, afterwards Viscount Rochford, through whom he gained introduction to public service; fellow of All Souls' College, Oxford, 1523; D.C.L., 1533; clerk of chancery, 1543; knighted and appointed secretary of state, 1543; ambassador to the Emperor Charles V, 1545; retained public office under Edward VI, Mary, and Elizabeth; gained large estates in Essex at the Dissolution; married, first, Gertrude, daughter of Sir John Tyrrell of Warley, secondly, Anne, widow of Sir John Tyrrell of Heron; *Custos Rotulorum* of Essex, 1556–71; generous benefactor of Exeter College and All Souls' College, Oxford; built Ingatestone Hall, and died there, January 1572.

PETRE, WILLIAM, FOURTH BARON PETRE OF WRITTLE (1622–1684), great-great-grandson of Sir William Petre; accused by Titus Oates, son of the Anabaptist leader at Chelmsford in Dr. Michaelson's time, of complicity in a popish plot for the invasion of England; committed to the Tower, 1678; allowed to languish there without trial till his death five years later.

PLUME, THOMAS, OF MALDON (1630–1704), vicar of Greenwich, where Pepys heard him preach, 1658–1704; Archdeacon of Rochester, 1679–1704; endowed chair of astronomy and experimental philosophy at Cambridge; generous benefactor to Maldon, his birthplace; bequeathed to a school he endowed there his library and other papers, including interesting commonplace-books.

PURCHAS, SAMUEL (c. 1575–1626), writer of travels; born at Thaxted; presented by James I to vicarage of Eastwood, near Southend-on-Sea, 1604; became interested in tales of travel told by mariners in his parish and neighbourhood; compiled *Purchas, his Pilgrimage; or, Relations of the World and the Religions observed in all Ages*, 1613; fourth edition, much enlarged, 1626; published *Purchas, his Pilgrim*, etc., 1619; and his greatest work, *Hakluytus Posthumus or Purchas his Pilgrimes, contayning a History of the World in Sea Voyages and Lande Travells*, etc. (4 vols.), 1625; is said by some to have died in a debtors' prison; his son, also Samuel Purchas, was parson of Sutton, and author of a quaint work entitled *History of Bees, or A Theatre of Political Flying Insects*.

QUARLES, FRANCIS, OF ROMFORD (1592–1644), poet; son of James Quarles of Stewards, Romford, who held public offices under Elizabeth; cupbearer to Princess Elizabeth, Electress Palatine, 1613; secretary to Archbishop Ussher; returned to Essex before 1633 and spent two years composing his *Emblems*; many of his poems written while staying with his friend, Edward Benlowes, at Brent Hall, Finchingfield; appointed chronologer to the city of London, a post previously held by both Ben Jonson and Thomas Middleton, 1639; published pamphlets in defence of the king; his house searched and papers taken or destroyed by Parliamentary soldiers; by his wife, Ursula Woodgate, had eighteen children; his son, John Quarles, also poet, bore arms for Charles I at Oxford and afterwards was obliged to live in exile; returned to England at the Restoration and died of plague, 1665.

RAY, JOHN, OF BLACK NOTLEY (1628–1705), naturalist; son of a blacksmith of Black Notley; educated at Braintree grammar school, Catherine Hall, and Trinity College, Cambridge; fellow of Trinity, 1649–62; commenced botanical tours, 1658; took holy orders, 1660; preached frequently before his college in the chapel and before the university in Great St. Mary's; some of his discourses collected and published in *The Wisdom of God in the Creation*; unable to subscribe to Act of Uniformity and deprived of fellowship, 1662; made extensive tours with his generous friend, Willughby; elected F.R.S., 1667; retired to

Falkbourne Hall, 1677; removed to Dewlands, Black Notley, the house he had built for his mother, 1679, and spent the last twenty-five years of his life there; his works, many of them written at Black Notley, entitle him to be regarded as the father of English natural history.

RICH, CHARLES, FOURTH EARL OF WARWICK, OF LEIGHS PRIORY (1636–73), second son of the second Earl of Warwick by his first wife; succeeded to the title at his brother's death, 1659; married Mary Boyle, seventh daughter and thirteenth child of Richard Boyle, first Earl of Cork; their only son predeceased his father; suffered from gout and was a helpless invalid for the last twenty years of his life; maintained a doctor to assist in the care of the sick while Braintree was afflicted by plague, and sent two oxen each week to feed the poor; said to have been a querulous patient during his long illness, but it is doubtful which suffered most, he from his wife's piety, or his wife from his complaining.

RICH, MARY, COUNTESS OF WARWICK, OF LEIGHS PRIORY (1625–78), daughter of Richard Boyle, first Earl of Cork, and sister of Robert Boyle, principal founder of the Royal Society; married Charles Rich, afterwards fourth Earl of Warwick, second son of the second Earl of Warwick; came under the influence of the numerous Puritan ministers who frequented Leighs while the second earl lived; developed a pietistic temperament which expressed itself in diaries and devotional writings; a selection of her work was published in 1686; her diaries are in the British Museum.

RICH, PENELOPE, LADY RICH, OF LEIGHS PRIORY AND WANstead (c. 1562–1607), daughter of Walter Devereux, first Earl of Essex, and sister of Elisabeth's favourite; was the Stella of Sidney's *Astrophel and Stella*; the love between her and Sir Philip Sidney was frowned on by her family after the death of her father, who had desired the match; married, against her will, Robert, third Baron Rich, afterwards first Earl of Warwick, 1581; remained in love with Sidney until his death; afterwards left Lord Rich to live with Charles Blount, eighth Baron Mountjoy; favourite in the court of James I until divorced by Lord Rich, 1605, and married to Mountjoy, by this time Earl of Devonshire; dismissed from court by James for having broken a law of his Church; lived in retirement with the earl at Wanstead and died there prematurely.

RICH, RICHARD, FIRST BARON RICH, OF LEIGHS PRIORY (c. 1490–1567), lord chancellor; member for Colchester in Reformation Parliament, 1529; solicitor-general, 1533; acted contemptibly in the trials of both More and Fisher; knight of the shire for Essex and elected speaker, 1536; first chancellor of the Court of Augmentations, established to dispose of monastic revenues, 1536; helped himself to a large share of the spoil, including Leighs Priory and about a hundred manors in Essex; created Baron Rich of Leighs, 1548; appointed lord chancellor, 1548; signed proclamation in favour of Lady Jane Grey, 1553; when he saw how events were turning, welcomed Mary on her arrival in Essex, and gained her favour by persecuting Protestants; founded a chaplaincy with provisions for masses and dirges to be sung at Felsted; founded Felsted School, 1564, and diverted to it some of his recent Roman Catholic endowments, now become illegal; served under Elizabeth on a commission to inquire into grants of lands made under Mary; died at Rochford, 1567, and was buried in Felsted church.

RICH, ROBERT, FIRST EARL OF WARWICK, OF LEIGHS PRIORY (1560–1619), grandson of Lord Chancellor Rich; married Penelope Devereux, 1580; was associated with her brother, the second Earl of Essex, in most of his adventures; created Earl of Warwick, 1618.

RICH, ROBERT, SECOND EARL OF WARWICK, OF LEIGHS PRIORY (1587–1658), great-grandson of Lord Chancellor Rich, and eldest son of the first Earl of Warwick and Penelope, daughter of the first Earl of Essex; educated at Emmanuel College, Cambridge; member of Parliament for Maldon, 1610 and 1614; engaged in colonial adventures and privateering exploits that brought him into conflict with the great trading companies; associated with the foundation of New Plymouth, Massachusetts, Rhode Island, etc.; opposed the forced loan, 1626, ship money, and other measures of Charles I; became leader of the Puritan party, and by holding the patronage of many livings—acquired by his great-grandfather—was able to bring some of the most eminent Puritan divines of the day into Essex, who, during the civil wars, were in effect his political agents; married at the age of seventeen, Frances, daughter of Sir William Hatton, a wealthy heiress, secondly, Susan, widow of William Halliday, thirdly, Eleanor, widow of Edward Radcliffe, sixth Earl of Sussex; served as joint lord lieutenant, 1625; lord lieutenant from 1629 till, in 1635, the king appointed Lord Maynard, a Royalist; again lord lieutenant, 1642; active in raising forces for Parliament at the outbreak of war, and from that time to his death was a dominant figure in Essex; lord high admiral, 1643; head of commission for the government of the colonies, 1643; Speaker of the House of Lords, 1642 and 1648; against taking the king's life, and, though in the confidence of Cromwell, retired from public life during the Commonwealth; *Custos Rotulorum*, 1640–50; died in the same year as the Lord Protector, whose daughter, Frances, married his grandson and heir, Robert Rich, in 1577.

ROGERS, JOHN, OF DEDHAM (*c.* 1572–1636), Puritan minister; educated at Cambridge; vicar of Dedham, 1605–36; the most fanatical of the Essex Puritans.

SMITH, SIR THOMAS, OF SAFFRON WALDEN AND THEYDON MOUNT (1513–77); born at Saffron Walden; educated at Queen's College, Cambridge; lecturer in natural history and Greek; public orator at Cambridge, 1538; reformed pronunciation of Greek after long controversy; first regius professor of civil law and vice-chancellor, 1544; ordained priest, 1546; Provost of Eton and Dean of Carlisle, 1547; appointed secretary of state and knighted, 1548; lived in retirement at Theydon Mount during Mary's reign; occupied himself in rebuilding Hill Hall and writing *De Republica Anglorum*, completed in 1565, but not published till 1583; ambassador to France, 1562–6, and again in 1572; chancellor of the order of the garter and secretary of state, 1572; his life, written by John Strype, vicar of Leyton, was published in 1698; latest edition of *De Republica Anglorum*, 1906.

VERE, EDWARD DE, SEVENTEENTH EARL OF OXFORD (1550–
1604); born at Earls Colne; only son of the sixteenth earl;
succeeded to title, 1562; a royal ward in Cecil's household;
received early education from Arthur Golding of Belchamp
St. Paul, his mother's half-brother, scholar and friend of Sir
Philip Sidney, whose translation of Ovid appears to have
influenced Shakespeare; became a favourite at court and
married, 1571, Anne Cecil, daughter of his former guardian;
travelled in Italy, 1575–6; was patron of a company of players
known as 'The Earl of Oxford's Boys'; officiated as lord great
chamberlain, 1603; believed by many to be part-author of
Shakespeare's plays.

VILLIERS, GEORGE, FIRST DUKE OF BUCKINGHAM, OF NEW
HALL, BOREHAM (1592–1628), cupbearer to James I, 1614;
knighted, pensioned, and appointed master of the horse, 1616;
K.G., 1616; created Viscount Villiers, 1616, Earl of Buckingham,
1617, Marquess of Buckingham, 1618; achieved the overthrow
of Thomas Howard, Earl of Suffolk, and his son-in-law, Robert
Carr, Earl of Somerset, 1618; succeeded Carr as king's prime
favourite and became virtual ruler of England; bought New
Hall, Boreham, 1620; married the Roman Catholic Lady
Katherine Manners. 1620; dissuaded by Laud from professing
Romanism, 1622; assassinated by John Felton at Portsmouth.

VILLIERS, GEORGE, SECOND DUKE OF BUCKINGHAM (1628–
1687); brought up by Charles I with his own children; had little
connection with Essex; fought with the king in the civil wars;
estates confiscated, 1651; escaped to Holland, but returned to
marry the daughter of Fairfax, who came into possession of
much of his property, 1657; recovered most estates at Restoration, but not New Hall; associated in later years with Yorkshire;
a man of great gifts: playwright, chemist, philosopher, and of
great physical prowess; was the most reckless libertine of his
age, and as such figures in the writings of Dryden, Pope, and
Sir Walter Scott; left no legitimate children.

WALKER, ANTHONY, OF FYFIELD (d. 1692), country parson;
born at Connington, Cambridgeshire; son of William Walker,
vicar of Winston, Suffolk; educated at St. John's College,

Cambridge; curate to Dr. Gauden, 1646; chaplain to Robert Rich, second Earl of Warwick, 1648; carried MS. of *Eikon Basilike* to London and wrote in support of Gauden's claim to authorship; incumbent of Fyfield, 1650; ejected, 1662, but conformed immediately and was reinstated, 26th September 1662; D.D., 1663; died and was buried at Fyfield.

WASHINGTON, LAWRENCE, OF PURLEIGH, ejected minister; great-great-grandfather of George Washington, President of the United States of America; fellow of Brasenose College, Oxford; rector of Purleigh, 1632–43; ejected by the Puritans, probably because the living was too valuable to be enjoyed by one who was not of their party. His son, John Washington, who settled in Virginia, 1656, was joined later by his brother, Lawrence Washington. John was the father of Lawrence, the father of Augustine, the father of George.

WILLIAMS, ROGER, OF HIGH LAVER (*c.* 1604–83), pioneer of religious liberty; chaplain to Sir William Masham at Otes; married at High Laver before emigrating to become minister at Boston, 1631; assistant minister at Salem, 1631; chief teacher at Salem, 1635; incurred official hostility by entering into disputes on legal questions with the governing body of the Massachusetts Bay colony, and after a trial by the general court was banished; founded Rhode Island; visited England, 1651–4; associated with Milton, Cromwell, and many prominent Puritans; always tolerant in theory and the first great exponent in America of absolute liberty in matters of religion; in practice opinionated and doctrinaire. His successor at High Laver was John Norton, who also married there and afterwards emigrated to New England, and though in theory another advocate of religious liberty, instigated the persecution of Quakers in Boston.

WILSON, ARTHUR, OF FELSTED (1595–1652), historian and dramatist; gentleman-in-waiting to Robert Devereux, third Earl of Essex, with whom he travelled widely; gentleman commoner of Trinity College, Oxford; steward to Robert Rich, second Earl of Warwick; died at Felsted, and was buried there. His works include *The History of Great Britain, Being the Life and Reign of King James the First*, published 1653; an auto-biography, *Observations of God's Providence in the Tract of my Life*, first printed in Francis Peck's *Desiderata Curiosa*, 1735, lib. xii, pp. 6–34; *The Swisser*, 1631, first printed by Professor A. Feuillerat of Rennes, 1904; *The Corporall*, performed but not known to have been printed; *The Inconstant Lady*, printed 1814, edited by Philip Bliss; nothing he wrote appears to have been published during his lifetime, but a fragment of *The Corporall* exists in M.S., and the MS. of *The Swisser*, 'written in Wilson's clear and beautiful hand,' was purchased by the British Museum in 1903.

WROTH, LADY MARY, OF LOUGHTON, author of *The Countesse of Mountgomerie's Urania*, an imitation of *Arcadia*, by her uncle, Sir Philip Sidney; eldest daughter of Robert Sidney, first Earl of Leicester; married Sir Robert Wroth of Loughton Hall; received flattering tributes in verse from many of the poets of the day, including Ben Jonson, George Wither, and George Chapman; acted in Ben Jonson's *Masque of Blackness*, performed at Whitehall; one of the literary hostesses of James I's reign.

# INDEX

ABRIDGE, 105
Adultery, 81, 105–10, 112
Agricultural labourers, 94, 115
Ainsworth, Harrison, 101–2, 193
Aldeburgh, Suffolk, 199
Aldham, 233
Ale-houses, 150, 166–72
Altham family, 48
America, United States of. *See* New England
Apprentices, 117–19
Ardleigh, 214–15
Aubrey, John, 91, 233, 292
Audley, Thomas, Lord, 2, 312
Audley End, 2–15, 150, 238, 286, 312, 321
Aylett, Robert, 245, 312
Ayloffe, Henry, 216

Baring-Gould, Sabine, 209, 211
Barking, 192, 234, 254
Barrington family, 30, 46, 72–6, 83–97
Barrington, Sir Francis, 18, 19, 25–9, 33, 312
Barrington, Sir John, 33, 238, 244, 312
Barrington, Sir Thomas, 34, 86, 87, 90, 91, 248–9, 257, 312
Battell, Andrew, 196
Bays and says, 132–45, 184
Bell-ringing, 92, 175–8
Benlowes, Edmund, 297–8, 313
Benton, G. Montagu, 176
Billericay, 102, 118–19, 263
Blackmore, 150–1, 187, 303
Black Notley, 106, 291, 328
Blount, Charles, Earl of Devonshire, 20–2, 313
Bocking, 66, 134, 136, 137, 175, 188, 189, 226, 245, 246, 318
Boleyn, Anne, Queen, 2, 278
Boreham, New Hall, 23, 260, 277–8, 285, 325, 332
Boxted, 271
Bradfield, 36, 318
Braintree, 130, 134, 136, 137, 175, 189, 191, 245, 246, 250, 260, 263, 291, 293, 316

Bramston, Sir John, 192, 217, 219, 244, 254, 276, 283, 302–7, 313
Braybrooke family, 12, 14
Brentwood, 159, 165, 183, 191, 264
Breton, Nicholas, *quoted*, 126, 171, 206, 314
Brookes, Sir Robert, 286, 314
Buckingham, Dukes of. *See* Villiers
Bunyan, John, 175
Byrd, William, 121, 212, 314

Calamy, Edmund, 225, 314
Cambridge, 3, 12, 37–9, 92, 121, 220, 226, 256, 267, 291
Camden, William, 196, 200
Cammocke, Thomas, 203–4
Canewdon, 215
Canvey Island, 200
Capel, Arthur, Lord, 260–76, 298, 314
Capel, Sir Gamaliel, 25–8
Carr, or Ker, Robert, Earl of Somerset, 8–10, 23, 315
Catherine of Braganza, Queen, 14
Cecil, Robert, Earl of Salisbury, 16–17, 179
Chamberlen, Hugh, 56, 315
Chamberlen, Peter, 55, 315
Charles I, 29, 34, 36, 66, 243, 246, 277
Charles II, 13, 195, 281, 283, 286, 295
Chelmsford, 26, 38–9, 116, 119, 120, 148, 163–6, 181, 183, 191, 217, 218, 231, 249, 260–1, 285, 300, 304, 306, 324
Chesterton, G. K., 146
Chigwell, 69, 157–8, 173
Child, Sir Josiah, 54, 285–9, 315
Chingford, 301
Christmas, festivities at, 91
Clacton, 236–7
Clarendon, Earl of. *See* Hyde
Cokayne, Sir Aston, 206
Coggeshall, 49, 100, 117, 134, 142–5, 240, 246, 264, 270, 320
Colchester, 49, 92, 134, 139–40, 147, 161, 176, 186, 206–8, 214–15, 243, 246–9, 256–76, 285, 303, 312

335